(For Review – 1983)

Tries to provide theory by analysis 'cont' metaphysical underpinnings. Cf. p. 128.

Discipline and Authority in School and Family

Discipline and Authority in School and Family

John Martin Rich
The University of Texas at Austin

Lexington Books
D.C. Heath and Company
Lexington, Massachusetts
Toronto

Library of Congress Cataloging in Publication Data

Rich, John Martin.
Discipline and authority in school and family.

Includes index.
1. School discipline—United States. 2. Discipline of children. 3. Home and school—United States. 4. School violence—United States. 5. Authority. I. Title.
LB3012.R53 371.5 81-47962
ISBN 0-669-05168-3 AACR2

Published simultaneously in Canada

Printed in the United States of America

International Standard Book Number: 0-669-05168-3

Library of Congress Catalog Card Number: 81-47962

Contents

Preface and Acknowledgments

Various opinion polls indicate that the public and educators recognize discipline as a serious problem. To handle this problem, most books about discipline focus on specific techniques to reduce school disruptions. Some of these studies are useful, and a plethora of materials is currently available.

Yet if our understanding of discipline is to advance significantly, a different approach is sorely needed. Discipline raises many complex problems and, consequently, diverse fields of knowledge need to be considered in order to understand the problems, place them in perspective, and offer possible solutions. This book explores the interrelations and conflicts between the public schools and the contemporary American family, the two institutions responsible for handling disciplinary problems. The book also investigates the changing concept of authority and offers suggestions for improving relations among students, schools, and families.

Early patterns of authority in the home are examined as well as how they shape student attitudes toward school authorities. Also explored are the ways that different forms of authority promote and inhibit the young's quest for independence and autonomy. A theory of authority is presented, authority problems are examined in the family, and new policies are proposed for reducing disciplinary problems and incidents of violence in school and family.

This book is intended for teacher educators and school administrators. I would be pleased if the book also stimulated parents, classroom teachers, and others who work with youth to rethink the issues raised.

I have been aided in this project by a Special Research Grant from the University Research Institute. Edmund Pincoffs and Betty Sichel made helpful critical comments on an earlier paper on school violence. And I appreciate the skillful manuscript typing of Amy Keene and Marian Morse. Caroline McCarley and Margaret Zusky of LexingtonBooks have offered encouragement by their conviction of the project's merit.

The following journals have kindly permitted me to reprint some of my previous publications:

"Glasser and Kohl: How Effective Are Their Strategies to Discipline?" *NASSP Bulletin* 63 (September 1979):19-26.

"Discipline and the Shape of School Environments," *The Review of Education* 7 (Winter 1981):99-100, 104-107.

"School Violence: Four Theories Explain Why It Happens," *NASSP Bulletin* 65 (November 1981):64-71.

"The Libertarian Challenge to Public Education," *The Educational Forum* 45 (1982).

1 The Tasks Ahead

The public's perception of education as a glowing source of hope and faith for the nation's progress and a brighter future for one's children has diminished. Public-opinion polls indicate an erosion of confidence in public education. Public schools now face inadequate financial support, declining enrollment, teacher burnout, alarmingly high levels of violence and vandalism, and conflicting demands from an impatient public. At the same time a consensus is lacking on what schools should do and how best to do it. American public education appears to be at a turning point in its history as organized movements have sprung up urging parents to educate children at home, in special private schools, or by means of a voucher plan. The erstwhile faith in public education as a bulwark to American democracy and essential for a better life for one's children has been seriously shaken.

Discipline was chosen by the public as the most significant problem in education in nine out of the last ten Gallup polls of public attitudes toward education.[1] Some of the erosion of confidence in education could be ascribed to citizens' perceptions that schools have inadequately handled discipline. Administrators and teachers, though differing with one another and with the public about how to define and overcome this problem, are also seriously concerned about discipline. In a survey by the National Education Association of teacher attitudes and practices, 54 percent said that student behavior interferes with their teaching.[2]

Violence is no stranger to schooling. Since violence has a long and varied history in American life, it is not surprising that it would spill over into schools. What is surprising is the rapid growth of violence, delinquency, and crimes despite concerted efforts during the 1970s to recognize student rights and develop educational alternatives. Yet violence continues to grow.

Nationwide figures show as many as 65,000 teachers and twice the number of students were seriously assaulted in school in 1974. School crimes are costing the American taxpayers an estimated $500 million a year.[3] From 1971-1975, assaults in school increased 58 percent; sex offenses, 62 percent; drug-related crimes, 81 percent; and robbery, 117 percent.[4] The Senate Subcommittee to Investigate Juvenile Delinquency warned that "these problems are reaching serious proportions on a nationwide basis" and added that "the range and type of violence and crime found to exist in our schools include virtually every type of crime found in the streets."[5]

What can be done about these trends? A common solution is to offer teachers specific techniques to handle classroom disruptions or provide administrators definite plans and proposals for reshaping the school environment to alleviate discipline problems. These approaches to discipline have a place for practitioners; unfortunately, they do not usually get at the root of the problem or present discipline in its full range and ramifications in the interaction of school and home or show discipline in relation to changing patterns of authority.

Rationale

By viewing discipline problems exclusively from a classroom perspective or even in terms of the overall school system overlooks some of the most significant influences in the shaping of these problems: the home environment's great influence on children and youth. Educators have long recognized that home life has an important effect on academic achievement, and they have also recognized the need to secure parental cooperation in dealing with chronic cases of student misbehavior. However, in studying disciplinary problems, too often insufficient attention is given to the family's role in this area, and therefore, a careful examination and analysis of the role of the family in creating disciplinary patterns and how these patterns reinforce or negate the school's role in discipline is searched for in vain.[6] Moreover, the American family is rapidly changing, and the nuclear family is only one among many current forms; observers, in fact, are no longer in agreement on criteria for what constitutes a family.

Thus the scope of this study is not only broader than previous ones in its examination of a far greater range of vital interrelationships and influences, but it rests as well in a framework not customarily provided for studies of discipline. Most of these studies present a plan or approach for coping with disciplinary problems. What is really needed is a framework for generating more powerful explanations of disciplinary phenomena. Thus this book examines discipline within the framework of authority.

Problems of discipline grow out of an institutional framework in which patterns of authority can be discerned. Disciplinary problems, in other words, can be located within a social context where roles and status exist and where norms are employed to prescribe and regulate role relationships. Authority is the framework within which discipline is defined and acceptable behavior is prescribed. Parents, teachers, and administrators constitute authority figures holding varying amounts of power and whose authority is recognized as possessing different degrees of legitimacy. Thus power and legitimacy, among other conditions, are needed to exercise disciplinary controls (the precise nature of this relationship will be discussed in chapter 3). Authorities exercise power, impose sanctions, and thereby seek to regulate institutional structures in order to achieve selected ends.

With industrialization and urbanization, the American nuclear family increasingly succumbed to individualism and the self-interest of individual members. Parental authority attempted to rest on the provision of services, but as such erstwhile services families provided—religious, economic, educational, and recreational—were increasingly taken over by other institutions and agencies, families without property could exact obedience only through affection, deference, and a sense of duty. Yet as outside economic values pervaded the family, former traditions and hierarchal structures no longer seemed legitimate to youth, especially when these forms seemed to conflict with their own social and economic interests. The decline of parental authority reduced dependency and weakened the affective bonds between generations. The family's role in socialization subsequently declined, and the school, media, and peers have imperfectly substituted.

In the past two decades, public-education officials have confronted crises in the legitimation of authority: increasing emphasis has been placed on due process, community participation, and the protection of student rights. Thus questions about the legitimacy of authority were prominent in the community-control movement of the early seventies when the authority of an allegedly unresponsive centralized administration were challenged, and during the seventies when many court cases further clarified the basic rights of students. Growing cases of student alcoholism and the spread of the drug culture created problems that most teachers and school officials were unprepared to handle. The rise in violence and vandalism aroused fears among teachers and students and provoked some school boards to employ such stern measures as stationing uniform policemen in school. Other school systems attempted, with varying degrees of success, to employ measures more consonant with the aims of educational institutions. The authority of local school officials was further circumscribed and limited by a welter of state and federal regulations. Authority was clearly more divided than ever before, and a coordinating center of authority was difficult to discern. Thus educators in the 1980s are not altogether clear whether it would be more accurate to speak of a "breakdown of authority" or an "emergence of new authority patterns of power and control."

The scope of this study of authority will include both the classroom and local school policies (within the context and limitations of federal and state regulations) relative to discipline problems. Second, this study focuses on the changing authority patterns of the home in connection with the pluralistic forms of family life in modern America. How in turn do these early disciplinary experiences in the home shape the attitudes and behaviors of students in terms of school disciplinary regulations and expectations? A theory of authority will be developed to help explain these relationships and behavior problems.

Types of Questions

It is important to focus on the questions to be examined because correct answers or solutions to the wrong questions are otiose and diverting. The chief questions will be presented in forthcoming chapters; however, some of the different types of questions, which are samples of a range of concerns, can indicate more tangibly some of the problems to be explored.

The questions are of four types: conceptual, empirical, explanatory, and normative. *Conceptual* questions focus on key terms and the meaning and use of statements and propositions within a given context. "Conceptual inquiry" would not only aim for clarity but also indicate and set the parameters of a study.

Empirical questions would include not only questions about data, trends, and numerical patterns but also some pertinent historical data. What data are important and worth selecting are determined by a normative or valuational position that determines what is worth investigating and the relative weight to be accorded various findings.

Many questions are *explanatory* in character. People want to know the causes for the rise of violence and vandalism in some schools so that something can be done about it. They also want to know why there may be a greater incidence today of teacher burnout and whether the cause may lie with disciplinary problems, inadequate teacher-education programs, or from some other source.

Normative questions contain a value dimension. They can be divided into three principal types: prescription, justification, and evaluation. Prescriptive questions usually take the form of what should be done to remedy some problem. For instance, "should corporal punishment be used in handling classroom disciplinary problems" is a prescriptive question. Justification questions, on the other hand, ask for the grounds or the bases of support for claims or for a position taken; they call for a rationale to be offered. "Why should our school continue to use corporal punishment" asks for the reasons or grounds for the practice and whether the grounds are adequate. A third type of normative question is evaluation. This question asks for the worth or relative worth of a program, process, procedure, or outcome. Thus when teachers ask about what sorts of disciplinary procedures would best control classroom disruption, it may be thought that they are asking a methodological question (which, in part, they are asking); but the question is largely evaluative because it would be necessary to provide information of the relative effectiveness of different procedures, which is an evaluative activity. Thus it is an evaluative question about appropriate methods and procedures.

Of course, these four principal types of questions do not exhaust the types of questions capable of formulation; rather, the types previously discussed are the most prominent ones explored in this study. Further examples of these questions will show some of the range of concerns to be found in subsequent chapters.

With conceptual questions, it is important to explore the meaning of such key terms as *discipline, violence, authority,* and *family.* It is also important to uncover whether some conceptual connections exist between discipline and authority and between discipline and violence. Other conceptual questions are: Is the apparent inability of experts to reach a consensus on what constitutes a family in itself a generator of social problems? In what sense does a notion of "democracy," or democratic life, influence our conception of authority? Ultimately, we want to know whether the problems of discipline and the alleged breakdown of authority are genuine problems or only, at least in part, considered so because of their stipulative definitions.

In any study of this type, pertinent empirical data are selectively drawn, and the types of empirical questions for which answers are needed depend considerably on the objectives of the study and the other types of questions deemed worth pursuing. Obviously, information is needed about discipline problems, trends, types of schools involved, nature of the offenses, consequences of the problems, coping strategies and remedial measures, and other pertinent information. Who are the youth involved, and what are their backgrounds? Are some teachers more prone to experience classroom disciplinary problems than others? What effect does certain types of crime and delinquency in the community have on the schools?

Some empirical questions overlap with explanatory ones. Are there certain structural or organizational features about school systems themselves that may precipitate discipline problems? The same question could be raised about the family. Perhaps discipline problems are symbolic of some deeper malady in our institutional structure, or are these problems largely what they seem to be and no more? Maybe disciplinary problems could, at least in part, be manifestations of some important functions that remain largely unrecognized. Could it be that certain types of disciplinary problems are ways that youth initially assert their independence from adult authority and thereby develop a sense of autonomy and social responsibility? Thus convincing explanations are needed for a host of puzzling questions.

When questions are raised about what specifically should be done about problems of discipline, violence, or vandalism, such questions are normative of the prescriptive variety. In other words, recommendations of various types, either about policies, plans, or techniques, are prescriptions stating what should be done or proposals outlining acceptable patterns of behavior likely to bring about desirable ends. Thus when disciplinary classroom problems erupt, a teacher may accept prescriptions that endorse certain plans for restoring order and better learning conditions. Administrators disseminate regulations that prescribe acceptable student conduct. Some parents have a list of rules for their children to obey; other parents let the rules emerge out of the situation as conditions seem to warrant; and still others are largely permissive and nonprescriptive.

Questions of justification and evaluation are also normative but serve different functions. What should be the purpose of disciplinary measures? Of authority structures? Acceptable answers to these questions need to be more than a bold assertion; the answers need justification. In other words, cogent grounds are needed for any claims advanced before purposes should be adopted. Are there certain values to which teachers may appeal in support of certain disciplinary practices? If so, then on what grounds were those values chosen?

Evaluation questions, in assessing the worth of something, seek answers to the effectiveness of policies, activities, and programs as the following questions suggest. In what ways can typical disciplinary codes be improved? How can more cooperative and fruitful relations be developed between school and home by greater attention to patterns of authority? How can authority structures in the home coordinate more closely with those in school? Although the pursuit of these questions successfully would require data and would eventually result in prescriptions and recommendations for improvements, the questions are primarily evaluation.

Purposes and Scope

Since this book's purpose is to get at the root of disciplinary problems, it is necessary to show the problems in their full range and ramifications of school and home. Thus this book relates the problems of discipline and violence to changing conceptions of authority, and these problems are explained, at least in part, by the theory of authority advanced in chapter 3. The child's first confrontation with authority is in the home, and authority patterns established there can be highly influential in the student's attitudes toward school authorities. Changing conceptions of authority can be viewed by examining what it means to grow up in America today and why former patterns of authority have broken down. Because prevailing theories are inadequate to fully explain these disruptions, I offer an alternative analysis and explanation that culminates in specific proposals for improving relations between the school and family.

Violence is examined not only because it is a critical problem in some schools and families but because it represents an extreme case of disciplinary breakdown and therefore enables the reader to envision the full range of disciplinary problems and make comparisons with the more commonplace ones. Violence also tests the authority of school and family differently than ordinary discipline problems; it extends the scope and types of moral, legal, and educational issues with which these institutions must face.

In contrast to many writers, I do not assume that a breakdown of authority, growing disciplinary problems, or the increase in violence are always harmful or unwarranted. Institutions sometimes need disruptive conflicts whenever orderly mechanisms of change and reform prove ineffectual. Those cases in which certain forms of disruption may be warranted and the grounds for making such assertions will be explored in considerable detail and compared to more common cases in which such claims cannot be established.

Although I agree with the public that the problems in these areas are serious, they are not always serious in the way that the public or educators seem to think. My thesis is that the problems are incipient manifestations of rather large-scale changes in school and family as well as changes in ideologies and basic ways of thinking about these institutions. Whether these changes are desirable depend on our ideals for the future and what is considered worthwhile.

In the next chapter, a panoramic view, drawn from multiple sources, shows what it means to grow up in America today in relation to authority patterns. The meaning varies depending on social class, race, ethnicity, and other factors; but to the extent that a national culture is promoted largely by the media, certain commonalities can be found despite the intervention of these other variables. Both commonalities and differences will be considered.

Since the book's framework is built on authority, it is vital to evaluate carefully the leading interpretations of authority. Doing so in chapter 3 leads to my presentation and defense of the theory of authority to be employed throughout the book. This theory is used to answer the explanatory questions previously listed and others yet to be introduced; it will also provide a framework for placing discipline and violence in a broad, meaningful perspective; finally, it will serve as a connecting link to perceive interrelations and sources of conflict between school and home.

Chapter 4 examines problems of discipline in school and home and then evaluates promising theories of discipline and relates them to the conceptions of authority developed in the previous chapter. It will be shown that many leading theories fail to meet the criteria essential to render them fully defensible, and alternatives to these theories will be proposed. The criteria will emphasize neglected and overlooked educational, moral, and cognitive standards.

The extent of violence and the characteristics of violent behavior are explored in chapter 5. It is necessary to ascertain what counts as violence in contrast to such seemingly cognate behavior as force, coercion, and aggression. Different explanatory theories of violence are evaluated and the basis, if any, is assessed for morally justifying certain types of violence.

My theory of authority is then applied in chapter 6 to the restructuring of authority in the family and to doing so in the school in chapter 8. It will be shown how authority figures can reconstruct their thinking and attitudes and how their roles and relationships with children can also be modified. These changes should help get at the sources of and reduce discipline and violence problems.

In light of these predicted changes, a set of policy proposals and recommendations is made in chapter 7 for improving relations between school and family. This is done by applying my theory of authority to reduce conflict and unnecessary strain between parents and educators over the child's schooling.

The last chapter will draw on futuristic studies and project our findings through the 1980s to indicate possible opportunities and hazards and the likely changes in authority patterns in American schools and homes.

Notes

1. Stanley M. Elam, ed., *A Decade of Gallup Polls of Attitudes Toward Education 1969-1978* (Bloomington, Indiana: Phi Delta Kappa, 1978).

2. "NEA Survey Investigates Teacher Attitudes, Practices," *Phi Delta Kappan* 62 (September 1980):49.

3. School Law *Newsletter* 5 (1975):167.

4. National Education Association, "Educational Neglect: Research Papers for Conference on Educational Neglect" (Washington, D.C.: National Education Association, 1975), p. 1.

5. Birch Bayh, chairman, *Challenge for the Third Century: Education in a Safe Environment—Final Report on the Nature and Prevention of School Violence and Vandalism* (Washington, D.C.: Government Printing Office, 1977), p. 12.

6. Interested readers may want to check this claim by surveying recent publications. See the bibliography in Malcolm Saunders' *Class Control and Behavior Problems* (London: McGraw-Hill Company United Kingdom Limited, 1979), pp. 213-223.

2 Growing Up in America: Authority and Autonomy

For the young, growing up is a time of fears and tears, hope and exuberance, illusions and intoxication. For their elders, it is a time of joys and exasperations. And it is only natural, for parents to be genuinely concerned about their child's education. But as Paul Goodman observed, "Fundamentally, there is no right education except growing up into a worthwhile world. Indeed, our excessive concern with problems of education at present simply means that the grown-ups do not have such a world."[1]

Perhaps that is true for some adults, that is, they lack such a "worthwhile world" and seek to create a special province for youth, if only for a time; other adults, however, have fewer misgivings and seek to transmit and preserve worthwhile features of the world of past and present.

The problematic tasks of growing up in America today are structured within a framework of authority, and it is within the various forms and functions of this framework that the child eventually grows from dependence to independence, from heteronomy to autonomy. It is generally considered that before one can be said to have "grown up," to be thought mature, that one needs to become increasingly independent from parents and peers, to carve out the direction for one's life while still not renouncing or openly rebelling against authority figures and thereby calling the rebellion itself the proof of independence. Thus though the child faces many important tasks, one of the most important is the hazardous search for independence and a growing measure of autonomy within a normative framework of authority. Thus this chapter first examines this framework of authority before investigating some pertinent findings in the child's growth from dependence to independence. Then it looks more carefully at the concept of autonomy and to what extent it can be defended as a worthwhile educational goal and how the commitment to autonomy may involve youth in some difficult decisions.

Authority Types

Authority presupposes a normative order not only in which one can appeal in cases of dispute over rules and laws but one where social life takes place and models for codes of conduct are approved. This will be clarified as authority types are looked at in the life of the growing child. *Authority types* here means that authority serves different forms and functions; each function may be served by one person (as judge) or one person may perform more than one function (parents). Authority types serve the following functions: expert, counselor,. role model, legislator, disciplinarian, and office holder.

Expert

One appeals to an authority who has specialized knowledge of a subject, whose expertise has been certified by some appropriate public so that confidence is assured in the expert's knowledgeability, veracity, and reliability in reporting findings. Advanced industrial societies greatly depend on the testimony of experts, and no citizen of these societies is immune to their influence. Since experts do not always agree, disputes may raise difficult problems of adjudication. In some cases other experts are consulted and majority opinion is followed; in other cases policymakers choose the expert advice that accords more closely with the consequences sought; and in still other instances, as in some cases of political, economic, and religious questions, those experts are sought who support one's own ideology.

The skeptical, well-educated adult can usually sort out the claims of the so-called experts, but the young child is in an especially vulnerable position and must initially take on face-value what seem to be the all-wise and knowing pronouncements of parents. But by the adolescent years, some youth find their peers wiser and less foolish and certainly not old-fashioned like their parents; then in young adulthood parental experience and insight may be appreciated again while still recognizing its limitations.

The notion of expertise is usually that of appealing to an authority in one circumscribed area of competence and assessing, if not always utilizing, the competence of the authority. But for the child the parents are seemingly all-knowing: their expertise is encyclopedic in scope and gives them god-like qualities. However, a serious problem arises as to how authority is to be justified because authority introduces the child not only to information but language, logic, and method, which provide the indispensable basis for the formation of beliefs and the evaluation of the claims of authority.[2] It seems that in human development not only that many beliefs must be acquired without justification but it is problematic how the veracity of authority itself can be assured—and it would be circular to again appeal to authority. A certain degree of cognitive autonomy would be needed before authority could be adequately checked; however, if authorities provide the means for checking these claims, how can one even know with any certainty that the verification conclusions were not also preordained by the methods and content authorities instilled? The child is introduced by parents into a public form of discourse, a linguistic community, in which the proper locutions are approved and incorrect ones are disapproved or corrected. Of course, we could hypothesize that some experts may not want children to learn the skills needed to eventually check on their expertise, and therefore, when they teach, they speak falsely and instill rules that are not theirs. But if they acutally did so, it would lead to a state of confusion, and no sense could be made by the child of the larger community of discourse to which he is introduced. Thus without habitual veracity by adults, there could be no linguistic community in which the young would be inducted, and therefore the possibilities for education would vanish. This should not be confused with a different situation in which an expert may not reveal all she knows either because the information is classified, considered family secrets, or allegedly harmful.

Thus the growth from total dependence on parents to autonomy involves maturation, increased experience, and the cultivation of competencies needed to check the claims of authorities. It is through socialization and formal and informal education that these results are achieved.

Counselor

A counselor is an adviser. "Counseling" refers to many occupational roles: supervisory duties at a summer camp, a counselor-at-law, someone who advises students on academic matters, or on career choices, and someone who gives therapy. But parent as counselor does not exactly coincide with any of these roles, though obviously some may represent what some teachers do in their relations with students.

What is the difference between parent as expert and parent as counselor? Both relations presuppose that parents have knowledge and skills of some type to impart. In order to advise, one may give pertinent information about a problem or a decision that needs to be made, and recommendations may also be made as to the most appropriate or wisest course of conduct. What makes the parental-counseling relation unique is the affectional bond between parent and child. It is true that some teachers strive to cultivate humanistic relations with students, which may lead to caring and treating students as whole persons, but it does not lead to the affectional bonds that grow out of consanguine relations and a sense of ultimate responsibility for the child's welfare. These responsibilities are both legal and moral, and are tied rather closely to what parenthood means in a particular culture.

Parents as counselors are treated as authorities because children ask them for advice and judgment; the soundness of the advice and judgment is not the critical factor here but only the act of entering into a counseling relationship. To the child, the parent not only has expertise but can also bring this expertise to bear in a counseling relation in helping arrive at a set of recommendations. Sometimes parents do more than recommend: they admonish, criticize, order, threaten punishments, or promise rewards. Counseling can be considered part of discipline—at least in some of the modern forms of discipline, as discipline involves more than the application of rules and the use of rewards and punishment; it may also involve advice about how to organize one's behavior in a manner designed to achieve desired ends.

Parents may lose some of their authority function or see them erode as the child grows older and finds in peers, teachers, and other adults a source of authority functions to which she may turn. After the child enters school, authority as expertise may be transferred partly to educators as the child is introduced to organized bodies of knowledge. Counseling, in different forms, is not only offered by teachers and guidance counselors but by peer groups, and it is these latter groups that assume an increasingly large share of the counseling in the lives of youth as they question their parents' judgment, beliefs, and values. But even peers cannot usually provide the affectional counseling bond of the parents and the maintenance of this bond even when the young are not a "success" in the larger world. Thus the authority of parents as counselors may not only be an essential role in helping to form the child's judgment and decision-making ability but it may nourish a foundation of emotional health.

Model

A model is something or someone held up for purposes of guidance or imitation. A person may be considered a standard of excellence to be imitated. One not only ascribes certain desirable traits to the model but may give the model deference as one would do with other forms of authority. In contrast to appeals to authority from motives of obligation or fear, one may attempt to emulate certain aspects of admired behavior that an authority exemplifies. The young child may use older siblings, playmates, or parents for modeling.

Although explanations of the child's acquisition of language are still open to debate, Moerk analyzed the language interaction in middle-class homes in which the child ranged in age from twenty to sixty months and found that the mother provides modeling opportunities and assists language learning by expanding, correcting, and second-guessing what the child has in mind.[3]

A high degree of masculine-role adoption seems to be related to the father's presence or that of some significant adult male and the boy's receiving positive feedback for appropriate male-role behavior.[4] And when the father is not involved in the family, according to one study, his daughter is likely to have sex-role development problems.[5]

According to Bandura, social learning can be explained by principles of imitation and modeling. A child watches a person who serves as a model perform some act is more likely to behave in a similar manner if given an opportunity to do so.[6] Both the characteristics of observer and model influence social learning. The model must be a significant person in the eyes of the observer; and the observer needs to be attentive to what the model does and have the ability to perform the modeled act.

Whenever the modeled behavior is considered undesirable, the parents may likely discourage or punish the child for exhibiting it. But whether the modeled behavior is deemed appropriate or not, the child's social-learning pattern is to use the selected model as an authority for the imitated traits. Thus modeling can be a significant process in learning a language and acquiring character traits and acceptable behavior.

Legislator

A *legislator* is one who makes laws usually for a political unit. Clearly, one cannot participate in making laws unless authorized by one's position to do so. Similarly, parents and teachers impose law-like pronouncements on children that take the form of rules that serve as authoritative regulations of conduct, practices, and procedures. Whereas legislators leave the enforcement of laws to other bodies and agencies, parents and teachers usually attempt to enforce the rules they prescribe by imposing sanctions, though they may at times enlist the help of others in doing so.

Those who make the rules are establishing a normative network for conduct and utilizing rules as a source of control over others. To exercise control is to restrain, direct, or command; it is a case of having power over another. But one could exercise power over another without having the authority to do so, as in the case of abduction. Parents and teachers are authorized to make rules within a certain domain that may not always be clearly defined; however, they are unauthorized to develop rules whose responsibility lies with others (for example, administrators, school boards, social workers), or to make rules that violate children's rights. Thus the authorization to make rules is a use of legitimate power, and obviously, not all uses of power are authorized.

The child's understanding of rule-making functions varies, according to Piaget, with the developmental stage.[7] In the earliest stage, which is motor and individual in character, the rules are primarily those that grow out of the child's early neuromuscular development. Between the ages of two and five, the child imitates the rules of others but either plays by himself or he plays with others without trying to win. Thus he imitates rules but practices them in accordance with his own fantasy. Since at this stage the child regards rules as sacred and eternal, any attempted alteration is interpreted as a transgression.

Between the ages of seven and eight, a less egocentric and more socially oriented outlook develops. The child now tries to win, and he also shows concern for the mutual control and unification of rules—although his ideas about them are somewhat vague.

Mastery of the rules proceeds by degrees, and between the ages of eleven and twelve, the rules of the game have become fixed, and a high level of agreement on the rules can be found among the players. At this age children take pleasure in discussing rules and the principles on which they are based. They recognize that the rules are formed by mutual consent and that, once agreed to, they should be observed in playing the game; nevertheless, they realize that a majority can agree to change the rules. In other words, at this age children's attitudes and practices toward rules closely resemble those of adults.

Although other observers, especially Kohlberg,[8] have depicted these developmental stages differently, the important point is that parents and teachers, in exercising their legislative role, need to be cognizant of the child's distinctive conceptualization at the different stages; consequently, legislative authority, if it is to achieve its objectives, will have to be adapted to the child's emerging world view and thereby recognize that practices likely to prove effective at one stage will not necessarily prove so at another stage.

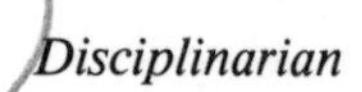

Disciplinarian

Legislators pass laws but delegate to other bodies the task of enforcement. Among the laws are those that establish the criminal-justice system and the law-enforcement machinery.

On the other hand, parents and teachers as authority figures not only serve in a legislative but also in a disciplinary capacity. Of course, it is true that the disciplinary function today is divided: it is not exercised solely by parents or localized in one institution. Parents have increasingly either delegated more disciplinarian authority or lost it to other institutions and agencies, and teachers have increasingly turned over recalcitrant disciplinary cases to administrators, truant officers, or juvenile courts.

Parents have the right to corporally punish their children so long as the punishment is reasonable and does not harm or injure the child. What is reasonable punishment would depend on the age of the child and the nature of the penalty. Sometimes the disciplinary function is voluntarily divided by the parents with the courts when parents need help to prevent their children from committing delinquent acts. This function is handled in all states by "disobedient-child" laws that permit parents to bring the child into court for failing to obey reasonable commands. But courts may refuse to intervene to regulate objectionable literature once it is brought into the home or require an adolescent to attend church, accompany parents on a vacation, or attend a private rather than public school.[9]

The decade of the seventies witnessed the greater recognition by the courts of student rights and the restriction of some disciplinary practices. Students could no longer be punished for public statements that administrators or teachers disapproved of because their right to speak is not only protected away from school but within school. Although some courts have ruled that students can wear their hair at any length they want, the courts have also held that school officials have the authority to establish reasonable dress codes. One area in which disciplinary powers of school authorities have been greatly limited is in the area of due process. Formerly, schools could develop rules, determine punishment, and administer it on the basis of decisions by school officials. Courts today have ruled that with serious offenses, due process must be observed. The form that it would take would depend on the seriousness of the offense, but in some cases school officials would be required to provide adequate notice, a hearing, the right to legal counsel, and the opportunity to cross-examine witnesses and challenge evidence.

One who is empowered with disciplinary authority may not necessarily be an effective disciplinarian but would expect her commands to be obeyed so long as the commands were reasonable. And what may count as "reasonable," at least in one sense, would be commands that are in keeping with the law. Thus any claims that a particular command (or a punishment) is unreasonable would be referred to the covering law. This process could be pushed back a step further, however, by challenging the law. It might be said that the law is not applicable in the case under consideration; it would then be necessary to show how the law actually applies to the disputed circumstances. On the other hand, the law may be said to be unfair, and if it can be shown to be unfair, it cannot be used to justify the particular disciplinary practice. What the courts could rule on would be whether the law is constitutional; it may be that the practice violates a constitutionally protected right. However, legal systems themselves do not inquire whether the distribution of a system of rights itself is just since the law is not the judge of the norm it defines. The law establishes a distribution of rights as a normative equilibrium for society. It is what those who legislate have stipulated as the normal condition of society, which they would by law preserve and, if lost, by law restore.

Revolutions, among other things, usually challenge the justice of the legal system. Other ways short of revolution, such as a constitutional convention, can challenge the legal system. More frequently, as with the civil disobeyer, the challenge is to a particular law and not the legal system as a whole. This was the case of the Amish, a religious group that migrated from Switzerland to the United States nearly 250 years ago in search of religious freedom. Education beyond the eighth grade, their religion teaches, is a deterrent to salvation and a violation of their community. Jonas Yoder and two other Amish residents of New Glarus, Wisconsin, refused to send their children to high school. A lower state court upheld the state requirements. The Wisconsin Supreme Court reversed the lower court and exempted the Amish from school attendance beyond the eighth grade. The case was appealed to the U.S. Supreme Court, and in 1972, in *Wisconsin* v. *Yoder*, the Court ruled that members of the Amish sect are not subject to the state compulsory-education laws. In order to deny the Amish their free exercise of religion, the state must show a compelling reason that their nonattendance would create a clear danger to society. The case was settled on the grounds of religious freedom and could in no way be construed as a *general* challenge to the validity of compulsory-education laws. Neither does it appear that any group or party who believes that the public schools are imposing an alien majoritarian doctrine on their children are likely, by this claim alone, to secure relief from observing compulsory-attendance laws.

The connection that this case has with disciplinary authority is its challenge to the law's application to the Amish on grounds of violating their First Amendment right to religious freedom. Thus this is a dispute that determined whether Amish parents or the state has the right to discipline and regulate the educational experiences of Amish children beyond the eighth grade.

Although disputes may arise over where lines may be drawn among the different authorities in their regulation of the child, anyone who holds disciplinary authority expects to be obeyed unless the right to exercise that authority can be successfully challenged. Commands are nugatory when given by someone not in authority and carry no legal or moral backing and can be enforced only through coercion. Thus disciplinary powers must be legitimized or else they are no more than coercive acts. In some cases the person may be exercising legitimate authority, but the youth being disciplined refuses to authorize or recognize the legitimacy of the disciplinarian. But this is not a legal or moral problem but a motivational one—a matter of the effectiveness of the authority (assuming none of the disciplinary practices used by the authority are morally questionable). On the other hand, those who are to be disciplined may participate in the legislative function with the disciplinary authority by cooperatively developing the rules by which they will be governed. Parents who use one of the modern techniques of child rearing and progressive educators would more likely employ this approach. But in many school systems teachers may be restricted in applying this approach because external authorities formulate rules and regulations to which teachers are expected to comply. Thus in most situations discipline in school and home is not an exclusive prerogative of any group but is divided among a number of authorities.

Office Holder

Generally, it is assumed that an office holder, at least in an industrial state, is a member of a bureaucracy. The objectives of bureaucracies, according to Weber, are to eliminate irrational and emotional elements, to elevate precision, speed, continuity, unambiguity, and to encourage the subordination of personnel to the administrative hierarchy in order to reduce friction and keep material and personnel costs at a minimum.

Following Weber's interpretation, bureaucracies organize their offices according to the hierarchal principle in which each office is under the supervision and control of a higher one.[10] The lower office has the right to appeal and issue a statement of grievance to the higher one. Qualifications for each office are specified in writing. The office is regulated by written rules that define the sphere of its authority. In order to meet qualifications for the office, one needs specialized training. The objective is to ensure that appointments will be based on merit rather than wealth, influence, or other extraneous factors. Promotion is based on seniority, achievement, or both; employment in the system constitutes a career, and the office holder is protected against arbitrary dismissal.

But the teacher's position is not entirely bureaucratically organized. The teacher's classroom, although under the authority of the principal, is not usually closely supervised and cannot be thought of as following orders or serving as a line for implementing policy decisions because the goals of the school system cannot be readily quantified and measured. Moreover, administrative rules (other than such things as taking attendance and monitoring students) are not applicable to teaching, which contains many unpredictable factors and numerous teaching judgments. Finally, in contrast to a factory in which there is quality control, evaluation of teachers is difficult to devise and interpret.[11]

Despite criticisms of bureaucracies, not all aspects of bureaucracies have been harmful to schools. Corwin notes that formal rules have kept schools free from the patronage of corrupt city governments, helped centralize and standardize schools that enabled them to accommodate diverse waves of immigrants, and have kept the schools from disintegrating during periods of rapid change and cultural conflict.[12]

The undesirable aspects of bureaucracies seem to be perpetrated upon the teacher's office when some techniques of industry are applied to school systems. Frederick W. Taylor advocated the scientific study of jobs based on time studies of tasks, leading to the establishment of a standard time for each job and payment of wages in proportion to output.[13] Following Taylor's study, more systematic treatments dealt with the division of labor, specialization and departmentalization of functions, and managerial supervision.[14]

American businessmen, from their positions on school boards, pressured educators to adopt industrial-management principles in operating school systems, and from 1910 to 1929 these values and techniques were widely adopted in American education. The justification for such procedures was greater efficiency and economy.[15]

The analogy, however, between industry and education is not close and when applied too literally, leads to abuses and distortions of the teaching-learning process in the name of efficiency. Only certain aspects of education such as the business operations of school systems can operate effectively on this model.

Another model—this one emerged during the 1970s—focused not only on efficiency and economy but on improving the quality of education. The accountability movement developed as a result of growing public dissatisfaction over rising costs for education and the low achievement level of some students. Accountability places emphasis on output over inputs. The public wants to know that proportional benefits are accruing for dollars spent, both in terms of school business practices and student achievement on selected standardized tests. No attempt is made to consider the full range of educational outcomes such as aesthetic appreciation, affective changes, and the development of novel and creative approaches to problem solving.

Once again, the assumptions underlying accountability may lead to a mentality alien to the educational process. Accountability overemphasizes measurement, efficiency, and competitiveness; it may usher in educational engineering: the application of technology and government cost accounting to the obdurate problems of education. Concern is not with purposes of education but with means and techniques. While means should not be ignored and a close connection should be maintained between means and ends, the technocratic model of accountability tends to shape the educational process to fit an efficiency mold and thereby may tend to become fixated upon objective data and measurable performance. Thus, in order to overcome these weaknesses, the accountability movement needs to alter some of its theoretical assumptions and broaden the range of evaluative procedures employed.

The relation that these movements have to the teacher's authority as office holder is that teachers are part of bureaucratic school systems that were shaped first by the scientific-management approach and later by the accountability movement. Thus what is important in the teacher's office is partly defined by accountability.

But teachers may be expected to humanize education, which runs counter the impersonality fostered by bureaucracies; to individualize instruction, which may conflict with bureaucratic insistence on following rules applicable to everyone or to classifying students into predetermined categories.

If students do not respect the office of teacher, they may respect the teacher's expertise; and if they lack respect for expertise, they may respect or, more likely, fear negative sanctions. It is usually more promising, whenever possible, for the teacher to establish trust and goodwill.

This chapter has so far examined various authority types: expert, counselor, model, legislator, disciplinarian, and office holder. The process of growing up is structured within an authority framework, and the child encounters in varying degrees each of these authority types in her growth from dependence to independence. This independence is achieved within a framework of, and sometimes in oppositon to, authority.

The Development of Independence

From Dependence to Independence

Each person is usually expected to move from a state of dependence to one of independence. What constitutes "independence" varies from one culture to another: American culture, for instance, expects a greater degree of independence than Japanese culture, where greater group and family consciousness and less individualism is generally deemed desirable. Since in American culture, independence is highly valued, we will examine it closely in terms of the development from dependence to independence, the characteristics of independence, and the relationship of independence to authority types.

The human infant has a longer period of dependency than most animals; not only the length of time but its critical effect upon later development makes it of considerable concern for all those involved with children and youth. Rigidity and severity in feeding and weening infants can lead to dependency in early childhood years.[16] The more rejected the child feels, the more dependent he is likely to be.[17] Before the child can demonstrate an initial need for some independence, he needs to gain some skills in motor control and language, which begins about six years old when he can state his wants, show he can be negative (refusing to do something his parents tell him to do), and exercise control over eliminative processes.

Parents may be ambivalent: they want their child to grow but also want him to be subservient to their expectations; they hope their child will do the right thing but worry that he may get into trouble unless carefully supervised. This parental ambivalence may continue through the adolescent period, taking different forms, and causing the young person consternation except when family rules are established, understood by the child, and consistently and fairly enforced. At any age level there is an optimum range of parental control where too much may lead to submissiveness or later to rebelliousness and too little may result in immaturity and irresponsibility.[18]

With the adolescent years tension over freedom develops when the youth wants to be allowed more freedom while his parents search for the proper relationship between freedom and responsibility in developing codes of behavior. Social-class differences can be observed in rearing youth. Middle-class parents encourage more autonomy for boys and a greater role in decision making for girls than do lower-class parents.[19] Middle-class parents are likely to begin independence training and continue it through adolescence.[20]

Studies indicate that parents more frequently influence educational and occupational choice, while peers influence appearance, dress, and customs that determine peer acceptance.[21] Family conflicts are more likely to be over money, homework, and hair styles rather than basic values.[22] More slavish peer conformity seems to occur whenever parents are either extremely permissive or authoritarian.[23]

Thus certain types of child-rearing conditions seem to support the development of autonomy. Parental warmth and concern, a democratic level of concern, and consideration and consistency in rule enforcement are supportive conditions.[24] Autocratic or very lenient parents usually have children who are low in self-confidence and either dependent or rebellious.[25] Thus for the development of more autonomous behavior, democratic controls are needed to provide opportunities to make decisions and to learn skills of independence and self-reliance. And this takes place best in home where rules are consisent and adequately enforced.

Characteristics of Independence

The concept of independence may be easier to pin down than autonomy, but some difficulties also arise with independence. By starting with certain developmental tasks, the problem will likely be clearer. Havighurst speaks of certain tasks that arise at different periods in an individual's life; the successful achievement of these tasks leads to happiness while failure leads to unhappiness.[26] The tasks may arise from physical maturation, cultural pressures, or the individual's aspirations. The tasks are listed for six periods of development. While successful completion of all the tasks may make some contribution to healthy attitudes toward either oneself or others, the following tasks for adolescence are directly related to the achievement of independence: achieving emotional independence of parents and other adults; achieving assurance of economic independence; selecting and preparing for an occupation; preparing for marriage and family life; developing intellectual skills and concepts necessary for civic competence; desiring and achieving socially responsible behavior; and acquiring a set of values and an ethical system as a guide to behavior. Let us examine each in turn.

Achieving emotional independence of parents and adults differs from some of the other tasks because it is not readily measurable, and standards of achievement vary depending on what view of the emotions is held.[27] But if we take a cognitive view of the emotions, independence would more likely be achieved when the young bring their emotional life under rational assessment and thereby begin to understand their emotions and decide how they want to relate emotionally to the world and to their own interior life. They will come to understand that emotions are not magical, mysterious, or strange feelings to which one suddenly and involuntarily succumbs but that they are created by one's assessment of situations and the subsequent reaction to the situation. Thus to plunge from the high diving board may evoke fear in the beginning swimmer yet generate no appreciable fear in an experienced diver. Whereas the latter swimmer experiences confidence when approaching the board and can picture in his mind's eye a graceful dive, the former swimmer may tell himself that the dive will likely be unsuccessful and may cause injury and pain; these thoughts in turn evoke fear. With some diving success and recognition that he is evoking fear by the way he defines the situation, he then can gain better control over his fears. Just as youth, while listening sympathetically to their parents' views, can learn to form their own independent judgments, so too can they learn to begin creating their own emotional life by deciding what it is that deeply matters to them and how greatly they will concern themselves over what they value. It may be that their emotional responses to some situations resemble those of their parents; however, if they have gained some degree of emotional independence, the resemblance will be by choice because they have decided to make an emotional investment in the issues. Whereas if they feel that they are reacting the way they do because of a lack of emotional control or because of early socialization practices, then they lack emotional independence on the particular issues. Emotional independence, however, is a matter of degree and is not a developmental task that is completed by young adulthood; it continues into the life cycle where increasing independence is gained with greater experience and maturity.

Achieving assurance of economic independence is far easier to ascertain than emotional independence because definite standards exist and the achievement of standards can be measured. Some variation in the standards are a function of social class, and occasional divergences are based on individual and family aspirations, but certain behaviors would generally be accepted as reasonably clear indicators of emerging economic independence: developing career goals; achieving occupational skills; growing financial independence from the family; demonstrating skills in successfully managing one's financial affairs; and evidence of assuming responsibility for one's financial decisions and mistakes.

Selecting and preparing for an occupation is essential in gaining independence from family, promoting one's abilities, and making some contribution to society. Although parents, teachers, and other adults may advise about an occupation, the ultimate choice should be with the adolescent. And the choice should be based on a realistic assessment of career goals, one's abilities, and the actual opportunities in the chosen field rather than on peer pressure or media images.

Preparing for marriage and family life, ostensibly a reasonable developmental task, has become ambiguous and perplexing. It is not only that marriage is being delayed and is no longer always looked on as the capstone of young adulthood, what constitutes a family is no longer clear: the nuclear family, though still the prevailing form, is only one form among many. Today we find single-parent families, extended families, living-together arrangements (which include either a heterosexual couple or a homosexual couple), one elderly man with two or more elderly women, communes, and various forms of group "marriages." The diversity, rather than offering the young greater opportunities, may cause further consternation and confusion over sex roles and personal identity. From this perplexing state of affairs, some opt to remain single longer than planned—or even indefinitely. Thus one may decide not to prepare for marriage and family life or prepare for a very different type of family than earlier generations would sanction. Decisions are not based only on choices available but on one's value system and self-concept; therefore, without a clearly conceived and supportable value system, a young person is likely to drift dangerously or become embroiled in traumatic relationships for which he is unprepared to handle.

The adolescent needs to develop intellectual skills and concepts for civic competence in order to assume her citizenship role in the community independently of parents. Opinion is divided as to how this task is to be fulfilled by the schools. Earlier thinking suggested that a certain curriculum content would most likely provide the needed intellectual skills. The Committee of Seven of the American Historical Association recommended in 1899 that high-school student study four years of history; subsequent reports of national commissions advocated study of a broader range of social sciences, and knowledge of academic disciplines were no longer considered an end in itself but judged worthwhile more for their alleged instrumental value. A structure of the disciplines approach became popular in the 1960s in which students would be taught basic concepts and generalizations and shown how to conduct research on a miniature scale like social scientists. Thus rather than the usual history lesson, the student may go to the local courthouse to uncover his roots (family tree). Teaching of these inquiry skills shifted somewhat during the 1970s to a study of values and attitudes because of a belated recognition of the importance they play in shaping decision making; this in turn led to programs that encourage students to clarify and think through their values. Thus, in light of these changing approaches, there is no single way to promote this developmental task but rather many programs that compete for allegiance and funding.

The task of desiring and achieving socially responsible behavior is culturally relative (as is civic competence). In other words, the culture defines what is socially responsible behavior; and although cross-cultural norms exist, some norms are indigenous to a culture. Although some form of family life can be found in all cultures, the form that it takes and the acceptability of practices vary (such as whether monogamy or polygamy is sanctioned). The extent to which deviance from social norms is tolerated will depend considerably on tradition and the form of government. For instance, a tradition of persecuting those who hold minority religious views will likely promote fear and conformity, whereas governments that provide constitutionally protected rights encourage its citizens to have less trepidation in deviating from established norms or engaging in civil disobedience. Compliance with norms out of fear is not a moral motive; therefore, it is necessary to cultivate the moral maturity to want to act in a socially responsible manner. Opinion is divided whether the best way to accomplish this task is to accept a developmental approach (as those of Piaget or Kohlberg) and try to advance the student to a higher level through various types of cognitive strategies or to interpret the problem as one of incontinence or weakness of will and seek to strengthen personal resolve, moral fiber, and the ability to resist counter-inclinations.[28]

The acquisition of a set of values and an ethical system as a guide to behavior is a vital developmental task that begins early in life after a premoral or amoral stage. Some youth, however, may fixate at a lower stage and never achieve independence; others may be more successful after a lengthy period of struggle and costly mistakes. Yet some youth may have accepted a set of values, whether from their parents or someone else, without giving the decision serious thought. In my own experience in working with youth, I have found that most of them have acquired a set of values, but they may have difficulty articulating them and have seldom sought to rigorously reflect on their values and justify why they subscribe to them. The reason seems to be not so much an indifference or lethargy as a lack of adequate guidance in conducting such an assessment. Some of today's values-education programs may help to overcome this deficiency.

Now that we have surveyed a number of developmental tasks that will likely promote independence, it may prove valuable to see how independence relates to authority. Thus in the next section the authority types discussed earlier will be related to independence.

Independence and Types of Authority

Each individual who strives for independence will not likely become independent without developing certain basic skills and competencies that are created within the framework of various authority patterns. Earlier it was observed that autocratic or very lenient parents usually have children who are low in self-confidence and are either dependent or rebellious; thus parental warmth and concern coupled with rules that are consistent and adequately enforced make for a healthier form of parental authority.

The process of becoming independent also involves assuming some of the different authority types for oneself, to increasingly become one's own authority and, as a young adult's new responsibilities should call for it (as when one becomes a parent or a teacher), to play the appropriate authority-type role to the young of the next generation. But how does one begin to assume the different authority types for oneself? The process is not an either-or one in the sense that either authority figures play these roles or else one does it for herself. Rather, it is a transitional period that may be gradual and relatively smooth for some youth and fraught with trauma and emotional conflict for others.

Specifically, looking at the different authority types in relation to growing independence, the adolescent faced with the need for expertise, has long passed the stage of virtual complete dependence on parents and now seeks expert knowledge from other sources: parents, teachers, older friends, the media, libraries and museums, and interviews or correspondence with experts. But increasingly the shift from adolescence to young adulthood means ultimately greater decision making for oneself and the growth in skills in the assessment of expertise. These skills are developed through a combination of personal experience and organized instruction designed to develop critical abilities. Thus the transition from dependence to independence is the shift from virtually complete reliance on parental expertise to the ability to select a variety of experts wisely, weigh their judgments, and make one's own decisions in light of those judgments and any other pertinent considerations.

Counseling goes beyond expertise and introduces elements of caring and empathy. Some youth experience ambivalence and tension in the authority relationship of counselor, which parents use not only to dispense advice and admonish offspring but to form emotional bonds of empathy and caring in times of trouble. But the counseling relationship may also be transferred in part to peers, older friends, professional counselors, and psychotherapists. Except during periods of emotional breakdown or trauma, the youth is less dependent on this relationship because he is increasingly able to handle his own problems. And when entering such a relationship, the counselor expects the youth to begin to assume adult responsibilities rather than maintain earlier dependencies. Thus one test of the counseling relationship is whether it promotes greater independence and personal responsibility.

Drawing on authority as models for one's behavior is not a process that is relinquished in young adulthood; rather, new and more appropriate models are chosen as guides for shaping appropriate behavior in emerging adult roles. Thus the task of preparing for a career leads to the choice of a successful person in the chosen occupation or profession. Upon entering the law, the neophyte would likely choose a prominent attorney on which to model behavior. It would be better that the model is someone who can actually guide the young person's career rather than someone in the media admired from afar. Once the neophyte gains a certain level of confidence, she may gradually or abruptly divest herself of the model and strike out on her own, developing her own style and approach to the field; later, there may be a reconciliation with the formerly treasured model and an affectionate recognition of the role the model has played in her career development. The problem for women is that female mentors are scarce, and those that could serve as mentors are frequently so occupied by the struggle for survival in a male-dominated occupational world that they are unable to be good mentors to younger women.

Levinson, in his study of young male adults, found that the mentoring relationship is often situated in a work setting, the mentor is usually eight to fifteen years older than the protégé and the relationship lasts two or three years on the average.[29] The mentor functions as a transitional figure and represents a mixture of parent and peer but not exclusively either one. The mentor can serve one or more functions: teacher, sponsor, host and guide, or counselor. The most crucial function is that the mentor support and facilitate "the realization of the Dream."[30] The "dream" is initially a vague vision, poorly articulated to reality, of what he would like to make of his life. Thus a developmental task is that of more clearly defining his dream and finding ways to realize it. It is the mentor who helps define the dream and provides needed moral support and encouragement. Thus the mentor serves as a vital model in the newly emergent developmental tasks of young adulthood.

Authority as legislator has been transformed from childhood to young adulthood, for in the latter stage it is generally recognized that rules are made by mutual consent and, though they should be complied with when one is engaged in activities that are rule governed, a majority can agree to change the rules. A rule is a type of generalization used to prescribe conduct, action, or usage. A distinction can be made, as John Searle notes, between "regulative" and "constitutive" rules.[31] *Regulative* rules regulate antecedent or independently existing forms of behavior. *Consitutive* rules not only regulate but also create or define new forms of behavior. Etiquette would be an example of regulative rules; sports or games such as football or chess are examples of constitutive rules because the rules make possible the playing of such sports or games. In other words, constitutive rules create the games, whereas regulative rules control preexisting forms of behavior.

The growing independence of youth places them in a position from which they can in some cases develop their own rules for activities and in other cases decide whether rational grounds can be found for the rules governing certain activities and, where options exist, thereby decide whether they want to participate in these activities.

Rule-governed behavior can be thought of as rational in the sense that reasons can be offered; reasons can be given for abiding by a rule in terms of its ability to achieve the desired end and its efficacy in doing so. Dispute at this point could arise over whether the claims for the rule can be supported. The dispute is settled by reference to authoritative case studies demonstrating that following the rule achieves the stated objectives.

Another type of dispute is one in which the ends, which rule following is designed to fulfill, are questioned. The question of the appropriateness of the rules and the reasonableness of following them is put aside until the question of ends is successfully adjudicated.

Thus the young adult finds herself in a world proliferated with rules; however, many of these rules are not applicable because they govern occupations, statuses, and role relationships of which the individual is not a member. Thus rules applicable to immigrants, airline pilots, or recipients of social security govern the specific activities of those who fall under those categories; other rules such as those pertaining to citizenship functions, are more universal. Independence, in this instance, is the ability to evaluate the grounds for rules, deciding which rules to accept and act on, and in some cases make rules for oneself or others (once the individual becomes an office holder).

It might be assumed that authority as disciplinarian vanishes upon becoming a young adult; but this would be to overlook the network of authority relations in which the young are embedded and the disciplinary functions, especially socialization, that these authority relations exact. Socialization does not terminate in adolescence but continues in young adulthood with the responsibilities of marriage, rearing the young, and gaining vocational competency.

Socialization in marriage is achieved more often by trial and error or the use of models than by any systematic instruction (in contrast to initial employment in some occupations). Young parents have to exercise disciplinary controls over their behavior if they expect to promote the family's common good. In other words, young adults learn new disciplinary controls because they relinquish their single status; now, as a newly married couple, their status is neither dependent nor independent: it is largely interdependent. It therefore requires self-discipline to adapt successfully to these new roles, which demand breaking any dependency relations with parents while cultivating more mature emotional bonds. With the birth of their first child, the young couple will learn to serve as a disciplinary authority to their offspring.

Authority, as noted earlier, is also a manifestation of the office held; and as the young person enters the occupational world and develops her vocational competencies, she will begin to assume offices—perhaps modest ones at first before making the long trek up the occupational ladder to those positions in the organization that carry more authority. On the way up, however, the person is subject to the use of authority by those in the hierarchy and must therefore decide whether the use of authority is rationally grounded and ultimately whether she wishes to comply with the requirements or pay the consequences for noncompliance. At the same time she may be groomed for a higher position and would need to learn and be socialized into appropriate role behavior befitting the new assignment. Thus at this stage of development, the young adult is probably assuming her first full-time office with all the rights and responsibilities it carries while learning new roles and expectations (as promulgated by higher-office holders) in order to advance in the system.

The process of becoming independent, therefore, involves learning to assume some of the various authority types for oneself while still being subject to various forms of authority with the authority no longer in the parental home but in the workplace and in one's own young family (although it should not be assumed, as has been the case until recently, that the choice to remain single is not a mature one or represents a failure to assume adult responsibilities).

But how does the growth from dependence to independence within frameworks of various authority types represent a growth as well from heteronomy to autonomy? To say that the individual has become increasingly independent may not be synonymous with increasing autonomy. Although we have tried to relate independence to developmental characteristics within various authority types, this approach has not been employed in the literature with the concept of autonomy. Yet autonomy is an important concept because some educators have viewed it as a culmination of a sort for the entire educational process. Thus we need to examine autonomy to see the part it plays in the lives of the young.

The Concept and Goal of Autonomy

Autonomy has been advocated by diverse groups, from analytical philosophers[32] to libertarians.[33] Autonomy has been variously expressed; but one of the more commonly accepted interpretations is Dearden's notion that "a person is autonomous to the degree that he shows initiative in making independent judgments related both to thought and to action."[34] Learning how to learn, he says, is valuable as a means to autonomy. Frankena holds that to be autonomous, the individual must increasingly make firsthand judgment; he is self-governing but makes judgments from the impersonal standpoint wherein judgments are open to independent appraisal by others.[35] For Peters, autonomy involves several conditions.[36] It not only means that one has adopted a way of life independently from the dictates of others but that it has been subjected to assessment and criticism; it also means that an autonomous person can uphold his position despite counter-inclinations and thereby suggests courage, integrity, and determination.

One can speak not only of autonomy in a cognitive sense but about moral and emotional autonomy as well. Some have suggested that it is not enough to say, especially with moral autonomy, that self-determination is equivalent to being autonomous. It is necessary, according to Greenville Wall, to construe autonomy as based on rational self-determination that presupposes the existence of public criteria of judgment.[37] This is closely related to Alan Gewirth's position in which he claims that to be autonomous is to act according to rationally justifiable norms that one accepts for oneself insofar as one is rational.[38]

In contrast to the preceding views of moral autonomy, Kohlberg's cognitive-development approach presents six stages in which the last two are autonomous, postconventional, and based on prinicples held apart from the authority of groups and individuals subscribing to these principles.[39] The fifth stage is a social-contract, legalistic orientation with utilitarian overtones in which right action has been construed in terms of basic individual rights examined and agreed upon by society. This stage is also relativistic and utilizes procedural rules for achieving a consensus, whereas the sixth stage is a universal-principle orientation in which what is right is established by decisions of conscience congruent with self-chosen ethical principles that appeal to universality, consistency, and comprehensiveness. The abstract ethical principles may take the form of the Golden Rule or Kant's categorical imperative.

Emotional autonomy, the third type, has been described by Brian Crittenden as not only self-mastery in the control of one's emotions, feelings, and desires whenever emotionally involved in situations but emotional detachment from persons and things.[40] It is an ideal in which one carefully avoids loving or loving too much. He cites the long history of this form of autonomy in the life of Socrates and the doctrines of the Cynics and Stoics.

Problems with Autonomy

Despite the attractive features of autonomy, each of the three types raise certain problems that are not readily resolvable. John Wilson notes in terms of cognitive autonomy that becoming an apprentice, where one takes advice and knowledge from others, would not count according to Dearden's definition (which, it will be recalled, it based on making independent judgments pertaining to both thought and action); yet we want to say that apprenticeship is a good thing.[41] Intellectual autonomy may also be very demanding—perhaps more demanding than most adults are capable of handling—if it means not only making one's own judgments but determining what constitutes adequate evidence and supportable grounds for truth claims. Most people fall back on the authority of experts without being able to evaluate the validity of their claims.

Autonomy as an education goal could not be universalized if it conflicted with the political principles of government, especially those of totalitarian states. In the Soviet Union, for instance, autonomy is considered to be largely an aberrration of capitalistic societies; instead, they would allow development to Piaget's second stage but discourage development to his third stage. Of course, it might be thought that this is a prima-facie case of the political system's weakness; however, to make that assumption, it would have to be based on having earlier established the universal validity of autonomy as a goal (which we have not done). All that could be concluded so far is that the goal of autonomy is more likely to be promoted in liberal democratic societies with a long tradition of individualism. The latter point about tradition is important because modern Japan, a democratic nation, does not advocate autonomy as an educational goal because of an extended tradition of group consciousness and loyalty that suppresses emergent propensities toward individualism.

Difficulties can be found not only for cognitive but moral autonomy as well. In Kohlberg's last two autonomous stages, only an isolated few have attained the sixth stage, and most people do not get beyond stage 4 (a "law-and-order" orientation that consists of doing one's duty, showing proper respect for authority, and helping maintain the social order for its own sake). Despite some success by Kohlberg in developing such thinking exercises as moral dilemmas to overcome arrested development or advance a young person through the stages more rapidly, only a minority actually reaches the autonomous stages.[42] Thus *ought* implies *can* and therefore moral autonomy, at least in Kohlberg's system, can be a goal only for a morally elite group or a select minority of any population that would promote this system of moral development. Nevertheless, there may be nothing wrong with this select goal, for schools with programs for the intellectually gifted have special goals for this group. What strikes some as objectionable with moral autonomy is that morality, in contrast to intellectual activities, is a shared goal that everyone is supposedly capable of achieving. But this is not entirely true, however, because different standards are developed for children, the mentally retarded, psychotics, and, to some extent, for alcoholics, addicts, and sociopaths.

Perhaps this question can be approached in a related manner. Kurt Baier argues that no one, even in a democracy, engages in universal individual self-legislation in moral matters (as Kant advocates), and therefore moral autonomy so interpreted cannot be the aim of moral education.[43] Baier contends that it is logically impossible for each citizen to be subject to the will of another and therefore there would be no laws including self-legislation. What would result would be independent individual's developing rules and maxims—not laws—to which each would subject himself and no other. A monarchy might have one person who was literally autonomous, but no one else would be. But in a democratic society, Baier notes, each member, even if she has a role in making the law has no more than a share and is therefore subject to the will of others. Only under the highly implausible condition of living in a society in which all legislative wills coincide would one have moral autonomy; thus the best one could hope for would be to be subject to legislative wills not greatly divergent from one's own.

In light of this conclusion, Baier proposes that moral autonomy be reinterpreted as a form of self-mastery, which he defines as a tendency to conform in one's behavior to decisions about what to do and to maintain control over impulses that would conflict with these decisions.[44] Self-mastery includes self-control, strength of will (resistance to temptations and threats), willpower (resistance to pain and fatigue), tenacity, and resoluteness. Moral self-mastery can still be a legitimate goal for moral education, he believes, without holding that everyone is capable of judging moral matters for himself. In other words, one could still maintain an elitist view in the realm of moral judgment.

Baier's belief, however, that it is logically impossible for each citizen to be subject to only the laws that she has made is technically correct but overlooks the freedom in democratic societies to make independent judgments. He overlooks the citizen's right to choose a way of life (so long as the way is not legally prohibited) and the opportunities to protest and repeal laws through established forms of grievance or through acts of civil disobedience. As for Baier's self-mastery as an appropriate moral goal, it would assure certain forms of behavioral autonomy but not cognitive autonomy. But such self-mastery, especially in light of Kohlberg's findings might be all that it would be reasonable to establish for moral-education programs, except that evidence from other programs such as values clarification indicate that students of various ages, when supplied with exercises geared to their interests and abilities, can clarify their own values and grasp more fully how their values influence their actions. Even Kohlberg's stages 5 and 6 may be examples of cognitive autonomy about moral decisions but not moral autonomy itself, which would likely require the ability to act regularly and consistently on the basis of those decisions—and there is no assurance that individuals would so act because insufficient attention is paid to moral motivation, the discrepancy between knowing the good and doing the good. Even to propose such a program for an elite assumes that moral autonomy is a worthwhile goal—an assumption that we have yet to show is entirely warranted. But such considerations will be temporarily deffered until problems with emotional autonomy are examined.

Emotional autonomy may include, in part, characteristics Baier cites as self-mastery, and it would be a kind of emotional detachment in relation to others and to things. It would offer the individual an emotional independence and self-sufficiency. And no doubt it would allow the individual to experience adversity in financial and interpersonal relations without becoming greatly disturbed, anxious, fearful, or grieved because of his emotional detachment. On the other hand, some may look on this detachment as a form of desensitization and indifference, if not callousness; it may, in other words, conflict with certain moral responsibilities toward others based on concern and commitment. Perhaps the emotionally autonomous person could perform his moral responsibilities out of a sense of duty or because he believes that the act is right but not from a sense of caring and commitment. Here again, the emotionally autonomous person may be better prepared to navigate the dangerous shoals of life and suffer less debilitating trauma as a consequence of his detachment and desensitization; yet he may also exhibit character traits that some would find unadmirable. On the other hand, the opposite extreme of failing to gain emotional detachment may embroil one so greatly in the lives and concerns of others' that one's inner emotional life withers along with one's sense of identity. Thus emotional autonomy would not in itself preclude the individual from fulfilling his moral responsibilities, but it would not result in entirely admirable character traits (at least in terms of certain prevailing Western notions of character). Thus our argument against emotional autonomy is culturally relative.

In conclusion, we have seen that emotional autonomy is not an entirely appropriate goal because it currently reflects certain culturally unacceptable character traits, whereas both cognitive and moral autonomy make demands that most persons cannot fulfill and therefore would be goals attainable and suitable to an elite (though the composition of the elite may differ according to the type of autonomy). Additionally, cognitive autonomy, even for an elite would not be a desirable educational goal in itself; it would need to be coupled with moral autonomy because intelligent hired killers and clever professional criminals could be cognitively autonomous. It would also seem that if emotional autonomy is to be encouraged that it would have to be connected closely with the development of moral autonomy in order to prevent emotional detachment from degenerating into insensitivity and unconcern for others.

This chapter has argued that independence based on the achievement of certain developmental tasks is a desirable goal. In contrast, the pitfalls found in the various forms of autonomy need to be guarded against; even then, autonomy cannot stand alone but needs to be supplemented with other worthwhile goals as long as educational systems seek to foster the full development of persons who can live fruitfully with others in democratic communities.

Notes

1. Paul Goodman, *Compulsory Mis-education* (New York: Vintage, 1964), p. 59.

2. A.M. Quinton, "Authority and Autonomy in Knowledge," *Proceedings of the Philosophy of Education Society of Great Britain,* Supplementary Issue, vol. 5, no. 2 (Oxford: Basil Blackwell, 1971), pp. 201-215.

3. E. Moerck, "Principles of Interaction in Language Learning," *Merrill-Palmer Quarterly* 18 (1972):99-106.

4. H. Biller and L. Borstelmann, "Masculine Development: An Integrative Review," *Merrill-Palmer Quarterly* 13 (1967):253-294.

5. H. Biller, *Father, Child and Sex Role* (Lexington, Mass.: Lexington Books, O.C. Heath, 1971), pp. 108-109.

6. Albert Bandura and R.H. Walters, *Social Learning and Personality Development* (New York: Holt, Rinehart and Winston, 1963); A. Bandura, "Vicarious Processes: A Case of No-Trial Learning," in L. Berkowitz, ed., *Advances in Experimental Social Psychology,* vol. 2 (New York: Academic Press, 1965).

7. Jean Piaget, *The Moral Judgment of the Child* (New York: Free Press, 1965).

8. See Lawrence Kohlberg, "Stages and Sequence: The Cognitive Developmental Approach to Socialization," in D.S. Goslin, ed., *Handbook of Socialization Theory and Research,* (Chicago: Rand McNally, 1969), pp. 347-480); and "Moral Development and Moral Education," with E. Turiel, in G. Lesser, ed., *Psychology and Educational Practice* (Chicago: Scott, Foresman, 1971), pp. 410-465.

9. Alan Sussman and Martin Guggenheim, *The Rights of Parents* (New York: Avon Books, 1980), ch. 4.

10. See *From Max Weber: Essays in Sociology,* translated and edited by H. Gerth and C. Wright Mills (New York: Oxford University Press, 1958); and Max Weber, *The Theory of Social and Economic Organization,* translated by A.M. Henderson and Talcott Parsons (New York: Free Press, 1975).

11. Robért Dreeben, "The School as a Workplace," in Robert M.W. Travers, ed., *Second Handbook of Research on Teaching* (Chicago: Rand McNally, 1973), pp. 452-453.

12. Ronald G. Corwin, *Education in Crisis* (New York: Wiley, 1974), pp. 7-12.

13. Frederick W. Taylor, *Scientific Management* (New York: Harper, 1911).

14. James D. Monney and Alan C. Reiley, *Onward Industry* (New York: Harper, 1931). [Later published by James D. Monney under the title *The Principles of Organization* (New York: Harper, 1947).]

15. Raymond E. Callahan, *Education and the Cult of Efficiency* (Chicago: University of Chicago Press, 1962).

16. Robert R. Sears, John W.M. Whiting, Vincent Nowlis, and Pauline S. Sears, "Some Child-Rearing Antecedents of Aggression and Dependency in Young Children," *Genetic Psychology Monographs* 47 (1953):184.

17. Robert R. Sears, Eleanor E. Maccoby, and Harry Levin, *Patterns of Child Rearing* (New York: Harper and Row, 1957), p. 525.

18. U. Bronfenbrenner, "The Changing American Child: A Speculative Analysis," *Journal of Social Issues* 17 (no. 1):6-18.

19. E. Douvan and J. Adelson, *The Adolescent Experience* (New York: Wiley, 1966).

20. Melvin L. Kohn, *Class and Conformity,* 2d ed. (Chicago: University of Chicago Press, 1977).

26. Clay V. Brittain, "Adolescent Choices and Parent-Peer Cross Pressures," *American Sociological Review* 28 (June 1963):385-391.

22. Leonard A. LoSciuto and Robert M. Karlin, "Correlates of the Generation Gap," *Journal of Psychology* 81 (July 1972):253-262.

23. Edward C. Devereux, "The Role of Peer Group Experience in Moral Development," in John P. Hill, ed., *Minnesota Symposium on Child Psychology,* vol. 4 (Minneapolis: University of Minnesota Press, 1970), pp. 94-140.

24. U. Bronfenbrenner, "Some Family Antecedents of Responsibility and Leadership in Adolescents," in L. Petrullo and B. Bass, eds., *Leadership and Interpersonal Behavior* (New York: Holt, Rinehart and Winston, 1961), pp. 239-271.

25. Douvan and Adelson, *The Adolescent Experience;* G.H. Elder, "Structural Variations in the Child Rearing Relationship," *Sociometry* 25 (1962):241-262.

26. Robert J. Havighurst, *Human Development and Education* (New York: McKay, 1953).

27. Several divergent theories of the emotions are outlined in Warren Shibles' *Emotion* (Whitewater, Wisc.: The Language Press, 1974) and William E. Lyons, *Emotion* (Cambridge: Cambridge University Press, 1980).

28. This latter problem is discussed in G.W. Mortimore, ed., *Weakness of Will* (London: Saint Martin's Press, 1971).

29. Daniel J. Levinson, *The Seasons of a Man's Life* (New York: Knopf, 1978), pp. 96-101.

30. Ibid., pp. 91-97.

31. John R. Searle, *Speech Acts* (Cambridge: Cambridge University Press, 1969), pp. 33-42.

32. R.F. Dearden, "Autonomy and Education," in *Education and Reason,* part 3 of *Education and the Development of Reason* (London: Routledge & Kegan Paul, 1972), ch. 3.

33. John Coons and Stephen D. Sugarman, *Education by Choice: The Case of Family Control* (Berkeley, Calif.: University of California Press, 1978), ch. 3-5.

34. R.F. Dearden, *Problems of Primary Education* (London: Routledge & Kegan Paul, 1976), p. 74.

35. William K. Frankena, "Toward a Philosophy of Moral Education," *Harvard Educational Review* 28 (fall 1958):300-313.

36. R.S. Peters, *Psychology and Ethical Development* (London: George Allen and Unwin, 1974), pp. 340-342.

37. Greenville Wall, "Moral Autonomy and the Liberal Theory of Moral Education," *Proceedings of the Philosophy of Education Society of Great Britain,* Supplementary Issue 8 (July 1974):222-236.

38. Alan Gewirth, "Morality and Autonomy in Education," in James F. Doyle, ed., *Educational Judgments* (London: Routledge & Kegan Paul, 1973), p. 41.

39. Lawrence Kohlberg and Richard H. Hersh, "Moral Development: A Review of the Theory," *Theory Into Practice* 16 (April 1977):53-59.

40. Brian Crittenden, "Autonomy as an Aim of Education," in Kenneth A. Strike and Kieran Egan, eds., *Ethics and Education Policy,* (London: Routledge & Kegan Paul, 1978), pp. 108, 116.

41. John Wilson, *Philosophy and Practical Education* (London: Routledge & Kegan Paul, 1977), p. 97.

42. Here, for the sake of discussion, it is assumed that it is desirable, as Kohlberg claims, to develop to the autonomous stages. Some researchers,

however, have had serious misgivings. See the list of critical studies in my *Innovations in Education: Reformers and their Critics,* 3rd ed. (Boston: Allyn and Bacon, 1981), pp. 269-270. Kohlberg has recently presented stage 7 to accommodate theories of religious transcendence. Here religious development presupposes moral development. See his *The Philosophy of Moral Development* (New York: Harper and Row, 1981).

43. Kurt Baier, "Moral Autonomy as an Aim of Moral Education," in *New Essays in the Philosophy of Education* (London: Routledge & Kegan Paul, 1973), pp. 101-106.

44. Ibid., pp. 106-107.

— no mention of Peters, Authority, Resp & Ed

3 Dimensions of Authority

In the last chapter authority was shown playing a vital role in the process of growing up in a culture, of moving from dependence to independence and interdependence. Authority was envisioned in terms of various types: expert, counselor, model, legislator, disciplinarian, and office holder. Authority could take different forms depending on its purposes, role relationships, and social context.

This chapter, however, approaches authority in a different but more systematic way by examining the generic factors in authority relations and distinguishing them from relationships that have an outward resemblance to authority and are consequently sometimes confused with it. Ultimately the specific connection of authority and discipline must be established; yet before doing so, a basis must be developed for understanding and justifying authority.

First, it is necessary to be clear about authority by distinguishing it from the apparent relationships of moral persuasion, coercion, and power. Next, different aspects of authority will be presented in order to further clarify and delineate authority relations. This section will culminate in a model of authority. The third section of the chapter explores the possible grounds for justifying authority. Then the final section turns to the relation of authority and discipline by applying our previous findings on authority.

Moral Persuasion, Coercion, Power, and Authority

Moral Persuasion and Authority

Would it be accurate to say that whenever someone exercises authority, she may at some point use moral persuasion, coercion, and power? And if so, are all those processes merely different features of authority? Or is authority entirely separate from these processes? For those who may wonder what difference it would make, let us take an example. Would it be accurate to say that a government official could legitimately coerce a citizen to act against the citizen's will because coercion itself is merely another way of exercising authority? Or perhaps authority does not have anything to do with coercion but instead is a form of moral persuasion.

A great deal of moral persuasion takes place between parent and child; it can also be found, but on a more limited scale, in teacher-student and administrator-student relations. Moral persuasion is concerned with right and wrong behavior and is based on a code of conduct or an ethical system. To persuade someone morally is to try to get the person to do something or adopt a course of action by using arguments, promises, entreaties, or expostulations. Moral persuasion may appeal as much to feelings and emotions as it does to reason. Thus, could it be that whenever authority is exercised, it is moral persuasion that is being used essentially? This seems plausible in Weber's account of charismatic authority, which is based on heroism, exceptional sanctity, or exemplary character,[1] characteristics that may be found in outstanding religious and military leaders. But moral persuasiveness could be attributed to charisma rather than the converse; thus since most authority figures lack charisma, this interpretation is inapplicable to them even though it does not rule out the possibility that they use moral persuasion as a legitimate exercise of their authority.

One can attempt to persuade another morally without occupying an authority position, as with friendships in which a friend pleads with another to act a certain way or to avoid doing something because it is allegedly morally wrong. Thus friendships are usually egalitarian, rather than authority, relationships. Moreover, it might be claimed that if one were really in authority, it would not be necessary to resort to moral persuasion; that is, an authority is obeyed because the person is actually in authority. In an ideal relationship—at least from the view point of many authority figures—orders or commands are followed because one is *in* authority: it legitimates them. Bureaucratic authority is based on rules rather than charisma; it requires followers to obey rules because their duty as organizational members are designed to promote organizational goals.

Thus moral persuasion is not part of the successful use of bureaucratic authority; but, as is well known, not everyone willingly complies with rules, at which point an authority figure may likely invoke sanctions or engage in moral persuasion. The types of sanctions that are permissible are organizationally defined; however, though moral persuasion is used, is it permissible? This is a question of justification. With the young, persons who hold a paternalistic relationship (parents, teachers, guardians) can under many circumstances utilize moral persuasion—not necessarily because of their superior moral knowledge but because they have been entrusted in certain situations to care for and protect the young. With adults, however, the problem is more complex becaue they are supposed to be independent moral agents and would not be expected to listen to moral persuasion unless they volunteered to do so, were in a legitimate paternalistic relationship (such as a mentally retarded person under adult supervision), or it was someone's duty to listen (as a judge or a social worker may talk to abusive or negligent parents). Some authority figures are in a paternalistic relationship and could employ, on those grounds, moral persuasion; other authority figures such as in employer-employee relations are not paternalistic because the employer's principal interest is to increase profits and promote the firm's growth. Thus bureaucratic authority, especially among adults, could not legitimately employ moral persuasion unless the worker volunteered to listen and to consider it. In contrast, moral persuasion is a legitimate part of charismatic and paternalistic forms of authority; moreover, moral persuasion is not some technique external to authority but is, in the case of charismatic authority, part of its distinguishing characteristics. Thus there can be no charismatic authority without moral persuasiveness.

Coercion and Authority

What is the relation of coercion to authority? Does it mean that a person in authority has the capacity to coerce and that capacity is one of the distinguishing marks of authority? If so, does that also imply that coercion is a legitimate use of authority? Or is the use of coercion both an abuse of authority and an indication that authority has broken down?

First, the concept of coercion must be clarified. Lasswell and Kaplan view coercion in relation to constraint and inducement.[2] They hold that constraint is employed by threats of deprivation and inducement by the promise or prospect of indulgence. Thus coercion is found whenever constraint and/or inducement is high and choice is low.

But some have viewed coercion differently. McCloskey claims that inducements are separate from coercion.[3] Since he thinks that whenever someone is coerced, they still have a choice to act otherwise and inducements sometimes evoke irresistible desire, then the person in the latter case is not coerced. This is based on a distinction between force and coercion, as noted by Hayek.[4] The coerced person is someone who becomes the tool of another; he still has the choice, under the constraint, of choosing the least undesirable course of action. Or, if speaking of laws as coercive, one can still choose not to obey the laws. But when subjected to force, one does not act but is acted upon; certain things are done to the individual. Thus when one is forced, he can be excused because he does not act and therefore cannot be held responsible; in contrast, one can be held partly responsible for acts under coercion with responsibility determined by circumstances of the case. Yet McCloskey does not make a plausible case for holding that inducements may be irresistible whereas constraints are not. It would seem that constraints that are serious threats to one's well-being and inducements that purport to alleviate great suffering or deprivation both carry the weight of force. A person who is threatened with death may feel under force rather than coercion, just as one whose life is seriously endangered and consequently turns over his worldly goods to someone who promises to save him (as in the case of victims of natural disasters). One test for distinguishing coercion from force would be the extent to which the victimized person could be held responsible.

Returning to our opening questions about the relation of coercion to authority, a person in authority usually has the capacity to coerce; it is the capacity itself rather than actual coercion that may render an authority effective. Authority carries with it certain symbols: the prestige and traditions of the office (especially high political office) and the regalia, ceremonies, and various trappings of the office or those of the charismatic leader. Some tacit symbols surround the potential power and coerciveness that the office holder exercises, and the knowledge that these tacit symbols could be employed if necessary are frequently sufficient to ensure that they need not be used. On the other hand, the frequent resort to coercion is usually indicative that authority is insufficiently respected and the symbols are neither revered nor feared. Coercive potential varies with the office: principals usually have more of this potential than teachers, superintendents more than principals. In the past decade the teacher's tacit symbols, generally speaking, proved less effective so that, with increased disruptions, some teachers have had to exercise their full coercive potentials.

Although authority in many instances is more effective when coercion is not used, it is not an abuse of authority unless coercion violates basic rights of subjects. In the former case, if a teacher utilizes corporal punishment in class but is prohibited from doing so (either by a rule of the school system or by state law), then this would be an abuse of the teacher's authority. And if the use of corporal punishment could be shown to violate a basic right, the teacher would also overstep authority. In some cases the rules of the school system may compel the teacher to take actions that violate human rights. Technically, the teacher is fulfilling her professional responsibilities by complying with the rule until it is successfully challenged and repealed. Yet some teachers may not wish to wait until the rule is repealed and may refuse to comply with it. In such instances, however, the teacher would not be exercising officially prescribed authority.

What is the relation between coercion and power? Is coercion synonymous with power, separate from, or an aspect of power?

Power and Authority

Power is the ability to get someone to carry out one's will despite resistance on their part. Thus *A* has power over *B* if *B* resists *A* but still acts in the way *A* prescribes. Power may also take the form of participating in the decision making of others so that the person exercising power influences or controls the other party's decisions. If the power figure controls a sufficient number of key decisions—as in parent-child relations—then the power figure dominates the subject by determining his life plan. Other examples of determining the subject's life plan would be in a totalitarian state, in prison, or in a prisoner-of-war camp.

The use of coercion would be a form of power (if the coercion were successful), but power is the more encompassing of the two terms and therefore has forms other than coercion. Power may be exercised by the use of force—and we earlier observed how coercion and force differ. Power may also be used in conditioning, behavior modification, hypnosis, personal charisma, propaganda, and other devices—at least in those instances where these devices render the subject incapable of resisting.

Power is also closely related to *influence*. In influencing another, the influential person sways, affects, or alters another by indirect or intangible means; it may be exerted consciously or unconsciously. In contrast, power is exerted consciously, is tangible, and usually direct (though there are exceptions, as in the case of propaganda). Power also differs from influence because the power wielder can invoke sanctions but the influential figure cannot do so. As an example, a leading movie star influences countless fans to see his latest motion picture without invoking sanctions; the influential personality features of the star, which create a wide following, may frequently be intangible or ineffable.

Power can also be viewed from two perspectives: First, the amount of force that A can use against B regardless of the resistance of B and the overall effects.[5] Second, the ability of A to get B, despite the latter's resistance, to act on A's decisions.[6] Assuming some way is available for measuring force and the standards of measurement are commonly agreed on, then an index of power is the sheer naked power that one party can bring to bear on another. This type of power conjures images of one military power arrayed against another or the amount of force riot police can employ to quell an outbreak of violence. The other part of the equation, however, is the resistance to force that lowers its effectiveness and the potential of great force used ineptly (as some commentators have claimed about the American military mission in Vietnam and the failed mission to rescue the American hostages in Iran). Resistance to power and the effectiveness of power can both be clarified by placing these two variables in a contextual relation. B is able to resist A (where B and A are armies), and fight to a stalemate, but C (another army) is unable to resist A. Thus, is A a powerful army? Here it would depend on criteria of what counts as power—and certain numerical factors would be used independently of one army to rout another, especially in those instances in which the two armies had never clashed. But suppose A is claimed, on numerical grounds, to be a far more powerful army than *D*; yet when they eventually clash, a clear-cut victor is not established. In that case, a revision of relative strength would be needed to gauge power more precisely.

Thus we can come to some conclusions about these two aspects of power. By inserting the notion of potential, power would describe the force that *A* could possibly exert against *B*. Moreover, the resistance that *B* could possibly bring to meet *A* would also constitute potential power. The ability of *A* to get *B* to act on his decisions despite *B*'s resistance is *actual* power. Any discussion of power needs to consider both facets, distinguish them clearly, but not permit a conception of them to be restricted to one or the other.

It may be thought that teachers have little power because they usually cannot use force and therefore exert their will through expertise, influence, and the status of their office. Notable exceptions occur whenever teachers are legally permitted to use corporal punishment and exercise other forms of physical control over recalcitrant students. If propaganda, behavior modification, and conditioning are also considered forms of power, it would suggest that some teachers may exercise considerable power; yet, for the most part, the conception of power developed previously would apply in educational policy primarily to legislative bodies, law-enforcement machinery, and key administrative positions. For instance, those state officials designated to enforce compulsory school-attendance laws would have considerable power. But the scope of power must be distinguished. Obviously, officials empowered to enforce many state education laws would exercise more power than those who controlled only a few; once again, however, it would depend on the importance of the laws involved and the number of persons affected.

It would be misleading to suggest, however, that because education is a national activity, appeal is primarily based on authority and that therefore power is infrequently employed. It is true that authority may first be appealed to; however, when citizens who do not accept the authority as legitimate or wise (as in the case of busing), then power may be used. Historically, though initial resistance to desegregation occurred in the deep South, most desegregation, despite lurid newspaper headlines, has been peaceable, and therefore, the exercise of power was avoided. A classic case of the use of power occurred where busing was resisted by citizens, and officials had to order in police or National Guard protection. To determine how much power officials possessed (as in Little Rock or Boston) would involve a case study to determine the force that was used (for instance, the number of troops or police, what type of aggression they used against defiant citizens, the resistance met, the success in overcoming the resistance, and eventually desegregating the designated schools). In desegregation violence, it is not the total amount of force that a government can bring to bear on the disturbance (since obviously only a tiny proportion of the total military force is used); it is a proportionate force wisely used that would most likely assure overcoming resistance with the fewest deaths and injuries.

In conclusion, we have looked closely at power and have mentioned it at times in relation to authority, but the precise relationship of the two has not been made fully clear. Before this task can be undertaken, however, it is necessary to elucidate some other aspects of authority.

Aspects of Authority

DeFacto and de Jure Authority. If *A* is in authority by, say, appointment or election to an office, then he is a *de facto* authority. And if his authority is recognized as justified or legitimate, then it is a case of *de jure* authority. For instance, when Juan Peron (1895-1974) was president of Argentina, he had de facto authority. Among his followers he enjoyed de jure authority; but those who wanted to overthrow him recognized only de facto authority (similarly with his second wife, Isabel Peron, b. 1931, who succeeded her husband as president after he had returned from exile). Or, to take another example, Mao-tse-tung (1893-1976) was recognized by the U.S. government as a de facto but not a de jure authority because of the U.S. position toward Taiwan (until the position changed in the early 1970s). In contrast, when Peron fled Argentina, he was recognized by his followers as a de jure authority despite his lack of de facto authority.

De facto authority is easy to discern, but de jure can be controversial. Any official, governing body, or nation may be rejected as de jure authority, as in the case of a ruler, a district federal court, or a nation (the Soviet Union vis-à-vis Poland). The problems of legitimacy and justification are complex and important and will be explored later in this chapter. For now, it can be shown that the recognition of de facto authority but the failure to accept de jure authority may likely lead to the use of power as the authority figure finds that his orders are not complied with and therefore other, sterner measures must be taken. Yet, psychologically speaking, the widespread use of power may alienate those affected and render it even more difficult to establish de jure authority. Instead, the development of influence would likely be more effective in creating legitimacy.

Authority and Orders

It might be said that when someone is in authority, she is entitled to give orders, commands, directives, and make pronouncements. Others not in authority may also attempt to do these things; the difference, however, is that only one in authority may realistically expect to be listened to and obeyed. Is it a distinctive feature of authority to give orders? And if that is the case, why should authority expect to be obeyed?

Authorities habitually issue commands and orders. Commands differ from the latter in their peremptoriness and imperativeness (as a sergeant to recruits or a parent to a child) and their unquestioned nature. With commands, as R.S. Peters notes, no reason need be given, for once it is granted, the person has the right to occupy the office and is within his sphere of competence or not exceeding his prerogative, then there can be little question he is entitled to issue commands.[7] In contrast, orders are given to subordinates in the form of instructions that may use explicit detail.

One way to identify de facto authority is to observe who is issuing commands or orders; and if obedience is given, de jure authority may exist for the observed followers (although it cannot be entirely ruled out that their compliance stems from fear of sanctions; thus more information would be needed before any firm conclusions could be drawn). Although others not in authority may occasionally issue commands and orders, they are likely to be discouraged from continuing because their utterances will likely be met with disbelief and resistance; consequently, their tactics would likely include moral persuasion and coercion (in the form of inducements).

But it might be said that the preceding model fits the authority of office far better than it fits expert authority. What is it that the expert commands or orders? The economist cannot "order" the government to adopt his ideas; nor can the nuclear physicist order others to believe in quantum theory. Usually, the weight of ideas, their cogency, and the evidence marshalled in their support create persuasiveness. Even a nuclear physicist does not order a nuclear plant closed upon discovering uncontrolled dangerous radiation; rather, she presents her findings to government officials who, in light of their office, issue an order to close the installation until the leakage is corrected. The epistemic claims must first be carefully examined before the person is considered an expert in the matter. Or at least some previous history of expertise must be achieved before one would be asked for a judgment.

Should authority, then, expect to be obeyed? Not unless the authority is entitled to give commands or orders. But how else, other than followers accepting the authority's legitimacy, can authority receive obedience? Since the authority of office is governed by the applicable rules of the organization or bureau, then those entitled to prescribe rule-governed behavior within the organization are expected to be obeyed if it can be shown that the rules are effective in advancing organizational goals, that the goals are worthwhile, and the means used to attain them are not contraindicated because of their deleterious or dehumanizing effects on the participants.

But obviously one is not expected to obey unless he falls under the authority's jurisdiction; thus one must be a member of an organization or a worker in a business firm and fall within a superordinate-subordinate relationship before obedience can rightfully be exacted. Or one must be a pedestrian or a driver of a vehicle before a traffic official can issue commands.

Once again, obedience does not apply in any strict sense to expert authority but only the authority of office. Yet the expert does want his ideas to receive an ample hearing and be examined for their merit; and if the ideas are sound, he expects others to adjust their thinking, when necessary, to take them into account and to act on them whenever they can be applied.[8]

The teacher's authority, as indicated earlier, rests upon both the authority of the office and expertise (although the elementary or secondary teacher would not literally be an expert in a discipline but, presumably, a knowledgeable person who would operate with students in a semiexpert relationship, at least in more traditional classrooms). Can teachers legitimately give orders and expect them to be obeyed? They do. But perhaps they do this out of desperation rather than from the sanction of authority. When classrooms become disruptive, teachers frequently give commands; and when making assignments and organizing student activities, orders are commonly given. The legitimacy of their doing so rests upon their office and the expectation that teachers will enforce school rules. On the other hand, they want to be listened to because they believe the curriculum is important and their knowledge claims are supportable; yet they cannot order or command students to accept these things, though they can order them to pay attention, except that doing so will not assure acceptance, only that they may get a hearing.

Thus the picture of perfect authority of office is when an authority figure enjoys both de jure and de facto authority, can justify the grounds for authority, and commands and orders are obeyed without resort to power or coercion. Of course, this seldom occurs—not only in the case of classroom teachers and school administrators but corporate heads and political leaders as well. The costs of attaining perfect authority of office may be too great, thereby leading some authorities to rationalize the use of power and coercion as a stopgap measure only to find it has become an addiction. It may seem that charismatic authority fits perfect authority insofar as followers may exuberantly or mesmerically obey; yet such figures may not be de facto authorities, and they frequently use coercive techniques (based on promises about a more glorious future). In contrast, the perfect expert authority is one whose ideas have great epistemic support, are disseminated on the widest scale, discussed intensively, and prove highly influential.

In conclusion, the issuing of commands and orders is not one identifying characteristic of all forms of authority. But where such activities are important in the very meaning of exercising authority, the commands are obeyed not only because of the fear of sanctions or for reasons discussed earlier surrounding roles, rules, and norms of the office holder but because, as Carl. J. Friedrich has suggested, they hold "the potentiality of reasoned elaboration."[9] In other words, rational grounds can be offered that may further incline one to accept (though frequently the grounds are not demanded).

Failure to obey an order or command is not in itself an indication that de jure authority is rejected, as it may be attributable to one of the following conditions: (1) inability to fulfill an order because it lies beyond the person's physical or intellectual ability; (2) a lack of understanding or a misinterpretation of the order; and (3) ambiguity or conflict over to whom the order is properly addressed.

A Model of Authority

At this point it is necessary to pull together some information already given and present them in a more convenient and comprehensible form. An authority may utilize or appeal to: truth claims, rules, symbols, influence, coercion, or power. This is illustrated in table 3-1 for three types of authority.

Authority as expertise is highest of all variables in terms of truth claims because such authority is established by the persistent ability to make assertions that can be corroborated by other experts. Experts use symbols, influence, and rules to a medium extent. They cannot avoid the use of symbols insofar as their discipline requires the use of linguistic, scientific, or mathematical symbols in order to communicate their knowledge effectively. Yet, in contrast to some other authority types, they do not employ symbols chiefly to persuade, sway, and overcome resistance; therefore, the use of symbols is not readily separated out as a tactic to win adherents, though occasionally it is used in this manner. As for influence, it is important not to confuse the fact that most authority would like to *be* influential with the use

Table 3-1
Authority Variables

Types of Authority	*Truth Claims*	*Rules*	*Symbols*	*Influence*	*Coercion*	*Power*
Expert	High	Medium	Medium	Medium	Low	Low
Office	Low	High	High	Low to medium	Varies	Varies
Charismatic	Varies	Low	High	High	Moderate	Low

of influence as a device. Experts do affect or sway others by indirect and intangible means, especially literary and artistic experts rather than scientific ones (where direct and quantifiable evidence is presented); the expert also cannot usually apply sanctions—and it would be thought inappropriate to do so—when others refuse to accept their claims. Experts, depending on the discipline, ask the hearer or reader to accept or employ certain rules that arise from the discipline (as in mathematics and languages); however, the rules are integral to the discipline and not an external device to achieve compliance. Coercion and power are seldom employed by experts not only because they have little but because it would be considered improper, inappropriate, or unprofessional (though there may be notable exceptions).

The authority of office, as seen earlier, is high in the use of rules and symbols. The office holder is expected to enforce the appropriate rules designed to achieve organizational goals and to issue orders to ensure that designated tasks are performed according to rule-governed behavior. And although the number of rules and the range of persons to whom they apply differ according to the size and type of organization as well as job descriptions, rules are seldom abolished but tend to multiply; appealing to them may mean that sanctions will not need to be used. Authority of office ranges from low to medium on influence even though some authorities would prefer that it be higher so that there would be less recourse to coercion or power. But since such authority is largely direct and tangible, only the more subtle office holders utilize considerable influence. Truth claims are low because this type of authority appeals to the office and its legitimacy for backing. As for the use of coercion and power, it varies depending on the office and the leeway exercised by the office holder. But generally other devices are used first (those stated previously) before employing coercion or power, with inducements likely to be used first and force as a last resort (though this varies with actual conditions).

Charismatic authority is high on symbols and influence. The symbols of charismatic religious leaders are vested in sacred documents, prayers and incantations, holy garments, the icons of the church, religious ritual, and the like. Similarly, the charismatic military leader has a host of symbols: love of country, secret codes, uniforms, medals of valor, rituals of demonstrating respect for military hierarchy, deference to higher officers, and obedience to commands. Influence is usually high because, as with the charismatic religious leader, his presence and holiness are intangible and indirect means for inspiring obedience and altering behavior. Of course, some charismatic leaders employ more direct approaches, but they usually have at their disposal a wide range of techniques for exerting influence. Such authority is moderate in the use of coercion, which may take the form of inducements based on promises that the faithful, loyal, or dedicated will reap a bountiful harvest when the mission is accomplished, the opponent is vanquished, or the promised land is reached. Since these measures are usually effective, the charismatic leader seldom resorts to the use of power—and for many such leaders, it would be contrary to their style and mission; moreover, they usually have little power in a formal sense. And they cannot appeal to the rules of an organization because they are commonly outsiders and any rules, should they create a movement, are developed de novo. Their truth claims vary: some may appeal to righteous hopes and fears; other pronouncements may be apocryphal or cryptic; while still others may insist that they are the Messiah or God incarnate.

Using this model, how does it help to explain parent-child and teacher-pupil relations? Obviously, few if any parents or teachers represent charismatic authority; yet both groups represent, in varying degrees, expert authority and authority of the office.

Parents, as we saw in chapter 2, represent expert authority to the young child. Initiation of the child into the use of language is primarily handled by parents who in turn largely shape their offspring's world view by the concepts and values transmitted and the relative weight ascribed to them. Parents may induce respect by their superior knowledge and experience, which serves to gain the child's compliance except where sufficient self-control is lacking or when the truth claims are rebelliously challenged.

But a parent does not fit the profile of expert authority very well not only because their expertise may be increasingly challenged or ignored as the child grows older but as a consequence of having access to coercion and power far more than most experts. Of course, as indicated in chapter 2, there are legally defined limits to the parent's power; yet many forms of coercion and power are permissible within those predefined limits. The parent's authority, it would seem, is not primarily based on expertise.

Then, is the parent's authority based on office? Technically, parents do not have an office but a legally recognized role; however, certain features of parenthood may resemble authority of office: predefined (though not as precisely stated as the function of most offices), a superordinate-subordinate relationship exists, orders are frequently given, and rules are applied. In contrast to most office holders, parents make more truth claims and employ more influence, coercion, and power.

The expertise of the teacher relies on greater claims than do parents and depends more on epistemic assertions in exercising authority. Yet for those students who lack motivation and interest in the subject, the teacher will need to employ other devices. Teachers are faced with two types of rules: academic and institutional. The former relate to the discipline's structure and intellectual operations; the latter relate to the rules that are used to implement school and classroom policy. The scope and extensiveness of the rules vary by academic discipline and by school. The symbols at the teacher's disposal are moderate, as they would be for an expert, rather than high, as for some office holders (such as political, military, or religious). The extent of the teacher's influence, coercion, and power is debatable, but it could generally be said that teachers have low to moderate influence, use moderate to high coercion, and low to moderate power. In the incidence of the latter two devices, teachers depart sharply from experts, who are low in these characteristics. Teachers may frequently employ coercion (depending on the seriousness of the discipline problem) in the forms of constraints and inducements. Enforcing rules and regulations against resistance, withholding privileges, imposing punishment, and using grades as a threat or reward may all be, in varying degrees, coercive acts. Teachers, on the other hand, have less power, in the form of force, than they do coercion.

It could be argued that the lack of power is no serious deficit and that even the reliance on coercive techniques is largely unnecessary to gain students' respect for the teacher's authority. The fact that students sometimes do not comply with duly constituted teacher orders in some cases stems from students' wanting to know the grounds or justification for the orders that in turn may be pushed back to a wider questioning of authority. So far this chapter has looked at characteristics, dimensions, and operations of authority; now it turns to the normative issues.

The Justification of Authority

Authority needs to be authorized before it can be legitimated. Two terms associated with authority during the Roman Republic were *author* and *authorize*. These terms refer to the source of a doctrine, rumor, or decision with the implication that its source, independently of its moral qualities or legal functions, was sufficient for others to conform voluntarily to what the source authorized.[10] But today this ground no longer seems sufficient for authorization.

In some usages, *authorization* may refer to authorization of the office holder by the organization whereas the term *endorse* refers to authorization by followers.[11] In other words, power may be authorized but not endorsed, or it may be endorsed but not authorized (when a leader is singled out in an informal group to assume authority functions). With this terminology, the objective would be to gain both authorization and endorsement.

Are there certain essential features of authority that would offer justification, or does justification lie in some way external to authority? R.S. Peters believes that justification may lie in appealing to such principles as fairness and consideration of interests.[12] Others suggest that authority has no intrinsic worth but would be justified in terms of the functions it serves. Hobbes commends it for providing order and protection from violence; Locke and Rousseau suggest that it helps promote the common good; and with the French Revolution, a new authority would, it was believed, promote justice and welfare. Since there are different forms of authority, they would differ in the functions that they would be capable of serving. And justification may vary according to political persuasion: an anarchist may deny legitimacy to imperial authority whereas a democrat would deny it to a totalitarian form.

For John Wild, authority conveys a value that calls forth the respect of others; thus authority must have access to the values it is conveying in order to be authorized and grounded.[13] But it would seem that Wild's explanation is not entirely satisfactory because not just any value can elicit respect—and it is not clear what values would do so. Moreover, respect, though admirable, may be excessive if authority could be justified more simply.

According to Richard Flatham, authority is justified when it contributes to the agency of its individual members.[14] The fundamental value of a society, Flatham contends, is the rationality, freedom, and moral integrity of its citizens. Yet he recognizes that the tensions that arise between authority and agency can be reconciled by a number of devices: draw on widely shared values, limit authority by formal principles, establish realms of action where authority is not permitted, and institute elections and rule of law. Some of these devices depend on authority or their exercise constitutes a form of authority. Thus certain forms of authority limit other forms; hence authority serves to assure legal justice.[15]

The Justification of Authority in Education

Authority can be characterized as both regulative and constitutive. Regulative authority regulates antecedent or independently existing forms of behavior. Constitute authority would be separate from the forms they are regulating and may also create or define new forms of behavior. Regulative authority, the more familiar type, would use rules, norms, and sanctions to control students' behavior. One purpose of doing so would be to ensure sufficient order for learning to take place and objectives to be pursued without excessive interference.

In contrast, constitutive authority is embodied in the disciplines themselves. The sciences, for instance make certain important epistemic claims that rest on the expertise of the scientific investigator who in turn is expected to open his findings to scrutiny and corroboration. This is another name for "expert authority," but what is being claimed is that such authority is constitutive of the curriculum. The curriculum, among other things, embodies knowledge claims that may not necessarily be taken on authority (though younger students may have to do so) but sometimes offers these for checking by students; therefore, to be involved in the learning process means to check epistemic claims constitutive of the curriculum or else accept them on expert authority. In any study—physics, economics, art history—one confronts the authority of the discipline, which most students are not in a position to challenge. And though students can engage in independent problem solving, to be able to solve problems of a discipline requires initiation into the discipline itself—its basic concepts, axioms, and postulates, its modes of inquiry and verification. If the student eventually makes a contribution to the discipline, this contribution becomes constitutive of the discipline and carries with it expert authority.

But it might be objected that the preceding notion of constitutive authority rests on a certain type of curriculum (subject) and would not apply to certain other curricular forms. It would not apply to the experience curriculum because it does not rest on disciplines but is based instead on students' interests and experiences. Since such a curriculum emerges from the ongoing activities and interests of the young, it would not appeal to the epistemic claims of the disciplines.

This argument is partly true, but it goes too far. An experience curriculum is not prohibited from drawing selectively on the disciplines; it is based on the assumption that learning is fostered more effectively through experiential, rather than subject-matter, units. Even then one would still need some way to sort out experiences in order to make sense out of them, to place them in perspective, and to draw warranted inferences. The rules and principles by which these activities are performed would constitute the authority; however, some of these rules and principles may be external to the experiences themselves and therefore when applied serve a regulative function. But if the rules and principles define what will count as an experience, then they would act as constitutive. Some examples might be in order. "Teach the child to use her senses in all early forms of learning" is a regulative principle; whereas conceptions about time such as a beginning and an end are constitutive because the notion of "experiences" would make no sense if they could not be separated out and distinguished, and it is done, in part, by time concepts.[16]

These examples could be contrasted to some from the disciplines or subject curriculum. Rules in mathematics governing operations are constitutive (addition, subtraction, and so on). A regulative rule: Take a short break at the end of every hour when studying mathematics.

It could be concluded that although a subject curriculum contains more constitutive principles and rules than an experience curriculum or cognate plan, the latter features an essential minimum, or the experiences themselves would not make much sense; moreover, teachers and students make claims about the verisimilitude, significance, and value of experiences (though these criteria may also be regulative). The overall conclusion is that it would be a contradiction in terms to say that one gained an education free of authority. Constitutive authority, therefore, can be found, in varying degrees depending on the form, in the curriculum. Regulative authority is found in all formal education and, to a lesser extent, in informal education. Even those who claim to be "self-educated" (who have had little or no formal schooling) have experienced the authority of their parents or guardians in helping them learn fundamental processes.

Those who object strenuously to authority are not actually intent on abolishing all authority. For Marx, capitalism rationalizes material exploitation and oppressive power; through revolution, the dictatorship of the proletariat would arise (another form of authority) and would eventually lead to a classless society that would allegedly dispense with political power but would need some authority for distributing basic goods and services. Anarchism, another political doctrine and social philosophy, despite its rejection of all coercive authority of institutions, does not reject all authority whatsoever but seeks to maximize freedom through a decentralized economy of cooperatives and trade unions. A philosophical anarchist in education as Ivan Illich, though he would deschool society, would transform and shift education authority to informal learning networks that would include apprenticeship and skill exchanges.[17] It is actually the quality, character, and scope of authority that is disputed, not the abolishment of authority altogether.

It would obviously be impossible to maintain classrooms without some regulative authority, despite disputes over its form and scope. Today's reformers generally object to bureaucratic school systems and the proliferation of rules and regulations that may tend to stifle, rather than promote, learning. The last chapter demonstrated that though some school systems could be considered bureaucracies, the teacher's position is not entirely bureaucratically organized.

Such regulative authority of teachers can also be used to help develop or modify the curriculum, organize instruction, conduct evaluation, and counsel students. It may also be used to promote and maintain discipline.

Authority and Discipline

Authority's relation to discipline needs to be explored. A problem, however, is that my conception of discipline has yet to be elaborated; yet rather than delay, I will relate authority to popular notions of discipline and in the next chapter make the connection with my own conception. This will provide some tentative grounds for thinking about the relationship.

Several popular notions of discipline are prevalent. One view holds that discipline is orderly or prescribed conduct. Thus conduct that is in disarray, confused, and chaotic is antithetical to disciplined behavior; prescriptions would seek to promote desired uniformities and regularities of conduct.

This view relates to the teacher's office and her regulative authority. Although at times there may be goal displacement and discipline may be sought for its own sake, discipline, in this view, is designed to maintain a form of order that will best promote learning objectives. Regulative authority enables the teacher to provide a classroom atmosphere conducive to learning. The authority, in this case, stems from the predefined rights, privileges, and duties of the office. Thus the authority of the office authorizes (though some students may not endorse) the teacher's prescription and enforcement of school regulations and the creation of classroom rules, either independently or in consultation with students.

This view assumes discipline to be of extrinsic value. Complying with *R* (rule) is instrumental to *G* (goal). Or *R* is instrumental to *O* (order), which helps achieve *G*. In the first predication, following the rule is instrumental to achieving the goal or a desired learning outcome. In contrast, the second predication states that observing the rule promotes order that is a necessary condition in attaining a desired goal. In both predications the goal may be thought to be intrinsically worthwhile, which thereby would justify following the rule; whereas the rule has no value in itself. If we apply these formulations to discipline, it can be seen that discipline in this interpretation, has no value in itself but only to what it may lead.

A second popular view of discipline is that of treatment that corrects or punishes. Discipline is commonly conceived as the means of rectifying errors and meting out appropriate punishment for wrongdoers. Teachers are empowered to correct and punish, though the scope of teachers' punitive authority and how punishment is to be administered are usually prescribed by courts and school boards. Historically teachers have been expected to exercise this disciplinary function, and their ability to do so according to prescribed standards has often been viewed as a hallmark of their overall effectiveness; it has only been in recent decades that growing concern has been expressed over children's rights—and a number of court cases have either proscribed formerly acceptable acts or limited the scope of the teacher's authority. Disciplinary codes must meet the demands of due process. Students must be warned that certain infractions warrant a spanking, a spanking can be used only after the failure of other measures and should be administered before another staff member.[18] Surprisingly to some civil libertarians, paddling does not violate the Eighth Amendment's cruel-and-unusual-punishment clause.[19]

In contrast to the regulative authority exercised in the preceding two disciplinary views, constitutive authority pertains to a different, but well-known, interpretation. It holds that to discipline is to train or develop by instruction especially in self-control. If the instruction embodies more than adherence to rules and regulations but involves study of a subject or a body of knowledge for the purpose of bringing about certain desirable habits or forms of conduct, then this might be a case of exercising constitutive authority. For instance, novels or short stories may be assigned because of the "lessons" they teach and their purported good influence; similarly, the study of history and contemporary political affairs may be used to show examples of desirable and undesirable behavior. Thus certain epistemic claims are advanced, and by so studying these subjects, it is believed that one's behavior will be changed for the better—an important historical justification, whether or not entirely warranted, for requiring certain subjects.

In conclusion, authority is the framework in which discipline rests. Ultimately it is necessary to look to the forms and grounds of authority in evaluating and adjudicating controversial disciplinary issues. The relationship will be refined in the next chapter, which diverges from common-sense views of discipline.

Notes

1. Max Weber, *Theory of Economic and Social Organization,* translated by A.M. Henderson and Talcott Parsons (New York: Free Press, 1957), pp. 358-363.
2. Harold D. Lasswell and Abraham Kaplan, *Power and Society* (New Haven: Yale University Press, 1950), pp. 97-98.
3. H.J. McCloskey, "Coercion: Its Nature and Significance," *The Southern Journal of Philosophy* 18 (fall 1980):338-340.
4. F.A. Hayek, *The Constitution of Liberty* (London: Routledge & Kegan Paul. 1960), p. 336.
5. Sanford M. Dornbusch and W. Richard Scott, in their *Evaluation and the Exercise of Authority* San Fransisco: Jossey-Bass, 1975), p. 33, take this approach.
6. Lasswell and Kaplan, *Power and Society,* ch. 5, seem to take this approach.
7. R.S. Peters, "Authority," Anthony Quinton, ed., *Political Philosophy* (Fair Lawn, N.J.: Oxford University Press, 1967), p. 95.
8. Some writers limit expert authority to "knowing that" as in R.T. De George, "Epistemic Authority," in R. Baine Harris, ed., *Authority: A Philosophical Analysis,* (University, Ala.: University of Alabama Press, 1976), p. 80.
9. Carl J. Friedrich, "Authority, Reason, and Discretion," in Friedrich, ed., *Authority* (Cambridge, Mass.: Harvard University Press, 1958), p. 35.
10. Leonard Krieger, "Authority," in Philip P. Wiener, ed., *Dictionary of the History of Ideas,* vol. 1 (New York: Scribner's, 1973), pp. 143-144.
11. Dornbusch and Scott, *Evaluation,* p. 61.

12. R.S. Peters, *Ethics and Education* (Atlanta: Scott, Foresman, 1967), p. 159.

13. John Wild, "Authority," in Frederick J. Adelmann, ed., *Authority* (The Hague, Netherlands: Martinus Nijhoff, 1974), pp. 7-23.

14. Richard E. Flatham, *The Practice of Authority: Authority and the Authoritative* (Chicago: University of Chicago Press, 1980), p. 186.

15. Ibid., p. 222.

16. This is, at least since Kant, a controversial point. Some existentialists handle it by positing a dualism between clock time and lived or existential time. I have in mind Kant's *Critique of Pure Reason,* translated by Norman Kemp Smith (New York: Saint Martin's Press, 1965), A31, B46-A50, and B74; and Martin Heidegger, *Being and Time,* translated by John Macquarrie and Edward Robinson (New York: Harper and Row, 1962), pp. 329-333, 349.

17. Ivan Illich, *Deschooling Society* (New York: Harper and Row, 1971).

18. *Baker* v. *Owen* (1975).

19. *Ingraham* v. *Wright* (1977).

4 Perspectives on Discipline

Discipline has long been a problem for educators. Authoritarian and harsh punishment can be found from ancient Jewish and Egyptian education to the modern period despite opposition from Erasmus, Ascham, Montaigne, and others. Flogging was commonplace; other forms of punishment included memorization or copying of lines, wearing a dunce cap, fines, expulsion, and imprisonment. By the sixteenth century, in some European schools punishment had become associated with Calvinistic beliefs in original sin and absolute obedience to parents and elders. By the seventeenth century, Massachusetts and Connecticut ratified laws for rebellious children, that after failure to comply with due corrections from parents, offspring could be put to death. The *New England Primer*, the most widely read American school book for a hundred years, perpetuated Puritan influences.

As a counterforce, liberalizing views of the child came from Anglicans, Quakers, minority religious sects, and also from deistic and secular outlooks. By the middle of the nineteenth century, newer child-nature views began to emerge from Rousseauan romanticism, growing humanitarianism, and political conceptions of democracy, which claim that the child needs greater liberty to be prepared for citizenship responsibilities. Bronson Alcott, Samuel R. Hall, and Horace Mann proposed more temperate discipline policies. Later Colonel Francis Parker and John Dewey created some advanced ideas that found expression in early progressive education. By the 1890s school practices exhibited greater leniency with students and wider use of positive rather than aversive types of control.

More recently discipline has been viewed again as a serious problem. Although many administrators may find school finance of more concern than discipline, the public and teachers in general are considerably concerned. In nine out of the last ten Gallup polls of public attitudes toward education, discipline was chosen as the most significant problem.[1] Also a National Education Association survey of teacher attitudes and practices indicated that 54 percent held that student behavior interferes with their teaching.[2] A sociologist claims that discipline in today's schools may be at "the lowest point in our history."[3]

To understand discipline better, one must be aware of the wide and varied ways in which it can be viewed. To explore more carefully these different perspectives will convey a range of possibilities and explanatory approaches. Thus this chapter will examine four representative perspectives that cover a full range of ideologies and policy proposals. The ideologies range from reactionary to radical, and the policies are diverse. After an exposition and evaluation of these four perspectives, I will present my own position.

Stern Discipline

Stern, harsh discipline, as noted previously, was characteristic of much formal schooling in the past. To speak of it in this manner, however, is to make a value judgment that may not always be shared by proponents of such practices; nevertheless, many observers today would likely concur with me (although, of course, readers must draw their own conclusions). Such stern practices may not be localized in any one system—public, private, or parochial—but some examples could be found in each one. The example that will be used here is the current back-to-basics movement, which is found largely in public schools. The movement will not be discussed, only the discipline practices associated with it. And although these practices are not as stern as found in earlier periods, they will probably be of more interest to the reader and still illustrate our point.

In the United States today, there is an ever-growing number of new fundamental schools. These schools are usually supported by parents and local citizens who are alarmed over declining achievement-test scores, devaluation of the high-school diploma, and an allegedly overly permissive atmosphere in regular classrooms. As examples, Myers Park Optional School in Charlotte, North Carolina, teaches arithmetic and penmanship, good manners and patriotism, and it emphasizes grades, report cards, and rules of deportment.[4] At the John Marshall Fundamental School in Pasadena, California, stress is placed on the three Rs, teacher dress codes, ability grouping, strict rules of conduct, homework, character education, and corporal punishment.[5] Teachers enforce class rules that include talking only when called upon, no flip answers or sarcasm, and putting trash in trash cans.

These rules do not seem overly stern, and it could be plausibly argued that sound discipline may be impossible without some rules. What is debatable is the content of the rules and who participates in their formulation. Among other things, rules should not violate students' rights. In fundamental schools students do not participate in the formulation of rules, which some observers would consider a shortcoming because students are more likely to comply voluntarily with rules that they have had a hand in shaping. Even then, there are limits as to the extent to which students could engage in rule development—limits in terms of maturity, time, and feasibility. Yet the principle of participation is not observed in fundamental schools.

However rules might be developed, it is wise to have as few rules as possible: those that clearly contribute to educational objectives should be retained and others eliminated. The reasons for keeping or establishing rules should be explained so that students will be aware of the underlying purpose. It is better to state rules positively (what is to be done) rather than negatively (what not to do). Above all, rules need to be enforced promptly and fairly; thus teachers should not make idle threats, nor should they fail to act on infractions.

The use of corporal punishment raises some problems, some of which have long been recognized. Quintilian (c. 35-95 A.D.) opposed the customary flogging of his day because he thought that it was only suited to slaves, that it would harden boys, and that no one should be given such unlimited power over them.[6] Other famous educators, for varying reasons, opposed corporal punishment. Although, as noted in the last chapter, corporal punishment may be used in school under certain strict conditions—and by observing these conditions, likely assuring no serious physical harm—its use may create resentment, damage interpersonal relationships, and force obedience (a case of the use of teacher or administrator power rather than authority). Some observers oppose not only corporal punishment but the use of punishment in general; they claim that it may contribute to school absenteeism, dropping out, vandalism, and excessive anxiety and conformity.[7] Punishment, of whatever type, is best justified whenever persistent misbehavior leaves no alternatives, whenever it is combined with positive statements of expectations and reminders about rules, and only after the student has been told what specific behavior is being punished.

But even rewards have their problems as a device for classroom management. Praise from a teacher (as a reward) may cause some students embarrassment and result in their being teased or taunted by classmates; other students who are accustomed to success and who are strongly self-confident may be better motivated by mild constructive criticism. Thus it is necessary to know which students are motivated by praise. Reward, as with punishment, is an extrinsic device rather than intrinsic: it is used to motivate because the student lacks interest in the subject for its own sake. Though it may be more difficult to bring about, it is generally thought that intrinsic interest rather than extrinsic devices are better and the latter should be resorted to when the former fails.

Although we began by exploring and questioning some practices in back-to-basics programs, our doubts spread to regular classroom activities that employ punishment and reward; and although it may not be possible to dispense with these devices altogether, certain serious limitations have been noted.

Natural-Development and Deficiency Models

Herbert Kohl is well known for his innovative ideas about teaching and William Glasser for his "reality therapy"; both also have developed influential discipline theories. Neither Kohl nor Glasser bases his theory on the use of punishment. Rather, both place discipline within the wider context of a learning environment and the life of the student; but, their differences are greater than their similarities.

Natural-Development Model

Kohl is committed to open education and child-centered learning. What is important, he believes, is to discover the student's needs and build a learning environment that emerges from these needs and fosters them. In other words, the teacher must be responsive to the way students naturally grow and develop.

For Kohl the emphasis is on observing, listening, and understanding youngsters so that a suitable and flexible environment can be established. "Openness, naturalness, and closeness," along with "consistency and strength," are necessary traits in working with young people, even though, admittedly, they are difficult to develop.[8] One does not permit personal problems to become an excuse for abandoning students or expecting them to handle problems that adults may not handle well. Although it is threatening to some teachers, students should be treated as "moral equals." In other words, the same rules apply to both teacher and students. The open teacher does not bully but is responsive to criticism and changes behavior whenever the criticism is sound.[9] The teacher should also have the strength to admit failure.[10]

Kohl believes that the total classroom environment as well as teacher-student relations are important; therefore, he does not hesitate to modify classroom arrangements and time tables. Classroom furniture can be arranged to ensure greater privacy, which Kohl considers necessary for student development. Private places are needed for both small-group work and solitary places for thought. This privacy can be built into classrooms by using fabrics, rug dividers, clothing closets, and the like.[11]

The student should not be squelched by unnecessary regulations, which should be reviewed by teachers. Why, for instance, must students line up the same way every day, raise their hands, or not talk to each other? In an open classroom the teacher has to abdicate some power; yet this does not mean permissiveness, for the teacher should express feelings forthrightly about student behavior and teacher concerns.

The teacher's objective is to create an environment in which trust and responsibility can evolve.[12] Each teacher must decide to what extent the school system will permit an open classroom. Compromises—with one's principles, other teachers, and administrators—are necessary in order to survive; but in some schools survival is undesirable, Kohl insists, and therefore it is better to resign or be terminated.

Despite the fact that the teacher should question practices and techniques, there are some limits that should be set. Students should not be permitted to bully or injure another, injure or maim themselves, interfere or prevent others from working, or destroy another student's work or classroom materials.[13] It is the teacher's responsibility to see that these rules are consistently enforced, although ideally it is the responsibility of the entire class. At one time or another each student in an open classroom will attempt to test these limits; it is the teacher's task to respect the student's strength while consistently enforcing these limits. When a discipline problem arises that concerns the entire class, the best way to handle it is by using a fable or story that can be discussed without anyone being embarrassed.

Thus for Kohl, discipline evolves out of open-classroom interaction fostered by the teacher's naturalness, consistency, and strength, traits that do not resort to numerous rules but rely only on establishing outer limits beyond which student welfare and growth would be endangered.

Deficiency Model

Glasser uses a deficiency model to explain discipline problems. Disciplinary problems, he believes, arise out of need deficiencies and can be overcome by fulfilling certain essential needs. The deficiency model is part of Glasser's "reality therapy," which states that anyone requiring psychiatric help suffers from an inability to fulfill needs. One reason that people do not fulfill their needs, Glasser claims, is that they deny the reality of the world around them; therefore, they must learn to face reality and be shown how to fulfill their needs. Needs are fulfilled by being involved with people—at least one person but preferably more; and these other people must be in touch with reality and able to fulfill their own needs. "Therefore, essential to fulfillment of our needs is a person preferably [sic] a group of people, with whom we are emotionally involved *from the time we are born to the time we die*."[14]

All people have the same needs, but they vary in their capacity to fulfill them. Reality therapy focuses on helping patients fulfill their need to be loved (from friendship to conjugal love) and the need to feel worthwhile to others and to self. The two needs are interrelated insofar as one who is loved will usually feel worthwhile. Even though there may be persons in our lives who claim to care for us, one may not care for them or be able to accept their love.

Responsibility is a key to understanding reality therapy. Glasser presents a stipulative definition of responsibility as "the ability to fulfill one's needs, and to do so in a way that does not deprive others of the ability to fulfill their needs."[15] Therefore, with this definition in mind, the responsible person has good mental health and the irresponsible person is mentally ill. (Glasser prefers to do away with psychiatric terms associated with the mentally ill.)

Glasser approaches classroom discipline problems by insisting that the teacher should try to change behavior rather than attitudes; for if we wait for attitudinal change, it stalls behavior improvement, but not the converse. The student must first succeed in one important aspect of life in order to succeed in general.

Irrespective of the child's background, Glasser believes that it is possible to succeed in school—and school success, he claims, gives one an excellent chance for success in life. But deficiency needs of love and self-worth preclude success. These needs are related to the concept of identity, which enables each individual to feel of some importance. One gains an identity through the home and school, and the acquisition of a successful identity motivates the student toward goals. Parents should help their children but let them take responsibility for finding personal goals; this can be facilitated by relating the good feelings about one-self to reasonable goals.[16]

In handling disciplinary problems, the teacher should help the student plan a better course of behavior, and once a student makes a commitment to change, then no excuse is accepted for failing to do so. Punishment, Glasser contends, is usually arbitrary and does not work. Discipline, in contrast, asks the student to evaluate and take responsibility for behavior.

The teacher should make learning experiences relevant by relating subjects to the lives of students and avoid conveying the idea that there is one right answer and that everything worthwhile can be measured and assigned a value. Glasser is opposed to tracking, grades, sarcasm, and ridicule.

Students should have a voice in developing and applying classroom rules; there should be reasonable rules that are firmly enforced and supported by brief periodic classroom meetings to discuss discipline problems. Although he favors abolishing rules whenever students show sufficient maturity to do without them, he believes that a permissive classroom is destructive for unsuccessful students because it generates student antagonism and a feeling that the teacher does not care about them.

Glasser believes that the teacher should relate personally to the student and set firm disciplinary limits. Minor disciplinary problems can be handled in home-room meetings; special groups, however, are necessary to handle major problems. Few meetings should be held with parents about discipline because parents usually get upset and punish the child. Whenever such meetings are held, they should be restricted to finding ways to solve the problem rather than finding fault. "Teachers have the responsibility for making education relevant and interesting; students have the responsibility *to attend class, to study, and to learn.*"[17]

Reassessment of the Models

Besides the fact that Kohl and Glasser are utilizing different models and assumptions, another difference is that while Kohl sees the system and the teachers creating many of the disciplinary problems, Glasser views student failure (caused by inability to fulfill needs) as much or more the responsibility of students as it is the parents and teachers. This difference stems largely from Kohl's child-centered approach as opposed to Glasser's behavioristic tendencies.

Both positions offer teachers, counselors, and administrators useful ideas about discipline and provide a more integrated and consistent view than usually found in the literature; on the other hand, there are certain weaknesses that should be noted. Kohl's approach provides a flexible, open-classroom setting in which the teacher displays such positive traits as responsiveness, openness, naturalness, closeness, and toughness. The teacher observes the natural development of youngsters and tries to provide an environment that will best nurture it. One is left with the impression of a humane atmosphere in which there is much freedom to learn, explore, and create. Most likely, especially under Kohl's guidance, the students will find it a happy atmosphere and will usually enjoy their school experiences. Discipline is a natural outgrowth of such a healthy learning environment.

But the natural development model tends to break down in several places. If we provide an atmosphere in which the child can develop naturally and only few disciplinary limits are set, it is still not evident where the teacher will end up by following the sequences of development stages as they unfold. Moreover, as some potentials develop they conflict with others and some criteria are needed for adjudicating the conflict. The teacher needs to offer direction and make critical decisions about which growth tendencies are to be nurtured and which are to be curbed. Growth itself exhibits and sets limits on what the child can do; it does not prescribe, however. The need for direction is not rectified by Kohl's vague statement that "the main goal of schooling is to enable young people to get out of school able to do something they value and can give to others."[18]

Student interests play a large role in determining Kohl's curriculum. But such interests cannot determine content because students have interests that are educationally undesirable (such as tying tin cans to a cat's tail), and there are things that they need to learn in which interest may be largely absent (for example, learning computation and writing skills). The task is actually that of taking sporadic interest of youngsters and broadening and deepening them in those activities in which they ought to become interested. Kohl attempts to do this to some extent, but he still views the curriculum as emerging out of student interests.

Kohl's role for the teacher, admirable as it may be, is difficult for many teachers to emulate. It is demanding to teach in an open classroom and manifest "consistency," "strength," "naturalness," and "closeness" in which teacher and students are moral equals. Most teachers prefer a more structured classroom environment wherein teacher-student relations are more clearly delineated. Until there are more successful programs preparing teachers for open classrooms, Kohl's type of teacher will be a minority.

Glasser's model also has a number of significant strengths and weaknesses that should be carefully considered before implementation. Glasser's program, in contrast to Kohl's, is more structured and more easily put into practice; it is clearly stated and reasonably well organized. Another strong feature is that it shows how to cultivate discipline without resorting to punishment. Glasser also recommends that the teacher should relate personally with the student and teach relevant material. Kohl would concur with Glasser about punishment and generally about the teacher's role, except Kohl would emphasize in greater detail the precise traits of openness needed.

One of the chief differences, besides the matter of Glasser's structure, is the emphasis on students' making a commitment to be "responsible" for their behavior. Glasser achieves a greater balance than Kohl for learning failures by having both teachers and students share distinctive responsibilities, whereas Kohl seems to believe that bad environments, created by teachers, administrators, parents, and the community, are the cause.

Glasser's approach, however, is afflicted with several related problems. He talks about people denying reality and therefore having to be taught how to face it. But to talk in this manner is to glibly gloss over some exceedingly complex problems that philosophers have struggled with for generations. What he probably means is that when an individual is acting responsibly, then that person is surely in touch with reality. This way of phrasing it, however, tells us more about psychological adjustment than resolving any questions about what is reality.

In contrast to Freud, Glasser wants to judge maladjustment and school failures in moral terms. This raises two questions over which there currently is a division of opinion. Is it ethically right to do so? And even if not unethical, is it pedagogically and therapeutically sound? Since Glasser is deviating from established practice here, he should offer a more complete and adequate justification.

Central to Glasser's system is the needs-deficiency model. These needs, Glasser holds, are deficiency or basic needs rather than derived needs (activities or processes used to satisfy basic needs such as learning to handle money or how to cook). In making statements about what an individual needs, the need actually exists to fulfill some objective ("he needs to learn to read in order to hold a job"). In such cases a need is recognized as such only if it fulfills a desired objective. Whether an objective is desirable is determined by a set of values or a philosophy of education. Glasser, unfortunately, has focused primarily on the needs and not the objectives and has spoken of objectives often in negative terms of eliminating school failure rather than a set of positive outcomes supported by a justifiable set of values.

Glasser fails to demonstrate that the two needs he cites are actually deficiency needs and that their fulfillment will overcome psychiatric problems and school failures. Psychologists who use a needs approach often disagree on basic needs. For instance, Abraham Maslow has postulated a hierarchy of needs that largely differs from Glasser's approach.[19] Some psychotherapists would also disagree that a deficiency in affection or love from another significant person or a group will inevitably lead to emotional illness or, in Glasser's term, "irresponsibility."[20] Empirical evidence is mixed. Some research studies do not support the use in classrooms of reality-therapy methods for improving self-concept, whereas other studies do provide some support.[21]

In conclusion, both Kohl and Glasser offer significant alternative approaches to classroom discipline, and their models can be used profitably as long as the preceding shortcomings are kept carefully in mind.

The Social-Literacy Approach

Alfred S. Altschuler bases his social-literacy approach[22] on Paulo Freire's educational philosophy, problem-posing processes, and dialog relationships.[23] His approach is organized into goals and methods. The goals section presents a synopsis of Freire's philosophy and some theoretical and strategic considerations; the methods section attempts to show how to resolve conflicts through dialog, raise consciousness, utilize the problem-posing process, and even handle mainstreaming, minimum competencies, and burnout. Social literacy focuses on prevention whereas most approaches, says Altschuler, are remedial and situation specific. This allegation seems to be essentially true about the weaknesses of other approaches; however, let us defer judgment momentarily on how well he has succeeded in his quest for prevention.

By posing questions with others, it should be possible to locate the conflict-producing roles and rules. By searching for generative themes (the central conflicts), it should be possible to show how the system victimizes those involved. And through democratic dialog, it should be possible to change the system by overcoming conflict and making it easier for people to love. The approach was initially employed in 1971 in the Springfield, Massachusetts, schools where observations were made to identify key variables; then in 1976 funding was obtained from USOE, which was used for training one hundred teachers from ten schools in an intensive three-week workshop; but no follow-up by independent evaluators was reported.

One objective of social literacy is to move participants from either a belief that the situation of oppression is an unchangeable fact of existence or that the problem lies in individuals who deviate from the rules and roles of the system to the critical-transforming stage where the problem is recognized in the conflict-producing, oppressive roles and rules of the system that victimize participants. To help individuals, the following activities are employed: a five-step process to identify central conflicts, consciousness-raising exercises, and instructions for problem solving.

Whatever the merits of the methodology, it does not seem that it could be used successfully just by reading the book; it would probably be necessary to listen to the eight audio-cassette tapes currently available and to participate in a social-literacy group, preferably under the supervision of an experienced group leader.

Although he shows much imagination and boldness in deriving the social-literacy approach from Freire's philosophy of education, the problem may lie in uncritically accepting and adopting some of Freire's ideas. Freire's aim is to help people become more fully human and to help overcome the conditions of oppression that prevent its realization. The fully human aim, however, seems to commit the naturalistic fallacy. Nevertheless, it is still a seductive aim until one realizes how widely it has been resisted. Those opposing the fully human aim include those holding humans to be innately wicked or brutish (Calvinists and Hobbesians), creators of a higher man (Nietzschians and Shavians), self-transcenders (some idealists), opponents of shaping youth toward a desired end (some romantics), devotees of transcending humankind and merging with a higher being or consciousness (most mystics), and potential transformers of human nature (eugenicists and genetic engineers).

Freire says that "any situation in which 'A' objectively exploits 'B' or hinders his pursuit of self-affirmation as a responsible person is one of oppression."[24] But he still needs to state criteria for oppression in order that its determination not be left to the judgment of each individual or group. Altschuler accepts Freire's notion by stating that "Oppression exists whenever there is economic exploitation or whenever an individual's development is blocked."[25] Dividing the world into oppressors and oppressed, as Freire has done, greatly oversimplifies because it fails to consider sufficiently the distribution and uses of power, economic realties, and the operations of social-class systems. Thus the social-literacy approach of exclusively blaming the system is an oversimplification and a distortion. More suitable approaches are available to ascribe collective responsibility.[26]

Coupled with the concept of oppression is Altschuler's widespread employment of a war-game metaphor of classroom conflict. But this is an unconvincing and inaccurate metaphor, whether we follow Clausewitz or a more recent military strategist, because the objective of war is to bring the enemy into battle and to defeat him in battle. The mistake is a confusion between conflict (and sometimes violence) and war itself. Thus to the extent that the causes of discipline problems are inaccurately diagnosed, the system is limited as a preventive measure. But despite the misgivings just cited, it is still a bold and imaginative approach that merits considerable attention and field testing.

A Normative-Proactive View of Discipline

To begin an examination of my own model of discipline, the question of what discipline would be like in an ideal society must be addressed. Each of us may have our own utopia, and the characteristics of such a utopia would surely influence what discipline would be like. It is unnecessary to outline my utopia, however, before stating an ideal form of discipline.

Ideally, the failures in discipline found frequently today would be nonexistent or negligible. Instead, each child would learn discipline naturally and effortlessly. The rigors, demands, austerity, self-denials, stringency of rules and requirements would be a hallmark of an earlier age where such challenges were thought good for the individual—an example of character building. Not only because some cannot successfully undertake and withstand these rigors would I ideally propose that they be eliminated; in addition, these rigors are unnecessary in an ideal system. But it might be objected that what is being proposed is fallacious for two reasons. One is that what is called "discipline" is not discipline at all but some sort of license or anarchy. But this contention rests on conventional notions of discipline; concepts evolve, and discipline is no exception. In a more utopian society, present concepts may be discredited.

In the second place, it may be claimed that without the traditional rigors generally associated with discipline, the young will not develop good character traits; they will be wild and impulsive, disrespectful of legitimate authority, unproductive and shiftless. But it could well be that the relationship between developing discipline and shaping character is no more than an accidental connection established by the type of society and justified post facto. In other words, different types of societies, (for example, democratic as opposed to totalitarian) offer different models of acceptable discipline;

they then seek to rationalize the models by such devices as associating good character and sound discipline.

What is being proposed then is that not only the characteristics and competencies generally associated with discipline could be acquired much more effortlessly; it is also suggested that many of the manifestations of disciplined behavior would be less in evidence in an ideal society because one's actions would have greater continuity and integration, they would grow out of what is healthy, and what individuals genuinely want to do, and what is healthy would largely coincide. Tensions between the individual and society, destructive conflicts in interpersonal relationships, and wars among nations would become little more than curiosities of history. Nothing unusual here: utopian thinkers have envisioned some of these changes for centuries, with each offering his own way to attain them, whether anarchism, socialism, communism, or some other ism.

What is also being suggested is that some current forms of discipline may have a place and could be justified even though they might well be discarded in a more ideal society. They might be warranted because either they promote certain desired goals and in so doing do not violate rights or dehumanize. Or they may be warranted because it has been shown that it is the best way to build widely valued character traits. A character trait such as fortitude may best be developed through certain disciplinary practices, and this character trait may be valued by a number of institutions and groups. If society, however, needs reform, the way to do it is not by abolishing present forms of discipline because ultimately such forms would be substantially modified and some discarded in an ideal society. Rather, present disciplinary forms may well be needed to assure that the demanding tasks that lay ahead will be properly performed. During the transition period to the more ideal society, participants will be reminded that the purposes for which these disciplinary traits were originally established are being changed, but some traits can now be used for other purposes. If one use of fortitude today, for instance, is to compete unflinchingly in the rivalry among firms for new markets, fortitude in the transition period may be employed to assure that participants persist in pursuing the goals of the emerging ideal society despite adversity, discouragement, and setbacks.

This means that discussing discipline in connection with an ideal society will not in itself tell us how to get there (other than to catalog what traits possibly developed through discipline would be needed—which I will not do here). Creating such a society demands much more than these traits despite their importance. My purpose instead is merely to suggest that the traits currently honored may not be the ones most valued in the future; thus if that future is worth achieving, it may be wise to make some compromises between serving the present and the future. This would probably mean that in any normative schema both types of traits would need to be built in. But to make this suggestion may be misleading insofar as certain societal changes would first be needed before the new disciplinary traits would prove functional and worthwhile. The traits, in other words, are servants of society rather than the converse; they are created in response to new conditions. Since it would be folly to sacrifice people for a distant future that may never arrive—or at least not in the lifetimes of people living today—then it would be best to concentrate on a discipline schema that focuses on the demands of the present and immediate future with perhaps a few new traits for the transitional periods.

A Discipline Model

So far, in connection with Kohl and Glasser, natural-development and deficiency models were evaluated and their shortcomings noted. Other models (though not necessarily applied to discipline itself) have been used in various academic disciplines: homeostasis, the brain as a computer, man as a machine, evolution, society as an organism, and others. Various earlier models can be found in education: the mind as a muscle (formal-discipline theory); the mind as a receptacle or storage bin for knowledge; Rousseau's unfoldment model; and Dewey's growth model, to name a few.

The role of a model is to provide an interpretation of phenomena through a form of analogy. A model may suggest ways to expand the theory that the model is either a part of or in which the theory is embedded. An established model can help a new theory gain acceptance if it resembles the model.

A model of athletics, as an interpretive analogy, may promote a better understanding of discipline. *Athletics* refers to sports, games, and exercises that may require physical strength, skill, stamina, or speed. A *sport* is an atheletic act requiring skill or physical prowess and often performed competitively. A *game* is an activity engaged in for amusement or diversion; it may be competitively conducted according to rules. *Exercise* is bodily exertion for the sake of physical fitness; it may be practiced in order to develop, improve, or display a specific ability or skill.

Thus discipline is somehow like sports, games, and exercises; precisely what the analogy is will need to be shown by first looking more closely at the features of these three activities. These three activities are obviously active rather than passive, but the activity is not random, capricious, or accidental but is goal directed. Being goal directed helps impart meaning to the activities and aids the participants in knowing better the whys for their performances. The goals may differ, however. The goal of many sports and games is winning, though some games are played merely for amusement or diversion. The object is to win within the framework of the rules so that the opposing players or team will not question whether one won fairly and possibly issue a formal challenge to the "victory." For some, the goal in sports is to gain fame; and some professional athletes aspire to wealth while others will settle on sports as a desirable way to earn a good living. In such cases, winning is not the goal but the immediate objective necessary to secure the long-range goal of fame, earning a good living, or becoming wealthy. In contrast, the goals of exercise may be none of the above; instead, they may be undertaken to condition for better health, improve appearance, or to prepare to participate more effectively in a sport.

The participants in the three generic activities may be individuals (as in golf, tennis singles), teams (baseball, basketball), or a combination (amateur wrestling, boxing, and gymnastics, in which the participants compete individually but their performance is tallied with their team). Games, as well as sports, may be of one of these three types of participation. In contrast to sports, games are more diverse and numerous (if all physical games of all age levels, especially children's, are included; mental games are excluded in the model). Exercise may be solitary or in an exercise group; teams are not involved, and it is not usually competitive, though one will likely try to improve on her own performance.

Authority is found in various forms in the three generic types of activities. Sports and games are rule constituted. In other words, without the rules there would be no sports or games because constitutive rules define them: what constitutes a score, how one competes successfully, rules for the players, or the object or purpose of the activities. Authority enters insofar as the originator of the sport or game created the rules; in turn, the rules are interpreted, applied, and enforced by referees, judges, or umpires. Exercise, in contrast, relies less on rules and more on instruction with the object to perform the exercise correctly in order to attain the desired results. Athletics are governed by standards in the sense that participants have benchmarks to achieve and are informed about their performance and progress.

Sports get their structure not only by their goals, rules, and standards but by their timing. To participate, the athlete needs to know about the beginning and end of the match, contest, or event; rest periods too are part of the structure—many team sports having rest periods, and other sports (track and swimming) do not once the event begins. Thus the activity may either be continuous or discontinuous. Once the event begins the purpose may be to overcome certain obstacles (modern equestrian) or the obstacles may be besting the opponents, or some combination. Along the way, many sports impose penalties of varying degrees of severity for rule infractions. Thus a synopsis of our discussion is presented in table 4-1.

The discussion so far shows what it means to participate in athletics, but it does not directly explain failure. Perhaps there are games in which no one fails—and certainly new ones could be designed in such a manner; yet it is

Table 4-1
Athletics Model

	Participants	*Activities*	*Organization*	*Regulations*	*Goals*
Sports	Individual or team	Continuous and discontinuous	Constitutive rules	Refereed, penalties	Winning, fame, wealth, enjoyment
Games	Individual or team	Continuous and discontinuous	Constitutive rules	Usually not refereed, penalties	Winning, enjoyment
Exercise	Individual or group	Usually discontinuous	Instruction	Usually no referee or penalties	Conditioning

true that sports are prominent for placing emphasis on winning and avoiding losing; games and exercises may place less stress on failure, especially exercises that could be tailored precisely to the person's interests and abilities. Someone could fail in athletics by any one of the following reasons or combinations: lack of requisite attributes, insufficient or inappropriate motivation, deficiency in certain intellectual abilities (concentration, quickness of judgment and ability to note connected events and make rapid decisions, ability to follow directions), lack of self-control or incontinence, inadequate performance by teammates (in team sports and games), and adverse environmental conditions (excess heat or cold, wet track, and so on).

A further word about models and athletics as a model: Models may be "models of" or "models for." The former are isomorphic, as scale-model prototypes of new airplanes, whereas the latter are not isomorphic. Instead, "models for" are more like hypotheses or assertions about the expected behavior of certain phenomena. The model may have negative as well as positive analogies; the negative analogies, which are misleading, are merely discarded.

Now how can the model of athletics help explain discipline? Discipline, like athletics, is active rather than passive. It is, in other words, not something done to someone; it is "proactive" rather than passive or reactive. Although we can speculate about discipline as a concept or theory, discipline as an activity contrasts to a speculative or contemplative pursuit. The person is the doer of the action: it may involve physical movement, ranging from usual functioning to vigorous and quickened action. Agency for action is of primary importance. Agency is attributed to people and partly to animals, not things or events. Thus if after careful investigation we cannot identify who performed a so-called action, it might be assumed that no action was committed. For instance, if a house looks as though it has been burglarized but no evidence of an actual burglar can be uncovered, then the damage may have been caused by a storm or some other natural event.

Since discipline is active and therefore not something done to someone else, it raises the question, is it accurate to say that someone was disciplined for his misbehavior? Here punishment and disapproval should be distinguished from discipline. To be more accurate, what was taking place was punishment or disapproval either for misbehavior or some deficiency, a case of failing to meet approved standards. What is done to get people to observe the standards is not discipline itself but certain external devices.

Again, discipline, as with athletics, is not random or capricious but goal directed. One need not be concentrating on the goal at all times in order to claim that an activity is goal directed any more than an athlete must think about the goal at all times rather than focus on the action at hand. As long as the goal or goals are compelling motives for participating and give a reason for action, it is sufficient to say that it is goal directed. But what are the goals of discipline? Are they the same or similar to those of sports, games, and exercises? It is not necessary that discipline have the same or similar goals, only that it be a goal-directed activity. Instead the goals of discipline are diverse because they depend on the objective of the activity for which discipline is employed. Such goals can be divided into extrinsic and intrinsic ones. Extrinsic goals could include: bring about order, show an ability to follow rules or instructions, perform a task in a certain way successfully (so that it was evident that discipline largely made it possible). Intrinsic goals, in contrast, are about a well-disciplined person, a person who manifests a certain type of character or intellectual disposition.

That an activity is goal directed does not in itself make it desirable, as other conditions must also be met. Similarly, actions that are casual and capricious are not discipline, but not all capricious behavior is a discipline problem, just as all fast driving (as in professional auto racing) is not considered "speeding."

As in athletics, discipline may be individual, group, or team. The team is less frequent and found only where individuals define themselves as organized on a team basis, whether in sports, games, military maneuvers, life-saving groups, and the like. Discipline in school is more frequently an individual or group matter. The classroom itself may be viewed as a group, and the teacher a group leader who uses group dynamics. But some classrooms may also have subgroups and cliques that generate tension and conflict. Even when group leaders precipitate conflicts, the problem may still be analyzed from a group perspective in terms of how the other members react to the leader's instigation.

Problems become individual rather than group when the student formulates and acts on goals that conflict with legitimate disciplinary regulations. This would be the case if a student decided to bring a trombone to English class and play an impromptu solo, whereas it would be a group problem if the student got together with the students in her clique and each member decided to secrete musical instruments into class and begin playing with abandon upon a prearranged signal from the group leader. Thus it is not necessary to postulate some sort of group mind to distinguish the two; rather, with group acts, agency is consultive or by consensus and is coordinated rather than planned and performed independently.

Discipline activities are usually discontinuous rather than continuous. They would be considered continuous when they take the form of team activities that are conducted from beginning to end without breaks or rest periods. But since most home and school activities are discontinuous, more attention will be given them.

Are more problems created by their being discontinuous and, if so, should they be reorganized into continuous activities? This question bears on the organization of the school day, the structure of the curriculum, and the sequencing of instruction. This is a large and complex question that is raised now only to present the model; later, perhaps, it can be explored when it relates to other findings. But it can be noted that to the extent that a significant discrepancy exists between the way students learn and an environment structured discontinuously, then serious thought will need to be given to remedial action.

Discipline features constitutive rules as well as instruction. Since students do not always know what is best to do or how to do it, they receive instruction from teachers. Receiving and assimilating instruction is not an abridgement of agency as long as coercive measures are not employed; however, since coercion is common in some classrooms, then in such cases the student is subject to control, not discipline, because agency is lost. Of course, each case differs, and it will be impossible to claim all coercion as examples of control; yet, in general, without contrary information, coercion would not be discipline.

Constitutive rules would be found in academic subjects; and to the extent that students need to learn the rules in order to master the subject could be an instance in which discipline comes into play. It will be seen more clearly shortly why this is likely to be the case.

In athletics, sports are refereed and have penalties; in games, penalties are found, but they usually are not refereed; and in exercise, usually referees are absent and penalties are not imposed. Which then is characteristic of discipline? To ask the question in this way, however, is to assume that discipline is solely of one type. Discipline could take more than one form depending on the characteristics and purposes of the activity. In schools, *discipline* generally refers to students' behavior and to the study of the curriculum; within these two activities may be some subdivisions. For instance, with behavior we can speak about how well a student handles or conducts herself, how she relates to classmates, and how she relates to the teacher and other school authorities. On the academic side, different types of skills are called on in various subjects, and tools for study and investigation may vary, though they would have to share something to be spoken of as discipline.

To the extent that standards of performance are present, school discipline is largely refereed. But if what is meant by *refereed* is something more literal—that someone is there to see that the standards are observed—then this is the case in much discipline in home and school; it would vary with age and maturity of the learner as well as the activity. Obviously, there are not only referees but referees who enforce penalties. The penalties, however, as in the case of the earlier discussion of punishment, do not constitute discipline. Penalties, in the form of various sanctions, are imposed to get students to observe standards and regulations; however, the penalties themselves are not discipline but external devices. Of course, we do speak of someone's being disciplined by imposing certain sanctions; yet the discipline is not external to the person but a characteristic of his action—whether individual, group, or team. The teacher may say that she imposed discipline, but what is actually the case is that she employed certain devices (that could be specified) to help promote better discipline. Devices in themselves do not discipline because teachers have to solicit the cooperation of students; otherwise, there would be no student agency and therefore no discipline, although there may be coercion and consequently control.

A prominent feature in athletics is not only the referee but the coach. Teachers tend to combine both functions. Coaches try to bring out the best in their players: they help them to understand and use their abilities as fully as possible, and they seek to develop new athletic abilities. The coach instructs the athlete in the fine points of the sport, explains strategy, and diagnoses problems in the athlete's technique and prescribes how best to overcome these problems. The teacher in turn may seek to recognize individual differences and adapt instruction to the learner; the teacher also diagnoses learning difficulties and employs remedial devices. In athletics, both the referee and the coach can impose penalties, whereas those allowed the referee are carefully predefined in contrast to the coach who has a wider range of options. The teacher's options or sanctions are limited by school regulations and students' legal rights.

But why does discipline break down? Do the generic ways in which someone fails in athletics illuminate discipline problems? As noted earlier, an athlete could fail because of a lack of requisite ability. If discipline is required in mastering certain aspects of a subject and the student lacks the ability, then the student is unable, at least at that point, to complete the task successfully. Thus to speak about discipline, it is necessary to observe the abilities of students and set tasks that can be mastered within a reasonable period of time.

Just as with athletes, some students lack adequate motivation and self-control. They see little point in their studies and self-control. They see little point in their studies and consequently have difficulty concentrating and applying themselves; and their lack of self-control dissipates their energy and impulses in directions that may oppose disciplinary goals.

In team sports and games, athletes may fail because of inadequate performance by teammates. In classrooms, students who belong to groups or cliques may fail to observe rules because they are following their peers. The clique's goals may differ from instructional goals. Thus many discipline breakdowns arise from the influence of peers—and as long as the student was not coerced but chose to follow them, it would fit into our model.

Athletes sometimes fail because of adverse environmental conditions (excessive heat or cold, wet playing surface), and students may fail to exhibit sound discipline because of adverse classroom or school conditions: excessive noise, overcrowding, improperly ventilated rooms, and unsafe playgrounds may all contribute to certain disciplinary problems.

So far this section has explored the model; however, there may be some facets of discipline that either are not in the model or are present but not explicit. Is discipline an either-or-matter? Though it is common to speak of someone as disciplined or lacking in discipline, these locutions do not correspond with the way discipline is actually evaluated because it is unusual to find in a task that discipline is either totally lacking or is perfect. It is rather a matter of degree, which in some cases can be accurately assessed. Discipline implies intent in the sense that the individual had a choice and strove to complete a task in order to fulfill a goal. *Focus* means to fix or settle on one thing: to concentrate by bringing something to the center of one's attention by directing one's thoughts and efforts to the task. Inability to do so may signify a lack of sufficient or appropriate discipline.

To say that one is disciplined is to say that her habits are orderly, that she is able to observe rules of conduct, follow instruction properly, exercise self-control in learning tasks; it also signifies that the individual exhibits proper or appropriate mental training by completing desired tasks and fulfilling worthwhile standards. To speak of desired tasks and worthwhile standards brings us to certain normative features of discipline.

Normative Aspects of Discipline

The *normative* aspects of discipline refer to the moral grounds on which discipline could be based. When teachers or administrators take action to overcome discipline problems, they need to recognize what techniques will have dehumanizing effects or impede the pursuit of desirable learning objectives. Not just any methods for promoting discipline will do: the specific methods enter into discipline and can be as important as discipline itself. Thus what makes an objective legitimate and the moral grounds that should be considered are essential normative issues. First, however, the overall school and classroom environment in which dehumanization may occur must be considered.

Dehumanization may occur in many different situations and take a number of different forms. Traumatic situations tend to brutalize people and would be a case of extreme dehumanization. These situations cause shock, mortification, dismay, worthlessness, and other feelings. Acts of violence, harsh corporal punishment, and related acts may cause it.

Other dehumanizing acts would be humiliation in terms of one's sense of dignity, a situation in which one feels that he is treated as a thing or object, and a situation that causes the person to feel that he is not in control of his own actions but is propelled by known or unseen forces beyond his control. The case of humiliation occurs in many schools by the student who is well motivated but is embarrassed by the teacher before the rest of the class because he does not know the answer or told publicly he will "never amount to anything" because of his behavior. The reader, no doubt, can add many more instances.

The student may feel that he is treated as a thing or object by the teacher establishing a quasi-master-slave relationship or acting as though students are little more than machines to be properly programmed. The former occurs with authoritarian teachers, and the latter may arise when teachers utilize a psychology of learning that employs a programming model—whether it is a narrow behaviorism or whether it is viewing the brain as a computer.

When students feel that they are subject to large, unresponsive bureaucracies or an administration or school board that exercises stringent control over their lives, they may believe they no longer are the author of their actions—merely puppets whose strings are being pulled. In contrast, when student government works effectively and the administration observes and protects students' rights, it is unlikely that this form of dehumanization will occur.[27]

Thus any method or procedure to promote sound discipline must first meet the test of whether it dehumanizes students in any of the ways listed. But other safeguards must be observed as well. Sound discipline may be good for its own sake insofar as a person who exhibits such traits would be thought admirable or worthy of emulation. And discipline,as more commonly believed, is good for contributing to some objective external to it—which, in this case, would be a learning objective. Whether it actually contributes is an empirical question. Yet the learning objectives themselves must be worthwhile before practices, conceived instrumentally, could be warranted. In other words, to take an extreme example, the practices in the Nazi program were unwarranted because the overall learning objectives were unjustifiable. Of course, a case could probably be made for many different types of learning objectives; but rather than review a long list, it may be more fruitful to observe that if the learning objectives culminate in an educated person, that in itself would be sufficient justification because this is presumably what schools and colleges are all about. Yet, one may ask, what today is an *educated person*?[28] The criteria vary, and any set of criteria will need their own justification, but once they gain the needed support, the practices to promote sound discipline will in turn be justified as long as they do not dehumanize.

Thus how does the preceding discussion relate to specific practices to promote discipline? Quite simply, the analysis probably rules out what was earlier called "harsh discipline" and those practices based on conditioning, programming, and manipulating students. It obviously does not rule them out (eliminate them) legally or in terms of majority views (depending on the community surveyed); yet it is worth reiterating that disciplinary practices designed to promote learning objectives that cannot be adequately justified should be eliminated.

Authority and Normative-Proactive Discipline

In the previous chapter, authority was related to common-sense notions of discipline. This section can now relate authority to normative-proactive discipline.

It was concluded in chapter 3 that one cannot gain an education totally independent of authority and that authority is the framework for legitimating discipline. By saying that authority "legitimates" discipline signifies that the right of teachers and administrators to prescribe, prohibit, or permit acts in the name of discipline rests on authority. This in no way means that every act is automatically legitimated, as any act may be formally challenged; instead, only the right is established to take actions under a generic notion of promoting discipline.

It was noted in the last chapter that teachers have a moderate to high use of rules in exercising the regulative authority of their office. In instruction the teacher's authority is used to explicate the constitutive rules and modes of formal operations in the subject matter and to get students to comprehend and utilize these rules and operations in their thinking. When a student is able to do so, we may say that she exhibits certain characteristics that are generally associated with discipline. The student may be able to concentrate on the learning task, persevere, follow instructions properly, develop orderly procedures for handling symbols and abstractions. On the other hand, if the student is overly distracted, lacks impulse control, and dissipates his energy in fruitless diversions, then it is the teacher's regulative authority that is used to promote more desirable dispositions. The teacher's efforts then are to recognize the proactive, goal-directed characteristics of discipline and utilize authority to realize extrinsic and intrinsic goals. The teacher at times serves as a referee and coach and sees that the appropriate penalties are imposed; yet the teacher's use of coercion or power cannot be considered discipline because student agency is bypassed. These two devices, if successful, could be thought of as a form of control, not discipline. Control could also be gained by administering tranquilizers, using behavior modification, threats, and the like; yet none of these devices is an example of discipline. Of course, when disorder in schools becomes widespread and personal safety is endangered, control, understandably, is usually sought rather than discipline. What is less understandable is that control is sought in many everyday school situations. Authority then cannot in itself promote sound discipline if student agency is ignored and neglected. But it is through authority that student cooperation is sought and the legitimacy established for the teacher's expectations of students.

Our analysis, however, applies to discipline; another type of analysis may be needed for school violence, a cognate topic to which the next chapter turns.

Notes

1. Stanley M. Elam, ed., *A Decade of Gallup Polls of Attitudes Toward Education 1969-1978* (Bloomington, Ind.: Phi Delta Kappa, 1978).
2. "NEA Survey Investigates Teacher Attitudes, Practices," *Phi Delta Kappan* 62 (September 1980):49.
3. Edward A. Wynne, *Looking at Schools: Good, Bad, and Indifferent* (Lexington, Mass.: Lexington Books, D.C. Heath, 1980), p. 156.
4. J.S.Shaw, "New Conservative Alternative: Fundamental Schools," *Nation's Schools and Colleges* 2 (February 1975):31-34.
5. Shirley Boes Neill, "Pasadena's Approach to the Classic School Debate," *American Education* 12 (April 1976):6-10.
6. In Robert Ulich, ed., *Three Thousand Years of Educational Wisdom*, 2d ed. (Cambridge, Mass.: Harvard University Press, 1963), pp. 110-111.
7. M.L. Meacham and A.E. Wiesen, *Changing Classroom Behavior: A Manual for Precision Teaching* (Scranton, Pa.: International Textbook, 1969, pp. 64-65.
8. Herbert Kohl, *On Teaching* (New York: Schocken Books, 1976), p. 100.
9. Ibid., p. 84.

10. Kohl has admitted his failure and how he profited by them in the following books: *36 Children* (New York: Signet Books, 1968) and *Half the House* (New York: Dutton, 1974.)

11. Kohl, *On Teaching*, pp. 115-116.

12. Herbert Kohl, *The Open Classroom* (New York: New York Review Book, 1969), pp. 80-81.

13. Kohl, *On Teaching*, p. 82.

14. William Glasser, *Reality Therapy* (New York: Harper and Row, 1965), p. 8.

15. Ibid., p. 13.

16. William Glasser, *The Identity Society* (New York: Harper and Row, 1972), ch. 8; and Glasser, *Schools Without Failure* (New York: Harper and Row, 1968), ch. 2.

17. Glasser, *Schools Without Failure*, p. 201.

18. Kohl, *On Teaching*, p. 102.

19. See Maslow's *Motivation and Personality*, 2d ed. (New York: Harper and Row, 1970).

20. See "Rational-Emotive Therapy," as developed by Albert Ellis in *Reason and Emotion in Psychotherapy* (New York: Lyle Stuart, 1962) and *Humanistic Psychotherapy* (New York: McGraw-Hill Paperbacks, 1974).

21. Donald F. Shearn and Daniel Lee Randolph, "Effects of Reality Therapy Methods Applied in the Classroom," *Psychology in the Schools* (January 1978):79-83.

22. Alfred S. Altschuler, *School Discipline: A Socially Literate Solution* (New York: McGraw-Hill, 1980).

23. See Freire's *Pedagogy of the Oppressed* (New York: Herder and Herder, 1972); *Eduation for Critical Consciousness* (New York: Seabury Press, 1973); and *Education: The Practice of Freedom* (London: Writers and Readers Publishing Cooperative, 1976).

24. Freire, *Pedagogy of the Oppressed*, p. 40.

25. Altschuler, *School Discipline*, p. 84.

26. See my "Responsibility, Rights, and Accountability in Education," *The Educational Forum* 44 (March 1980):355-362.

27. For a further discussion of dehumanization, see my *Humanistic Foundations of Education* (Worthington, Ohio: Charles A. Jones Publishing, 1971), ch. 2.

28. I have explored this question in *Challenge and Response: Education in American Culture* (New York: Wiley, 1974), pp. 169-172.

5 Theories of School Violence

Violence has a long and varied history in American life. It is therefore not surprising to find it in schools. But it is surprising that school violence would grow during the early 1970s, a period when student rights were more widely recognized and many new alternatives were being developed.

According to the "Safe School Study," violence increased from the early sixties to the seventies but leveled off after the early 1970s.[1] When the amount of time spent in school is taken into account, the amount of violence to teenagers is greater in school than elsewhere. In a typical month about one-half of 1 percent of all secondary-school students have something taken from them by use of force, threat, or weapons. About 1.3 percent of secondary-school students surveyed in the study were attacked in a typical month, with about twice as many junior-high as senior-high students assaulted. As for public secondary-school teachers, the proportions are similar to those of students. About one-half of 1 percent of the teachers are attacked in a given month (about 5,200 teachers), and approximately 19 percent of the attacks on teachers required treatment by a doctor as compared to 4 percent of the students attacked who required such treatment. Estimates of annual costs of school crime, including vandalism, is about $200 million. Other costs that cannot always be measured in dollars and cents are the fears and tensions created, teacher burnout, and the breakdown of a healthy learning environment.

How can one make sense of these trends? It is first necessary to clarify the concept of violence to eliminate various misconceptions that tend to mislead inquiry. The first section in this chapter shows that *violence* is commonly associated with such cognate terms as 'aggression,' 'coercion,' and 'force,' and it is indicated how the concepts differ. Second, can violence under certain conditions be morally justified? In this section some theories of justification are applied to see if this is possible. Finally, the last section seeks explanations for school violence by examining theories of social deviance to determine how each theory helps us to understand violence.

The Concept of Violence

Violence is a widely used term about which some conceptual confusion still persists. Gaining an intelligible sense of the term, however, is not assured by consulting such renowned writers on the subject as George Sorel whose *Reflections on Violence* employs the term very loosely to cover a multitude of divergent social acts.[2] Violence could be associated with such cognate terms as *aggression*, *coercion*, and *force*. Aggression may characterize an individual who pursues activities boldly and vigorously; it may or may not be associated pejoratively with the desire to dominate others, but it does apply to persons who pursue causes and their ambitions zealously. An individual who is thought of as basically aggressive may rarely if ever engage in violence; conversely, a person may periodically engage in violence but not be considered a habitually aggressive person. Thus the belief that violence is merely an extreme form of aggressiveness obscures more than it clarifies. News reports of aggression of one nation toward another generally use *aggression* as a cover term to signify threatening, hostile, or violent acts.

Violence is also associated with such terms as 'coercion' and 'force.' But though it may seem that violence involves some element of coercion, it need not, as when someone sneaks up behind another and strikes him hard in the back of the head causing immediate unconsciousness. Coercion is found whenever constraint and/or inducement is high and choice is low. Coercion need not in any way be violent. A policeman can threaten to arrest a group of demonstrators (an act of coercion) without using violence. Usually coercion involves an action by an individual, organization, or government to get an individual, group or organization to do *X* when their intention is to do *Y*. If the coercer is in a position of authority or can exercise sanctions, then success may be more likely, especially when sanctions can be applied.

Certainly violence is closely related to force insofar as a violent act would seemingly be forceful in some way.[3] But violence need not be, as Ted Honderich has claimed, "fundamentally a use of force prohibited by law."[4] Although he is correct that laws would proscribe certain violent acts, many violent acts would not be so regulated as in cases of self-defense in which the victim's violence was necessary to protect or defend against serious harm. Some violence (corporal punishment, for instance) may be permitted by law but prohibited by certain moral codes. Force involves the use of physical strength or power to cause one to do something. When subjected to force, one does not act but is acted upon. Force, when successful, may have strong coercive effects, but coercion itself is not force. Someone subject to force cannot be held responsible, but with coercion one can be held partly responsible, depending on the situation.

In speaking of physical violence, it would make no sense to say that an act was "violent but executed without force." Anyone making such a claim would likely be questioned about speaking in contradictions. Yet not all force is violence: one may force open a jammed door, force ahead of someone in line, and forcefully restrain someone from striking another person. Physical violence is done with considerable or great force rather than just a little force; it is also done suddenly, vehemently, and explosively. Thus violence is a type of force, but whether it also coerces would depend on a number of situational factors. Violence can be and is directed toward people, animals, and things.

Is there, then, one or more than one generic form of violence? Is violence, in other words, strictly physical, or can it be psychological as well? Newton Garver says that violence amounts to violating persons; it causes psychological harm that is "covert and quiet" such as a Freudian rebuff of accusing someone of having "a terrible Oedipus complex."[5] And Robert Audi concurs that violence, in addition to physical attack, can be "highly vigorous psychological abuse of, or the sharp, caustic psychological attack upon, a person or animal. . . ."[6]

It is true that violence causes harm or suffering; otherwise, violence would be of much less concern if such outcomes were missing. Without harm or suffering, violence would merely be an act involving great, sudden force. But violence need not encompass both psychological and physical harm because so extending the concept renders it unworkable. Psychological harm, in contrast to physical injury, is usually much more difficult to diagnose; physical injury is more readily observable and measurable than psychological harm, which would vary subjectively with the individual; this difference has something to do with the present state of medicine as opposed to psychiatry and psychotherapy. Additionally, criteria for physical harm are more generally agreed on by authorities than those referring to psychological harm. Moreover, extending the concept to psychological harm may vitiate the concept by stretching it to cover a far wider range of phenomena than can reasonably be handled; for if violence refers to such an enormous range of acts, then it fails to differentiate sufficiently. In any case, it is not necessary to employ the concept in this way because it is possible to describe psychological acts more precisely without using the term. One can say that she spoke accusingly, abusively, slanderously, harshly, caustically, and the like. (This does not signify, however, a lack of concern about the psychological effects of physical attack.)

Thus *violence* can be defined as *a sudden and extremely forceful act that causes physical harm or suffering to persons or animals.* One qualification needs to be made for property. One could engage in a sudden and extremely forceful act that causes harm or utter destruction to one's own property or could contract to have a demolition team destroy a building one owned; yet the owner is entitled to do whatever he wishes with his property as long as it violates no law and no one is physically harmed in the act of destruction; the act, in other words, is thereby authorized (even though the act may be repugnant, as when a building of historical interest is destroyed). Thus violence in relation to property can be defined as *a sudden and extremely forceful unauthorized act that causes harm or destruction to property*.

But we still are left with some questions about the social characteristics and functions of violence. Violence may have a rough resemblance to what Durkheim calls "social facts." There are ways of thinking and acting, Durkheim contends, that are external to the individual and exert a coercive power. These social facts are not only religious observances, public morality, and rules of professional behavior but waves of enthusiasm and social indignation found in a crowd. Social facts cannot be discerned through introspections; they are external to the individual and significantly shape human actions.[7]

Violence is a social fact insofar as it cannot be fully understood through psychological investigation; it not only originates in a given society but gains its significance through social interpretation. Thus what is violence and how it will be defined, the extent and type of violence to be regulated, and the choice of acceptable sanctions are all socially determined. Still this does not carry us very far inasmuch as violence is one among innumerable social facts.

John Searle's distinction between "brute" and "institutional" facts may help.[8] *Brute* facts deal with concepts that are essentially physical ("This rock is next to that rock"); the model for such knowledge is drawn from the natural sciences and is based on empirical observation. A ballistics expert, for example, could describe the internal workings of a gun used in a violent act, the trajectory of the shell, distance traveled, and so on, and the angle at which it entered the person's chest. But something would still be missing. It could be asked what makes this act a violent act or why the act was committed. In other words, brute facts may be necessary in determining essential features of the case; they do not in themselves offer an interpretation of violent acts and, as will be demonstrated, interpretations are sorely needed.

Additionally, Searle's institutional facts apply partly to violent acts insofar as these facts involve constitutive rules that are characteristics of such social activities as marriage, football, and the monetary-exchange system. Various activities such as games are defined in terms of and owe their existence to rules; therefore, the rules do not merely regulate but make sense out of the activity. Violence in its most abstract form is not an institutional fact, but neither is a human interaction devoid of context. Within one context dealing cards is part of bridge; in another, fortune telling. In one context, violence is capital punishment; in another, a grizzly crime; in still another, corporal punishment.

Violence is largely governed by what Searle calls "regulative rules" that regulate independently existing forms of behavior.[9] Violence, in this instance, is not defined by but is regulated by rules and laws insofar as it is brought under the control of rules and laws in order to eliminate it or reduce its incidence. If it is admitted that, in light of our definition, one could commit a violent act against oneself (such as mutilation or suicide), then some violent acts may be unregulated in certain localities. Violent acts, whether regulated or unregulated, are either planned or spontaneous. Some involve simple or elaborate plans; others are performed impulsively or from sudden rage. Violence would either be defensive or offensive, though the latter is more common. And violence could be either through direct contact or at a distance through the employment of weapons. It is no less an act of violence because someone does not have direct physical contact.

Is all violence intentional or can there be cases of accidental violence? It would be misleading to say that "He committed an act of violence accidentally." Here a distinction is needed between violent acts and violent occurrences. Such occurrences, as a violent explosion, can be accidental; violent acts, however, are intentional.

Problems in the Justification of Violence

Can violence to property or persons ever be justified?[10] On prima-facie grounds violence tends to offend and repel both by its shock value from the sudden force and vehemence of the act and by its resultant harm and injury. But could there be cases in which violence is morally justified?

The question of harm or destruction to property is not usually controversial as long as one knows the condition of the property prior to the act (so that the damage can be accurately assessed) and who committed the act (it cannot be by the owner or her approved agent following the owner's orders because the act would be authorized). Property could be defaced, seriously damaged, or destroyed. To clarify these states, *defacement* is stipulated as minor damage that costs less than one-half the original price of the property to repair; *serious damage* would be more than one-half the original price of the property to repair; and *destruction* would obviously leave the property irreparable. Respective examples would be a dented car fender; damage that required replacement of the car's motor, axle, and steering column; and the fire bombing of a car causing a gasoline explosion.

A victim may be harmed when violent acts of others damage his property, prevent him from exercising his rights, or cause him physical injury that does not relate to property or rights. Physical violence, for instance, may cause the victim to lapse into a lengthy coma and therefore prevent him from exercising his rights as much as or even more than being forcefully impeded or imprisoned. In contrast, some violent acts may not interfere with the excercise of rights, as in the case of a minor laceration.

Violence to persons is either self-inflicted or inflicted by others. Some forms of self-mutilation and suicide are prominent examples of violence against oneself. Advocates of such violence might claim these acts to be morally justified when individuals are in full control of their rational abilities and have considered the significance of their lives and the consequences of their act. This is based on the notion that despite obligations to others, basic control over one's life is the individual's own decision. Outsiders can rightfully attempt by reason and persuasion to discourage the suicide because that would be entering into a rational dialog, but it would be illegitimate to use force or violence to prevent it unless the individual is irrational and thereby fails to meet the previously stated criteria.[11]

In schools, however, since minors are involved, school authorities can rightfully prohibit and attempt to prevent self-mutilation and suicide. They can do so on paternalistic grounds. A *paternalistic act* protects the subject from harm and/or promotes his welfare; it is the basic reason for attempted or successful coercive interference with the action or state of a person. Such an act is done in the person's best interest whenever the individual is unable or incapable of performing the act for himself.

The objective of paternalistic intervention in preventing violence to oneself is to prevent harm, which obviously consists of danger to life and limb but could also include serious dangers of mental and emotional harm. Thus harm would be those factors under the school's aegis that endanger well-being by rendering one temporarily or permanently incapable of benefiting from an education. Schools place safety restrictions on the use of certain power tools in machine-shop courses (though some students may contend that these regulations abridge their freedom) and quarantine students who have contagious diseases. Thus if such practices are warranted, certainly paternalistic intervention to prevent self-mutilation or suicide is even more justified to prevent harm and to avert temporary or permanent incapacity to benefit from an education. Even if the student claims to be rational and to fully foresee the consequences of her act (though some paternalists would contend that such acts are never rational), paternalistic intervention would still be warranted for the reasons previously noted. In the case of self-mutilation in which the anticipated harm would be minor, the student's education would not be interrupted; therefore paternalistic intervention may have to be justified on the ground that schools attempt to teach rationality and the act, which is irrational, should therefore be proscribed (assuming it can be demonstrated that the act is irrational).

The second and more common type of school violence is violence by others, whether it be one or several persons who attack another person or persons. Consequentialism is the most plausible form for justifying this type of violence. *Consequentialism* holds that the rightness of an act is to be judged solely in terms of its consequences, either actual or anticipated. Two major forms of consequentialism will be presented: egoism (individual and ethical) and rights rebellion.

The egoist claims that it is the individual's obligation to promote for herself what is in the individual's own interest. This does not mean that one cannot help others, for there are many altruistic acts that are in the individual's interest to perform; it only denies that one should help others when one would not benefit. The universal form of ethical egoism states that everyone should always act in her own self-interest.

A person inclined to violence or a member of a violent gang may use universal ethical egoism as a rationale for school violence. The individual might declare that each person ought to realize the highest-order life plan he is able to attain within his circumstances.[12] The violent-prone individual may then include violence as part of his life plan. Does this formulation avoid the weakness of inconsistency usually attributed to universal ethical egoism? The inconsistency arises when the egoist universalizes, for at that point others may have self-interests that conflict; and therefore to tell others that they too should pursue their own self-interests means that one's own self-interest is less likely to be fulfilled. But the preceding formulation recognized that within the circumstances in which each person finds himself, he should attempt to realize his life plan, which would likely result in varying degrees of fulfillment, with some persons unable to realize their life plan. Consequently, some persons who prefer a life of violence may be unsuccessful in pursuing it—at least for very long. Since violent acts may interfere with the freedom and well-being of others, he may hope that when conflicts of self-interest arise, others will not always pursue their own interests.

If each person ought to realize her own life plan as well as she can under the circumstances, but violence prevents those injured from realizing their life plan, then it would be acceptable for those attacked to try to prevent being harmed. To carry out a life plan successfully, one must, among other things, avoid an incapacitating injury. Thus this formulation of universal ethical egoism, at least when applied to violence, is inconsistent after all because as individuals resist interference with their right to pursue their life plan, they will in turn likely resist violence and probably endorse instead some system of fairness or justice in order to gain sufficient protection.

The violent-prone person would be better off to avoid universalizing life plans; in so doing, he may adopt individual egoism, which maintains that everyone ought to act in his own self-interest. And if the person believes his self-interest lies in a violent life, then others ought to do whatever the individual believes would help him to pursue this life. Although there is nothing inconsistent with this demand (as with the previous position), the attempt to universalize has been abandoned and, to the extent that an ethical system must be capable of being universalized in order to be considered ethical, then it is an incomplete position. Individual egoism entails an inequality among persons, for this type of egoist expects his own life plan to be fulfilled even at the expense of others. Why should the individual egoist's interests count more than anyone else's? If one has certain qualities some may not have, there are still others who may share these qualities; and others may also have qualities that the egoist lacks. Why should the latter group not be given special treatment? Although the individual egoist could point out some characteristic deserving special consideration, the possession of this characteristic would become the supreme value in his system, and he would thereby be abandoning ethical egoism. What he might be advocating at this point is either ethical parochialism or ethical elitism. Ethical parochialism maintains that only the good of one's in-group, class, race, or sex should be taken into account. Ethical elitism contends that the good of an elite is the highest good and should be maximized. This does not seem to be a promising turn for the violent-prone person because the arguments commonly used against racism, sexism, and colonialism could be employed here; and against elitism, various forms of egalitarianism could be marshalled. Instead, a more promising approach for justifying violence may be rights rebellion.

Rights rebellion is based on an argument given for some forms of revolutionary activity; namely, that a group of people or a nation is suffering from oppression and their rights are being denied. It is claimed to be futile to attempt redress of grievances through the courts because the courts themselves are products of the system; and since the oppressor will never voluntarily cease exploitation, one must collectively overthrow the oppressor by any means available, including random and organized violence.[13]

The effectiveness of this oppressor-oppressed argument rests on a tacit belief in certain universal rights; once these rights are established and it could be shown that a government or official body was denying them, then some system of redress would be called for; yet it would still not follow that violence was warranted. Although many revolutionaries speak as though the end justifies whatever means necessary to achieve it, not all radical political philosophers support wholesale violence. Herbert Marcuse contends that no revolution can justify arbitrary violence, cruelty, and indiscriminate terror.[14] These unwarranted acts, however, have been used for the preservation of the status quo as well as its overthrow; understanding the historical functions and the social contexts in which these acts are perpetuated may be an indispensable weapon for combatting them.[15] In any case, revolutions have established new ethical codes: tolerance in the English Civil Wars and the inalienable rights of man in the American and French Revolutions.[16] But as Karl Popper has noted, we must be careful not to sacrifice one generation for the predicted lasting happiness of later generations. Since all generations are transient, our immediate responsibility is to this generation and the next one.[17]

But what has all of this to do with school violence, which is not a revolutionary situation and, in fact, is usually not even over the defense of rights? The term *rights rebellion* indicates that such violence can be distinguished from a revolution, which involves violent change in the leadership, policies, values and social structure of a society; instead, such rebellion involves resistance or defiance to education authorities over the alleged denial of student rights. However, the basic revolutionary argument previously stated would be largely applicable to rights rebellion.

It should be noted that the more humane treatment of students in modern times through the activities of educational reformers came about without violence, that the wider recognition of student rights during the 1970s came about through judicial decisions, and many advancements in civilization were made without violent revolutions. For instance, the slave traffic was ended by a stroke of the pen by many European governments (for example, Denmark, France, England, and Portugal) and serfdom was abolished by decrees (in Prussia and Russia). The civil-rights movement in the United States which led to, among other things, the Civil Rights Acts of 1964 and 1968, was based largely on nonviolent protest. And since its founding, the United Nation's Trusteeship Council has been instrumental in abolishing colonialism.

Could rights rebellion be roughly analogous to a just war? Justifications for such war are self-defense, preservation of the union, keeping the world safe for democracy, preventing wholesale tyranny, enslavement, and lapsing into barbarism. Whether such wars can actually be justified morally or only prudentially is debatable. In any case, these conditions do not apply to educational systems.

Before school violence could be seriously contemplated, it would be necessary to show that certain basic rights have been denied and that peaceable protest, due process, and other channels for redress of grievances are unavailable. It would also be necessary to show that procedures that cause less harm have been tried and have failed, would fail if attempted, or, on the other hand, may eventually succeed, but the probability of harm and suffering would be very great in the interim—greater than the violence designed to overthrow these conditions. But two problems arise at this point. First, one can never know in advance the total consequences of any act, which depends on what others do and how they in turn take account of what we do. It is understandable that on many casual matters, our limited knowledge is not given a second thought; however, in the case of violence, the possible gravity of the consequences makes it essential to engage first in serious deliberation.

The second problem is that the argument seems to be saying that the end justifies the means, although this charge is mitigated by the failure of authorities, in the example cited, to leave other means available. One should also note a certain inconsistency in the argument: on the one hand, violence is necessary to establish rights; yet, on the other, it would deny the rights of the victims who were killed or seriously injured. Here the argument turns into a form of utilitarianism that by certain violent acts, it is predicted, the rights of the greatest number of persons will be assured. But it is still not clear why it is fair or just to sacrifice the rights of a minority for the alleged good of the majority. Thus some principles of social justice, whether Rawls' principles or other ones, are needed to protect minority rights. These principles would need to provide safeguards that human beings treat others justly and fairly in interpersonal relations and in the distribution of scarce resources.

In conclusion, it is clear that egoism, whether ethical or individual, is unable to support school violence; that the grounds for school violence differ in some important ways from violence in the larger society; and that rights rebellion only under certain highly circumscribed conditions could provide a rationale for school violence.

Explanations for School Violence

Explanations are needed for school violence before proposing solutions. One of the best ways to do this is to examine theories of social deviance and determine how each theory helps us better understand violence. Thus four leading theories of social deviance will be presented along with programs and practices consistent with each theory for ameliorating school violence; next, the strengths and weaknesses of each theory will be noted; and finally, some concluding recommendations will be offered. The four theories presented are the social-disorganization approach, conflict approach, labeling, and differential association.

Social-Disorganization Approach

One explanation for violence lies in understanding how the social system seeks to maintain itself. A social system is organized through a consistent set of norms and values that foster orderly and predictable social interaction among its members. Leaders of society try to foster a normative consensus. Social disorganization results whenever orderly social interaction breaks down and normative consensus fails to be achieved. Disorganization stems from anomie (literally, "a state of normlessness"), or, to be more precise, a lack of consensus on norms (since some norms, even when society is disorganized, can always be found). Whenever disorganization and anomie occur, deviant behavior is likely to result; and as disorganization grows, deviance and violence increase. Social disorganization is expressed in inadequate institutionalization of goals, inappropriate procedures for achieving goals, weakened social control, and deficient socialization practices. Urban areas are disorganized whenever there is a lack of neighborhood cohesion, broken families, weak social control, and shifting population.[18]

Thus this approach would predict that school violence would likely erupt whenever disorganization and anomie are sufficient to precipitate disequilibrium in the school system. But schools will unlikely experience much violence if they can create a normative consensus, developing compelling goals and consistent procedures for achieving them, and institute effective socialization practices. A number of specific practices will likely overcome violence if we pursue this approach. Schools need to improve the socialization of students through the cooperative efforts of administrators, teachers, guidance counselors, and parents. Teachers need to inculcate greater respect for authority and the values of our cultural heritage. Students can also become acquainted with local police in a friendly, informative atmosphere; and students need to be informed about school security personnel and their functions.[19]

Conflict Approach

The conflict approach views society as a struggle of contrasting and opposing groups. Each group pursues its own values, which may be in conflict with the values of other groups; therefore, from the perspective of one's group membership, other groups would appear to be deviant. But this does not mean that the other groups are disorganized or that overall social organization is threatened. Society is not an integrated system in which normative consensus is typical; rather, it is a balance of contending groups. In any group conflict the dominant groups are the definers of deviance. Thus deviance in public schools is usually defined in terms of breaches of white middle-class values. Juvenile delinquents and criminal gangs are viewed as minority groups out of sympathy with the norms of the dominant majority. Those belonging to groups considered deviant may suffer alienation and a feeling of illegitimate control and exploitation. If those presently considered deviant can become dominant, they can then consider the formerly dominant as deviant because deviance is largely a matter of whose values will prevail. Conflict develops whenever groups holding different values live in the same community and laws and norms of the dominant group are extended to cover the other groups. Violence may likely erupt from such conflicts.[20]

The educational implication of the conflict approach is that in order to reduce conflict and alienation, one should identify those groups in which such tensions are likely to be found. Various ethnic, racial, and radical groups find themselves in conflict with school rules. One way that violence may be reduced is to observe and enforce student rights and for students and parents to participate in the development of student codes.[21] Another approach is to support community control of schools. In that way those minority groups who believe that schools are centralized, bureaucratic systems unresponsive to the demands of parents and local citizens would be able to formulate their own norms and sanctions so that they no longer would be considered deviant—at least not while in school. Though some groups may be less intolerant of violence than others, under a community-control plan, violence would be reduced because the conflict and imposition of alien norms would be eliminated.

Labeling

The labeling approach claims that deviance can be explained by the interaction of an authority figure who imposes a label and the person on whom the label is imposed. Labeling consists of classifying an individual and attributing or implying negative status to the label, as in the case of the "drug addict," "alcoholic," "truant," "juvenile delinquent," or "vandal." Although deviancy is identified by the label, the act of labeling may aggravate the deviancy and make it self-fulfilling. Labeling stigmatizes the individual and may contribute to deviance; therefore, to label some students as "vandals" and "violence prone" is to place them in special pejorative categories where they will view themselves negatively and others will begin reacting to them differently. This creates secondary deviance, which is a reaction by those labeled "deviant" to the social-control measures taken to control their deviance. One form of secondary deviance is a deviant subculture. Thus social-control measures to curb student violence and vandalism may precipitate more widespread participation in deviant subcultures.[22]

If school officials take the influence of labeling seriously, then they will attempt to eliminate all labeling except that which is entirely unavoidable. This would mean that labeling, and any classification schemes that would have the effect of labeling, cannot be used for instructional, guidance or administrative purposes. This would place restrictions on the uses made of various psychological and standardized achievement tests, the handling of students who violate school rules, and many other practices where labeling is commonly employed. Preservice and inservice education programs can warn of the dangers of labeling and can show instead how the adoption of humanistic educational practices treats the student as a whole person and refuses to label. Those students who have already been labeled may need to be transferred to alternative education programs where labeling is prohibited in order to prevent the manifestation of further secondary deviance. These are some measures by which school violence can be reduced by observing the dangers of labeling.

Differential Association

A fourth and final approach to social deviance is differential association, a theory developed by Edward H. Sutherland.[23] It holds that deviant and unlawful behaviors are learned in the same manner: by association. Specifically, deviant behavior is learned through a process of social interaction in which language and gestures are employed, and it is learned within intimate personal groups. What is learned would include techniques for violating rules or laws and the motives, attitudes, and rationalizations needed to perform deviant acts. The deviant's primary-group associations encourage the violation of codes or norms, and the deviant is sufficiently isolated or has insufficient association with law-abiding patterns to counteract these tendencies. Whether an individual will become deviant depends on the frequency, duration, and priority given to association with law-abiding and deviant groups. If a person associates more with deviant groups or violent groups in early life, or with greater frequency and intensity, then there is considerable likelihood that she will become deviant or violence prone.

Educators who utilize this approach would want to exercise great care in seeing that students associate with people who are law abiding. Primary-group relations would need to be regulated, student subcultures more carefully supervised, and sound role models supplied. But since the differential-association problem extends beyond the school, administrators could establish after-school programs in high-crime neighborhoods to get students off the street and provide them with healthy recreational and learning activities. Educators should encourage and support government programs for neighborhood improvement and renewal. Greater parental and community involvement in schools may help to reduce violence.[24]

Evaluating Deviance Theories

Each of the four theories has certain strengths and limitations. The social-disorganization approach has the advantages, for those who believe in the basic worth of the present educational system, of explaining how the system can be maintained and those factors—anomie, inadequate socialization, improperly instituted goals, and procedures for goal attainment—likely to bring about various forms of deviance and the outbreak of violence. The theory, however, is better able to explain deviance and crime among the lower-class than white-collar crime because the latter type of crime does not seem to stem from anomie and other causes cited previously. Even under such socially disorganizing conditions as war and economic depression, the majority of the population still seems to conform. And the theory does not recognize that what may appear to the dominant group as normlessness and disorganization may not be so perceived by minority groups because they adhere to different norms.

The conflict approach is a corrective to the social-disorganization approach insofar as it affords greater recognition to cultural pluralism and diverse values in a complex society. It also contends that those who are called "deviants" and who feel alienated and exploited by the establishment are actually cases of the establishment's failure to recognize divergent values and the needs of the alienated groups. But one problem with this theory is that there are crimes—theft, for instance—that it fails to explain adequately. Theft is not sanctioned in any society and it cannot be explained by conflicting values. Violence, on the other hand, is tolerated more among the lower class than the middle class because it is a mechanism for the former of coping with what is perceived as a hostile environment. Even though society is heterogeneous it is actually constituted by more than various conflicting groups, otherwise it could not persist. American society, rather, is held together by such common values and norms as are found in democracy, capitalism, or Christianity. Moreover, the conflict approach does not explain why some people deviate from their own group norms or become violent against members of their own group. Additionally, the theory is much more suited as an explanation of political and ideological conflict than such common crimes and vices as theft, burglary, rape, arson, and alcoholism. Violence itself is reasonably well explained when it stems from ideological conflict but less so when the violence is directed against fellow group members.

Labeling directs the observer to the process by which someone is called "deviant," insists that deviance is a socially defined category, and that the label perpetuates and aggravates the problem. But since the label did not create the behavior in the first place, the theory only addresses itself to an alleged worsening of the behavior after it occurs; thus the behavior created the label rather than the converse. Moreover, some labels may have a positive rather than a negative effect. Many alcoholic- and drug-rehabilitation programs use labels to shock people into recognizing the seriousness of their habit. More knowledge is needed in cases of labeling to determine what conditions are likely to be harmful: how soon after the onset of violent behavior is the label applied; the publicity or confidentiality of the label; the relationship of the aggressor to the labeler; and how readily the label can be removed. Labeling also seems to remove responsibility from the aggressor and place it on the labeler; however, doing so may encourage violent students not to assume responsibility for their initial behavior.

The Differential-Association theory offers a straight-forward explanation that violent behavior is learned in communication with others in primary-group relationships. It emphasizes that, just as law-abiding behavior is learned in these relationships, so is delinquency. The theory is able to explain a wider range of crimes, including white-collar crime, than the other theories; it is also true that some empirical evidence supports the theory.[25] But since the theory places so much emphasis on learned behavior, it is challenged by views that hold that aggressiveness and related behavior is inherited.[26] The inheritance or biological view, however, has been largely developed from animal studies and extrapolated to humans. At least at this time Differential Association—or even the other three theories that rest largely on social and cultural influences—is not undermined; it does point up, however, that biological influences, whenever they can be accurately assessed, will need to be given a more significant place in any social-deviance theory.

Another problem with Sutherland's theory is that the techniques of many criminal acts—rapes, assaults, murders of passion—are not learned. Furthermore, some white-collar crimes could be learned in association with law-abiding persons by utilizing knowledge gained in accounting and computer-programming courses to defraud unwary victims and business firms. Additionally, Sutherland overlooks the potential of learning deviant  behavior from the media and other non-primary-group relations. It is true that his theory was developed before the widespread influence of television; however, radio and motion pictures played significant roles in the lives of millions of people at the time the theory was formulated. Finally, the theory does not specify the exact nature of the learning process in primary groups; it therefore needs to develop or borrow a learning theory that is consonant with Differential Association.

Recommendations

You are now in a position to choose a social-deviance theory and consistent remedial programs and practices most likely to curb school violence. If you are interested in emphasizing the student's free will, the Differntial-Association approach does this best because it suggests that each person chooses his own primary group relations and decides whether to continue or change these relations. In contrast, the other three theories tend to stress societal forces not fully under the individual's control. Daniel Duke, for instance, has pointed out that depersonalization of blame has increased by the use of labels like "determination of causation" and "the investigation of environmental influences"; student failures and disobedience are blamed on family background, peer-group influences, poor teaching, the school system, and society in general.[27]

Thus, for those interested in getting violent students to accept greater responsibility for their actions, a revised Differential-Association approach should be adopted that considers the learning impact of media and other salient environmental influences and utilizes a suitable learning theory.[28] Thus the application of a revised Differential-Association approach, along with appropriate remedial practices previously listed, would likely be effective in curbing violence and encouraging students to take more responsibility for their acts. Differential Association is a promising beginning and deserves thoughtful consideration.

Notes

1. National Institute of Education, *Violent Schools—Safe Schools: The Safe Study Report to Congress*, vol. 1 (Washington, D.C.: Government Printing Office, 1978), pp. 1-14.

2. Georges Sorel, *Reflections on Violence* (Glencoe, Ill.: Free Press, 1950).

3. The relation of violence to authority and power is discussed in Hannah Arendt's *On Violence* (New York: Harcourt, Brace and World, 1970), pp. 35-36.

4. Ted Honderich, "Appraisals of Political Violence," in Norman S. Care and Thomas K. Trelogan, eds., *Issues in Law and Morality* (Cleveland: Case Western Reserve University, 1973), p. 4.

5. Newton Garver, "What Violence Is," in James Rachels, ed., *Moral Problems*, (New York: Harper & Row, 1971), p. 243-247.

6. Robert Audi, "On the Meaning and Justification of Violence," in Jerome A. Shaffer, ed., *Violence* (New York: David McKay, 1971), p. 59.

7. Emile Durkheim, *The Rules of Sociological Method* (New York: Free Press, 1964), ch. 1.

8. John Searle, *Speech Acts* (New York: Cambridge University Press, 1969), pp. 50-53.

9. Ibid., pp. 33-42.

10. Violence to animals will not be discussed. For various positions, see *Inquiry* 22 (Spring-Summer 1979). A position I would largely accept is Peter Singer's *Animal Liberation* (New York: Discus, 1977).

11. Different positions on the ethics of suicide are presented in the following works: Samuel Gorovitz, ed., *Moral Problems in Medicine* (Englewood Cliffs, N.J.: Prentice-Hall, 1976), pp. 376-401, and Robert F.

Weir, ed., *Ethical Issues in Death and Dying* (New York: Columbia University Press, 1977), ch. 5.

12. This formulation is drawn from James P. Sterba's *The Demands of Justice* (Notre Dame, Ind.: University of Notre Dame Press, 1980), p. 15.

13. This type of argument can be found in Franz Fanon, *The Wretched of the Earth* (New York: Grove Press, 1963), pp. 27-83. Also see Jean-Paul Sartre's "Preface," pp. 7-26.

14. Herbert Marcuse, "Ethics and Revolution," in Charles King and James A. McGilvray, eds., *Political and Social Philosophy* (New York: McGraw-Hill, 1973), pp. 420-421.

15. Herbert Marcuse, *Studies in Critical Philosophy* (London: NLB, 1972), pp. 196-197.

16. Marcuse, "Ethics," p. 421.

17. Karl Popper, *Conjecture and Refutations* (New York: Harper Torchbooks, 1965), p. 362.

18. Examples of the social-disorganization approach: Robert K. Merton, *Social Theory and Social Structure* (Glencoe, Ill.: Free Press, 1957); Albert K. Cohen, *Deviance and Control* (Englewood Cliffs, N.J.: Prentice-Hall, 1966); and Reece McGee, *Social Disorganization in America* (San Francisco: Chandler, 1962).

19. For specific programs developed in various parts of the country, see Subcommittee to Investigate Juvenile Delinquency of the Committee of the Judiciary, U.S. Senate, *School Violence and Vandalism: Models and Strategies for Change* (Washington, D.C.: Government Printing Office, 1975), part 2.

20. The conflict approach is presented in the following works: Thorsten Sellin, *Culture Conflict and Crime* (New York: Social Science Research Council, 1938); George B. Vold, *Theoretical Criminology* (New York: Oxford University Press, 1958); and Richard Quinney, *The Social Reality of Crime* (Boston: Little, Brown, 1970).

21. For various legal decisions and model codes, see *School Violence and Vandalism,* part 3.

22. Examples of the labeling approach: Howard S. Becker *Outsiders* (New York: Free Press, 1963); and Edwin M. Lemert, *Human Deviance, Social Problems, and Social Control* (Englewood Cliffs, N.J.: Prentice-Hall, 1967).

23. The theory was first systematically formulated in Sutherland's *Principles of Criminology*, 3rd ed. (Chicago: Lippincott, 1939) and revised in the fourth edition in 1947.

24. Some of these programs are presented in G. John Barclay, ed., *Parental Involvement in the Schools* (Washington, D.C.: National Education Association, 1977); and Don Davies, *Schools Where Parents Make a Difference* (Boston: Institute for Responsive Education, 1976).

25. See James F. Short, "Differential Association as a Hypothesis: Problems of Empirical Testing," *Social Problems* 8 (Summer 1960):14-25; Victor M. Matthews, "Differential Identification: An Empirical Note," *Social Problems* 14 (Winter 1968):376-383; and Harwin Voss, "Differential Associated and Reported Delinquent Behavior: A Replication," *Social Problems* 12 (Summer 1964):78-85.

26. This evidence comes from such ethological and sociobiological studies as Konrad Lorenz, *On Aggression* (New York: Harcourt Brace Jovanovich, 1966); and E.O. Wilson, *Sociobiology: The New Synthesis* (Cambridge, Mass.: Belknap Press of Harvard University Press, 1975). A criticism of Lorenz's ethology is found in Ashley Montague, ed., *Man and Aggression*, 2nd ed. (London: Oxford University Press, 1973).

27. Daniel L. Duke, "Student Behavior, the Depersonalization of Blame, and the Society of Victims," *The Journal of Educational Thought* 12 (April 1978):3-18.

28. Behaviorism would have to be ruled out because it considers the individual merely a reactive organism rather than proactive and self-initiating. A promising learning theory that might be used is Albert Bandura's *Aggression: A Social Learning Analysis* (Englewood Cliffs, N.J.: Prentice-Hall, 1973).

6 Authority in the Family

The family can be a source of economic and emotional sustenance and a bond of continuing affection, encouragement, and, as Christopher Lasch called it, "a haven in a heartless world." It can also be a source of corrosive rivalries and jealousies, negligence, abuse, incest, and violence. Both little and much is expected today of the American family. On the one hand, a larger percentage of the population is choosing not to marry, more married coupled are electing not to have children, and an increasingly enlarging work force is seeking primary satisfaction outside the home. On the other, most of those who divorce remarry, and many new family arrangements other than the nuclear family are being tried. The family is probably not declining as an institution (as some charge) but is undergoing a period of rapid change and restructuring, as can be observed today in multiple models of what constitutes a "family."

As seen in chapter 2, the early years of the child's life have a vital influence on her future educational progress. It is during this time that basic authority patterns are established and the child's self-concept begins to form. Questions about discipline in the home will be presented in relation to patterns of authority and family power, whereas specialized problems of violence in the family will be examined separately.

Changing Patterns of Authority in the Family

In terms of family authority, three basic and important questions will be explored. First of all, who should be in authority? Here it may seem obvious that parents should be in authority; however, with some countries' adopting national birth-control policies and passing legislation as to who may have children (for example, feebleminded people might be sterilized), many value controveries arise over public policies and the divisions they sometimes create over the family's exercise of authority.

Second, there is a need to inquire how authority is actually exercised. This will involve a brief historical look at changes in the American family's authority patterns, followed by some observations on social-class differences in socialization and child-rearing practices.

Finally, the question of how authority should be structured and exercised must be addressed. This involves an analysis of the rights and responsibilities of government, the courts, and social-service agencies vis-à-vis the home. In addition, findings from the response to the two previous questions are brought forward to help make pertinent recommendations for improving authority networks.

Who Should Be in Authority?

The Right to Have Children. Parents may exercise authority in various ways with their children but still not have ultimate authority. This is evident insofar as the state can intervene and, where adjudged necessary, remove the child temporarily or permanently from the parental home because of neglect or abuse. Another way the state may determine matters that some parents would consider their own prerogative is by establishing national programs of family planning, which may conflict with the parents' belief that they have a right to procreate, have as many children as they desire, and space them as they see fit.

While many married couples may recognize the state's right to discourage illegitimate births, these same couples may reject the notion that the state can restrict their procreative rights. They would appeal that one of the grounds for marriage is to sanction procreation and provided needed sustenance and protection for children; thus such state policies, they could claim, restrict their rightful liberties. Some would claim that the state has no right whatsoever to intervene in making such fundamental decisions. It might also be thought that such intervention smacks of totalitarian practices.

Opposing positions would vary along a continuum in terms of the state's right to intervene, but it would be unlikely to find any nation today in which the state would deny parents all rights in such decisions. Two positions, each with certain variations, are evident today. One is government-encouraged family planning; the other goes further than family planning and uses inducements and penalities in order to reach certain population-control goals.

Married couples may have an inalienable but not an absolute right in reproduction.[1] It is inalienable so far as it is a human right; yet if rights are considered claims, they can be overriden by other claims. The other claims, in this instance, would be the public interest or the common good. In other words, if each family is left to its own devices in reproduction, they may or may not satisfy their own family goals (they may have unwanted offspring), but may not fulfill national goals, especially in underdeveloped nations.

Death rates have been dramatically reduced in many countries through the control of disease and improved ability to feed the world's people, resulting in more babies who will survive to become parents. It has been estimated that world population would range from a low of 6.4 billion to as much as 7.2 billion in the year 2000.[2] It took two billion years for the world's population to reach its first billion in the year 1830. Subsequently, the second billion was reached one hundred years later; the third billion in only thirty years.[3] The fourth billion was reached seventeen years after the third in 1977.[4]

The rate of population growth poses problems of malnutrition and famine, widespread illiteracy, rising unemployment levels, great demands on the physical environment for living space, arable land, industrial raw materials, energy fuels, and fresh water.

Family planning is the primary approach employed by those nations that are attempting to control fertility. It may take the form of establishing clinics for instruction, disseminating reliable information, distributing contraceptives, and other measures. Some observers object to family planning on its alleged ineffectiveness to bring about sufficient population control, whereas other groups—notably, Marxists and Catholics—would uphold, on divergent grounds, the rights of married couples to exercise primary control.

The Roman Catholic position claims that the population problem is one aspect of larger social, political, and economic questions at the national and international levels.[5] While acknowledging the existence of a problem, it is necessary to make the necessary changes that will lead to a more equitable distribution of wealth and resources. Except for the Church, the family is considered the most important unit in society. Catholic tradition includes both a private and public dimension. Though dispute exists among theologians, official teaching prohibits sterilization, abortion, and contraception; only the rhythm method is sanctioned. Every act of sexual intercourse should be open to procreation. Yet such injunctions may apply only to private morality and, though open to further interpretation, public morality may permit the state to intervene in population policy. In other words, while advocating a definite position on private morality, an openness is shown toward public morality by not attempting to establish public policies in a pluralistic society.

Marxists reject Malthusian dire predictions and contend instead that the imbalance between resources and population stems from colonialism, imperialism, and capitalism.[6] In underdeveloped nations, the poor need better education, nutrition, land reform, and income distribution; and without these changes it might be quite rational to have large families. Once socialism is established, a balance will be achieved between population and resources by natural processes; resources, it is claimed, are always adequate under socialism to support the population.

Thus Marxists and Catholics, for different reasons, do not endorse national family planning but advocate a more equitable distribution of resources. Marxists insist that socialism would resolve the inequities found in other systems. In addition, it may be necessary, as seen in the Soviet Union, to develop long-range economic plans to increase the level of resources. Catholic social teaching calls on the state to guarantee a basic minimum of material welfare but has not aligned itself with a specific political or economic system as did the Marxists. Another step when plans go awry is to redefine what is necessary for the good life, which is especially true in Iron Curtain countries. Once expectations and aspirations are lowered and citizens acquiesce to these changes, then a balance between resources and human needs can be made in peoples' minds if not in actual fact.

If governments in the developing nations could be induced to adopt policies that would redistribute scarce resources within each nation more equitably, some population pressures may be temporarily alleviated. But how would such redistribution affect these nations? Since their own resources are far more limited than the developed nations, any redistribution would not have any significant effect; and if natural resources and arable land are scarce (which is most likely the case), then these countries will need large-scale redistribution from the developed nations.

There are serious limitations in such expectations, however, even in the unlikely event that the developed nations would comply. Environmental activity depends on the earth's capacity to supply energy fuels, industrial raw materials and fresh water, and the ability to absorb hundreds of thousands of chemical-waste products. The environmental crisis has resulted from the serious depletion of irreplaceable natural resources and the inability of the biosphere to absorb many of the waste products. As for food supply, unused land in most nations that can be put into production is limited because of insufficient water, bad soil, or climate. Only ten nations produce more food than they can consume, and should India's population growth continue at its present rate over the next ten years, it would take the United States' entire grain supply to relieve India's food shortage. Optimists, however, point to green revolution, synthetic foods, and hydroponics; yet these new sources have yet to achieve their potential, and the problem of equitable redistribution of scarce resources has also to be solved. Even if priorities were established and funds were available, some demographers are uncertain whether we have the knowledge to expend these funds to produce adequate results.[7] Other observers point to nationalism and the nation-state as serious impediments and urge new types of political institutions.[8] Thus to follow the redistribution route exclusively will likely lead to decreasing the level of what is meant by the good life or else increasingly limiting the range of access to the good life.

But family-planning programs, despite the willingness of dozens of nations to try them, seem inadequate for the task. Kingsley Davis has indicted such programs for lacking long-term goals and for not leading either to population control or fertility control.[9] No government attempts to influence all aspects of population (genetic quality, age-sex structure, geographical distribution, and so on) and family planning does not lead to fertility control but usually attempts to reduce only the birth rate. Family planning may reduce unwanted births to the point at which wanted ones outnumber the unwanted ones. Yet because some unwanted births still occur because of failure of a contraceptive practice or its use, abortion could be used as a back-up; however, most family-planning programs do not advocate it. Since traditions in some cultures may still call for large families, then changes in traditions, family structure, the role of women, and the motivation for having children would be needed to exercise effective fertility control. Thus although family planning may free couples from some unwanted offspring, it is only the first step in fertility control. What those additional steps are is open to serious debate; but we cannot turn to family-planning advocates to find out. Numerous proposals have been made: exercise greater control over illegitimate childbirth, encourage the postponement of marriage until after age twenty, get more women in the work force, legalize and provide free abortions, provide financial inducements or financial penalties, and sterilization (either accepting government financial inducements or a mandatory government policy after an allotted number of children are born). This is by no means an exhaustive list, and the list is a mixed one, representing varying degrees of freedom of choice and coercion.

Some observers, who have been called "survivalists," are greatly alarmed over world-population problems, reject piecemeal proposals, and make dire predictions of what will occur if large-scale urgent programs are not undertaken.[10] This group emphasizes human survival as the highest value and tends to equate population-related problems to world overpopulation. Because of the urgency of the problem, they advocate a variety of coercive measures: the use of food aid as leverage to the developing nations to induce them to adopt a strong population policy, abortion, compulsory sterilization, licenses for having children, community pressure, contraceptive implants, and fertility-control agents (chemical compounds that would control fertility or induce sterility).

Despite the gravity of world-population problems, the survivalists may have misinterpreted some of them. Overpopulation is seen as largely cause, rather than the result, of hunger, poverty, and ecological imbalance. Marxists and Catholics have advocated redistribution of resources and various reforms. While these measures alone may be insufficient, just as family planning alone may also be insufficient, a combination of redistribution of resources and family planning may alleviate many of these problems. Survival itself may not be as gravely threatened as claimed, and therefore time exists for these other means to be used, means that allow greater freedom of choice. Survivalists are using a consequentialist justification based largely on utilitarian considerations; however, it is an empirical question whether their dire predictions are accurate—and many have not come to pass.[11] The extent of state intervention, at least in nontotalitarian nations, will likely be a function of the seriousness of the problem. Other factors will include whether procreation is viewed as an absolute or relative right, and the possible justification for infringing such other values as liberty and justice for the sake of survival.[12] *Survival*, as Martin P. Goulding has indicated, is a scare word.[13] It seduces others to follow the dictates of some policy rather than risk catastrophe; yet it is ludicrous to suggest that everyone will die unless certain measures are taken.

Who then should be in authority? Obviously married couples, at least in most nations, cannot exercise unlimited authority in decisions about procreation and the rearing of children. But, as part of the American tradition, a prima-facie case can be made for freedom so that the burden of proof lies with those who would restrict it. Yet even in developed countries unrestrained population growth could lower the quality of life, cause shortages of housing and vital goods, create further problems of pollution, ecological degeneration, and economic dislocations. Thus while survival is not a matter of concern in these countries, the quality of life for present and immediate future generations may be.

Family-planning programs would be the first step in reducing unwanted births; it would not be coercive, though perhaps persuasive, in providing information and aid. Thus opening greater options and using persuasion would not limit but increase choice since the persuasion can always be challenged and disregarded unless combined with coercion. Various coercive and compulsory policies may also be employed; however, whether they should be introduced would depend on the nature and seriousness of the population problems facing a particular nation. The general justification for using such policies is that they will preserve or restore certain values such as those associated with the quality of life and the general welfare and that other values (freedom in procreation) will have to be temporarily or permanently limited (a "temporary" policy, however, may affect an entire generation).

Coercive policies would use inducements or penalties. Abortion or sterilization upon request, though morally offensive to certain groups and individuals, would not be coercive. Since the rise of the proportion of women in the work force tends to reduce birthrates, government could encourage economic policies that expand the job market and provide daycare centers. For some women, at least psychologically, this may have some coercive import; however, since coercion is found whenever constraint or inducement is high and choice is low, this would not be coercion unless either great pressure from family members is placed on the individual to work full time outside the home or family financial exigencies allow little choice.

As for coercive inducements, various financial incentives could be used such as pensions or social-security bonuses, direct financial rewards, and income-tax advantages. On the penalty side, removal of income-tax deduction after the second child, a flat-rate tax on childbearing, restriction on maternity benefits or on welfare for excessive births, substantial marriage-license fees, reduction of paid maternity leaves, elimination of public housing on the basis of family size, and others have been suggested.

Besides their coerciveness, the difficulty with some of these proposals is that they may not be just. First of all, it is unjust for government to place penalties or burdens on children for something that their parents did or failed to do. Second, any provisions that fall heaviest on the poor would also be unjust, and therefore various financial penalties, when not adjusted for family income, place great burdens on the poor. Financial incentives, moreover, that may be attractive to the poor may not be to the middle and upper classes. Thus it is not surprising that some minority groups with high births and low income would feel discriminated against and threatened by some population programs. Some blacks even view U.S. birth-control programs as "genocide."[14]

Compulsory programs would consist of such practices as raising the legal age of marriage, compulsory abortion or sterilization whenever family size exceeds the allotted number, marketable licenses for babies, and placing fertility-control agents in the water supply (which has yet to be perfected or tried). Raising the legal age of marriage, as late marriages at one time in Ireland demonstrated, can be effective in reducing fertility, yet only as long as tradition and government discourage births outside of marriage. Marketable licenses raise thorny questions as to how such decisions could be used other than resorting to economic grounds. Compulsory abortion or sterilization would not only violate individual rights but conflict with family moral codes and may do psychological damage as well. Thus only in dire cases, as sterilization was used in India, would such practices be warranted. Such a dire circumstance could be the predicted threat to survival from famine or plague of a significant portion of a nation's population. Or, in terms of the general welfare, if it could be shown that without implementing such policies, a majority of the population would fall into the poverty level, then such practices would likely be justified but only after other measures had been explored, if not tried. Such measures include redistribution of internal resources, loans and trade with wealthier nations, family planning, coercive inducements and penalties, and greater emigration.

Parenting

Whatever the population problems of a given nation and the restrictions placed on fertility, other salient questions can be raised about parenting. Should every married couple be given the right to have children (even in those nations in which government policies restrict family size)? Is every couple who has children capable of becoming an adequate parent? Obviously, some are not suited for this vital role but do not discover their incapacity until after their first child—or even their second or third—is born; others never fully recognize their incapacity and therefore can do even more harm.

But one could say that procreation is a right, a God-given right, or a right assured by the state, and this right should not be infringed. Perhaps it may be considered a natural right because the biological ability to procreate is an inherited endowment, which is partly what it means to be a human being. Take away this right, therefore, and the individual is less human or somewhat dehumanized. Thus to be fully human, this right must be safeguarded.

Some may defend this claim on different grounds. They might say that they had long looked forward to parenthood and the many joys and sorrows of rearing a family and to deny them this right would seriously conflict with their life plan. Their strong desire to have children may have been motivated by certain emotional needs, a virtual maternal or paternal "instinct," family tradition, or religious teachings; these conditions in turn helped to shape their life plan.

Turning to the first procreation right argument, to say that something is God-given may either be sincerely believed or no more than a rhetorical flourish; in any case, whatever its alleged theological standing, it would have to become law before it could be adequately protected and enforced. A law can be successfully challenged and subsequently modified or repealed. If procreation is allegedly a natural right (which might be based on a theological position), it would be difficult to support because, though one readily grants the existence of this biological capacity, doing so does not tell us what to do with it any more than having arms and legs tells us to be track stars rather than business executives. Of course, it is known that having these appendages means that they will atrophy if not used, but it does not tell what type of activity in which they should be used. One could become a professional athlete or take a sedentary job, but one could not lie in bed indefinitely. The same does not hold for procreative abilities: one does not need to use these abilities to maintain sound physical health (psychological health is more complex and will be mentioned later), and therefore the alternatives are either to abstain or use contraceptive devices. (For those who claim that abstinence precludes optimum physical health, the second alternative remains open.)

It may be that some youth have considered parenthood as an integral part of their life plan and to deny any of them this so-called right would be disruptive to and cause emotional distress. Of course, it should be recognized that in the United States not just anyone can marry but only those of requisite age and, in most states, those who have passed a blood test. Moreover, even parental consent is insufficient below a certain tender age (varying by state) to grant a marriage license. But once the minimum age is reached and no communicable diseases are present, persons are allowed to marry, have children, but sometimes are subject to a population-control program. That to deny a couple the right to have children, even when grounds are definitive, may well conflict with their maternal or paternal propensities, emotional needs, family traditions, or religious teachings. The question then is whether the harms are sufficient to override the dangers and potential harm to the child of incompetent parents. Of course, it might be observed that juvenile courts remove children from their parental home in substantiated cases of neglect or abuse that clearly endanger the child's health or welfare. Why not leave such matters to the courts and let it be proved that the parents' behavior warrants the child's removal? From an evaluative point of view, however, there may be many potential parents who could be identified as incompetent for parenting and this incompetence could not be overcome; others might presently be identified as incompetent but could gain competency through an appropriate educational program.

Other than random observation, why would one think that a sizeable number of parents are incompetent for parenting? Could it be simply because they lack training and knowledge for parenthood or they fail to meet adequate standards? Some will be adequate parents, however, without a training program, and others may fail to pass such programs. But in looking at the typical preparation for parenthood, a glaring absence of preparation is usually evident. Alice S. Rossi notes that probably a majority of American mothers face maternity with no child-care experience other than occasional babysitting or sporadic care of younger siblings and perhaps a course in child psychology.[15] Parenthood is usually more stressful than initial marital adjustment because the engagement period allows the couple to develop some skills that may be carried into marriage, whereas with the child's birth, in contrast to an occupational role, full responsibility must be assumed immediately.

Many youth, some of whom stormed the barricades of the 1960s, were raised on Benjamin Spock's *Common Sense Book of Baby and Child Care*, which has sold over 23 million copies since 1946. Spock admonished parents that the wrong kind of discipline could turn the child into a passive follower or a demagogic leader. To develop responsible citizens and allay the child's insecurities, he advocated daily routines that, while occasionally seeking the child's opinion, would stake out the parents' leadership role and present to the child his duties in the most positive light (for example, if the child has to move from an accustomed room because of the new baby, the move would be presented as an act of graduation because he is now a bigger child).

But while some parents struggled to apply the ideas of Spock and other authorities, others floundered badly and seriously wondered whether parenthood was a mistake, while a significant minority was adjudged by juvenile courts to be negligent or abusive. The reason for some failures may lie with the great demands and responsibilities of parenthood.

What do children need for healthy human development? Urie Bronfenbrenner contends that a child needs an "enduring, irrational involvement" of one or more adults. In other words, someone has to be "crazy about the kid" and needs to do things together with the child. Moreover, public policies should provide opportunity, resources, and time for parenthood.[16] This same strain is echoed by the Carnegie Council on Children in their insistence that for decades authorities have claimed that children need "one-to-one relationships with caring adults" and a stimulating environment that will promote their growth and recognize them as separate individuals.[17] The United Nations Declaration of the Rights of the Child goes further by proclaiming that every child should be given opportunities under law and by other means to enable her to develop mentally, physically, socially, morally, and spiritually in a healthy manner under conditions of dignity and freedom.[18] The Declaration adds, among other things, that the child should be reared in an atmosphere of affection and material and moral security; he should receive a free and compulsory education that promotes his general culture, social and moral responsibility, and enabling him to be a good citizen.

The Declaration seems to be espousing optimal benefits and conditions while many countries may have to struggle to meet minimal conditions. In any case, before obligations can become enforceable, it is necessary to ascertain what is feasible for a given nation to do for its children, develop plans, and use them as a starting point to attain those conditions in the declaration on which a consensus can be reached.

But, returning to the conditions enunciated by Bronfenbrenner and the Carnegie Council, theirs are not optimal conditions but essential ones for healthy human development. It could be argued, however, that juvenile courts and social workers already handle cases of negligence and abuse; and for the interested parents, courses in child rearing and human development are available. What else is needed?

Perhaps an analogy with licensing motor-vehicle users would be apt. It is widely accepted that before a license to operate a motor vehicle is granted, the applicant must first pass both written and driving tests; those who fail are given additional chances to demonstrate the requisite knowledge and skills but will be fined if apprehended for driving without a license. Those who have a license but are arrested for a violation may have the violation recorded and after a number of violations or one major violation, the driver's license may be revoked (after a court hearing where the charges are substantiated). Once a person is granted a license, she must abide by the numerous rules and regulations of the highway and of automobile inspection.

Does this analogy apply to parenting? As we have seen, the granting of marriage licenses acts as a screening device of a type, but it does not screen out most incompetent parents while, at the other end, juvenile courts deal only with the most extreme cases, and some cases that should come before the courts go unreported. Incompetence takes many forms, but it would at least constitute inability to enter into a strong, caring relationship and provide a stimulating environment for growth, as Bronfenbrenner and the Carnegie Council previously stated. As Rossi notes, the parental role exhibits both expressive and instrumental requirements.[19] Expressive requirements include spontaneity, flexibility, tenderness, love, and sensitiveness to childhood fantasies. Instrumental requirements consist of the ability to manage time and energy; consistency and firmness; training the child in body controls, language, and motor skills; introducing the child to the natural and social world; and helping the child develop social relations and a value system.

Thus a consensus exists among authorities on some general competencies, although on Rossi's list some agreement would need to be reached as to specific minimum competencies. Various parenting programs could be designed, experimental and control groups established, and results gathered on the relative effectiveness of preparing persons to become more effective parents. Before a program could be adopted, it should clearly demonstrate its effectiveness over competing programs and over those who underwent no program. Even before entering such programs, diagnostic tests should be devised to assess the likelihood of having difficulties in the parental role and, as the tests are perfected, to spot more precisely what those difficulties are likely to be and prescribe appropriate remedial programs. Some aspiring parents, on the basis of diagnostic tests, will be adjudged good risks for parenthood and will not be required to enter and pass a designated program before being granted a marriage license, but most likely a majority of those contemplating marriage would likely be diagnosed as needing a particular parenting program. Since competencies not used regularly may tend to deteriorate, married couples who postpone having children may have to demonstrate the retention of initial competency or else take a program to reestablish those competencies.

At present such programs do not exist; whether current programs in sex education, family planning, marriage, and family living could be used as part of parenting education outlined here remains to be demonstrated—and it will not likely be demonstrated until objections to the preceding programs could be overcome.

It was indicated earlier why the natural-right-to-parenthood argument is inadequate, and some doubts were raised about the life-plan argument.

Specifically, those whose life plan includes parenthood, if they lacked the competencies, could be asked to acquire the competencies. For those persons, who despite repeated attempts to acquire the competencies were unable to do so, could be granted a marriage license without the right to have offspring. The confidentiality of marriage licenses should be assured by the issuing agency. This provision could be modified where communal or kibbutz arrangements are found (assuming no serious genetic defects are likely to be transmitted) because physical care and socialization are not the responsibilities of biological parents under such plans. Where no communal arrangement exists and the parents are incompetent, the courts could take the child and place him in the best possible environment available.

Pursuing the life-plan notion, objections could be made to the parenting education program. It might be argued by some couples that the denial of parenthood will cause great distress, perhaps even mental illness; consequently, the harm done the couple would be greater than the potential harm done the child. But the couple would have numerous opportunities prior to marriage to acquire the requisite competencies and would therefore enter marriage with forewarning and a full realization of the limitations imposed on the marriage contract. Since the terms of the marriage contract would remain confidential and since couples today are electing to have fewer children or no children, there would be no stigma attached and the forewarning would enable the couple to modify their life plan without great emotional distress.

Either tradition or religion may encourage large families. Where such traditions are strong, as in some of the developing nations, it may be necessary to change economic conditions first before such parenting-education programs could be successful. Such conditions where parents need to rely on offspring for support in old age need to be altered by adequate retirement provisions and medical care; and in rural areas where large families are economic assets, it may indicate a need to diversify economic opportunities and vocational training. Thus even sound parenting programs may not be feasible until some other significant changes take place.

Limitations on parenting may also be objected to on various religious grounds. Here the appeal could be to natural rights or on some other basis. In some cases religious doctrines may hold the church to be supreme in such matters and brook no interference. In a Supreme Court decision, however, state law prohibiting child labor was upheld against a challenge by the child and her guardian that their religious freedom was being denied.[20] The Court held that even the primary right of parents to care for and educate their child and the child's freedom of religion were subject to restrictions when the child's welfare was likely to be endangered by potentially harmful conduct. In any case, religious beliefs are not absolute rights that can be imposed irrespective of children's rights. Whether religious beliefs that conflict with the proposed parenting-education program could be restricted would depend on, first of all, the demonstrated value of such programs, the harms likely to result from the unrestricted right to parenthood, and the status of the law at the time such cases are heard.

Another objection, perhaps a less serious one but taken seriously by those who raise it, is that the proposed program would increase bureaucracy and the influence of government in the lives of people. It would be best to reduce bureaucracy whenever possible and carefully scrutinize any proposals that would add to the already inflated role of government in people's lives.

There is some truth to these remarks insofar as all levels of government have grown over the past several decades, but whether this is good or bad would seem to require an appraisal of specific programs and legislation rather than a wholesale condemnation of government on size alone. Those conservatives who become indignant over the growth of government are not always consistent in their targets: their animus is directed much more toward the federal than to state and local government. If the federal government, deservedly or not, is currently the *bete noire*, then parent education can be handled by state and local government, just as marriage and divorce is handled.

Second, not all new services by government, which lead to growth in functions, size, and budgets, were objected to when first proposed. Social security and medicare were eagerly accepted by most people, and opposition came from only certain special-interest groups. Many of the new functions that public schools have assumed during this century—driver training, health programs, federally subsidized lunch programs, special-education programs, and numerous others—have been welcomed by most parents. Though a backlash can be observed in several states against continual increases in taxes during a period of high inflation, voters, though increasingly skeptical over the performance of public officials, want to halt their eroding standard of living by requiring more spartan public budgets rather than actually do away with standard services.

Third, any harms from such growth will be outweighed by the good likely to be obtained. But how can such good be assured? The public would be protected because the program would not be fully implemented until its effectiveness had been clearly demonstrated in experimental programs; in turn, these findings would be widely disseminated and a sizeable portion of the public would eventually be convinced of the program's merits.

How Authority Is Exercised in the Family

Reconceptualizing Family Membership

It would be useful to see how authority was conceptualized and reconceptualized over various historical periods before turning later to socialization in child-rearing practices. Thus before further recommendations can be made with any confidence, especially those concerned with how authority in the family should be structured and employed, it will be useful to view selectively how authority is exercised. The way that it is exercised has a great deal to do with the way various family members are conceived; moreover, as these conceptions and viewpoints change, relations among family members are likely to alter.

Phillipe Aries shows that some earlier ages once had no conception of childhood.[21] He arrives at this astonishing conclusion after a careful examination of the records, paintings, and iconography of earlier periods. Medieval art did not portray childhood but instead depicted persons as men on a smaller scale, and would exhibit the naked body of a child with the musculature of an adult. Other than ancient Greek art, similar treatments were found in ancient civilizations. Beginning in the thirteenth century a few depictions of children appear to be a little closer to modern views of childhood, but it was not until the seventeenth century that the modern view would be fully formed. That the idea of childhood was absent in medieval society does not mean that children were neglected or despised; yet it did result in less parental solicitude as compared to the seventeenth century.[22]

The survival of children was far too problematical for parents to become overly attached to them. One had to have many children to be assured even of a few surviving, and no one would think of keeping a picture of a child.

During the seventeenth century the practice of wet-nursing developed. Should the mother's milk run dry, the use of cow's milk was unsafe and generally considered to be the poor man's fate; the child was sent to another home to be nursed. The practice of wet-nursing continued into the nineteenth century until animal milk was made safe; the only change during the interim was that the wet nurse stayed in the parents' house.

Most children in England during the twelfth century were neither in school nor at home but were sent at age seven to the household of others to learn various menial skills as a form of vocational training and did not return to their own homes for another seven or nine years. Apprenticeship was more broadly conceived than today; it became a form of general education by which the child learned through practice and was the chief form of education for many centuries until schools increased their enrollment, first with boys and then later for girls beginning in the eighteenth and early nineteenth centuries.

Despite the widespread belief that the extended family prevailed in agrarian life, scholars now contend that the nuclear family was the dominant form in America since colonial times.[23] The patriarchial family was the norm, and primogeniture was common. Flandrin reports that in some French provinces as late as the eighteenth century, if a woman were asked whether she had any children, she might reply quite seriously that she had none and then admit later that she has several daughters.[24] Peasant women would be expected to do arduous work in the fields; they were sought for marriage on the basis of their reputation as a laborer and household skills. Once a spouse died, the survivor quickly arranged for remarriage. But some restrictions were placed on patriarchal authority and power by Christianity in order to assure the conversion of women, children, and slaves. Authoritarian behavior was customary by the head of the household: the husband was expected to beat his wife when he deemed necessary, and community custom treated him sternly when he failed to impose his will. In a French province in the fourteenth century, it was the community custom to make the husband who allowed his wife to beat him to ride on an ass backward through the town to the amusement and scorn of his fellows. According to a sixteenth century maxim:

A good horse and a bad horse need the spur
A good woman and a bad woman need the stick.

But by the eighteenth century, especially in bourgeoisie society, such practices were frowned on and husbands were urged to be companions to their wives; the middle class took their new behavior as indicative of having attained a higher level of civilization.

In colonial America the chief duty of the wife was obedience to her husband. She was regarded as inferior to her husband in virtually every respect; moreover, she was viewed with an undercurrent of fear and suspicion because she was not considered entirely trustworthy.

The status of the wife changed in nineteenth century America. A rapidly expanding industrial nation offered many opportunities and considerable risks in a world of Darwinian struggle for survival of the heartiest. The breadwinner faced toil and economic dangers and increasingly saw the family as a refuge in a heartless world. The erstwhile reciprocity between family and community during colonial times changed to an adversarial relation in the nineteenth century. Despite the sense of openness and egalitarianism of the outside world and the opportunity to become a "self-made man," the threat to traditional values was real. Thus the society at large and the home became two different spheres with divergent values. Home and wife were highly sentimentalized: home as a sanctuary for protection and renewal; the wife as a preserver of the cherished home and family, a higher moral being than her husband who had to make many compromises in the marketplace. She was expected to nurture the children and prepare them for the world, to create a cheerful and tranquil home, and engage in selfless service.[25] A woman was not permitted to work outside the home, was expected to be obedient to her husband, a comforter who administered to family needs and morally uplifted the household. Although this ideal increasingly came under attack by feminists groups by the turn of the century, women entered a transitional period of struggle before new role models were finally forged.

Attitudes toward children changed as infant mortality was reduced. Parents could not develop a deep attachment to any infant if the likelihood of early death was probable. But the lack of adequate care also raised mortality rates; therefore, as knowledge of child care and hygiene improved and was more widely disseminated by the late eighteenth century, some reductions were made in infant mortality.[26]

High infant-mortality rates were only part of the story, however. The parents' conception of the child and their symbolic relation to him, both in law and theology, would change slowly. Infanticide was practiced in antiquity and in the early Middle Ages. Theologians in the later period held that children were things belonging to parents and God could punish parents through their children. Even in the seventeenth century it was believed that children owed everything to their father because he gave them life.[27] And obedience was demanded by the "stubborn-child" laws of early New England, which required the death penalty for persistently disobedient children. Although not actually invoked, it remained a statute as an example of the state's interest in maintaining domestic order.

But by the nineteenth century, many of these laws and attitudes were vestiges of the past. An unprecedented amount of time was given to child rearing. The new style of child rearing contributed to a more self-reliant individual who could take his place in the competitive marketplace. Since the child was no longer viewed as a miniature adult, she no longer was present in adult gatherings and activities but became increasingly segregated. It was now expected that the child would be given love and affection, opportunities for play and an environment in which her nature could unfold slowly and naturally. These additional parental responsibilities came at a time when outside help in child rearing, such as relatives, became more tenuous.[28]

By the 1840s, opinions varied about corporal punishment: some suggested that it be used as a last resort, while others claimed that it need not be used at all if parents would set a good example; the religiously orthodox, however, refused to relinquish it entirely. Whatever punishment used in the home should be used, it was urged, with proper understanding so that the child would be capable of moral improvement. Love and gentleness would help promote good character. The child, no longer punished harshly, may have suffered guilt for his misbehavior or hostility toward parents because strong punishment, whatever its shortcomings, may have given the child the feeling that he had paid his debts and the matter was thereby settled.[29]

This was a period of population growth, mobility, exploration, expansion of production, and accumulation of wealth in which, according to Riesman, an innerdirected society developed out of which an innerdirected personality was shaped.[30] This personality type, though outwardly an individualist, was not independent of the values and attitudes inculcated by parents. The innerdirected personality had his own internal gyroscope, created early in life, which helped him to cope with rapid change and sometimes violent upheaval; yet it still did not make him immune to the sway of mass movements and group ideologies.

The innerdirected personality changed by mid-twentieth century to an other-directed person, one who lacks an inner gyroscope and seeks instead the approval of others. The emergence of this personality is a product of teamwork, gregariousness, and group integration. It was the rise of what William Whyte dubbed "the organization man," one who eschewed risk taking for the security of the corporation. From the short-lived rebellion of the late 1960s to what Christopher Lasch has called "the culture of narcissism," we come to the types of socialization practices used today within the authority framework of the home.

Socialization and the Exercise of Authority

Socialization is the process by which an individual acquires the knowledge, skills, and behavior that will make him an adequate member of society. In the process one learns appropriate roles for his age, sex, social class, and personal responsibilities. The chief socializing influences in the nuclear family during preschool years would, first of all, be the parents, and secondarily, siblings, relatives, playmates, and the media.

One of the chief tasks in socialization is the learning of roles (son, daughter, friend, student, and so on). According to Brim, to perform a role satisfactorily requires knowledge, ability, and motivation.[31] Thus the child must know what is expected of her, be capable of meeting the requirements, and have a desire to practice the appropriate behavior. Childhood socialization emphasizes the shaping of primary drives into socially acceptable behavior and the control of basic physiological processes; these behaviors are shaped by the learning of roles. Goffman distinguishes two types of roles: situated and conditioning.[32] Situated roles are found in specific locales and are based on a division of labor. Conditioning roles are found in many settings and are organized around such social characteristics and life situations as sex, age, social class, physical appearance, widowhood, and alcoholism.

Parents initiate the role of socializing agents; the young child, however, is unaware of his own role as neophyte and therefore is limited in the ability to cooperate in the process. In contrast, an older child or adolescent, cognizant of the process, can cooperate to foster the socialization process; yet this growing awareness can also be used to resist or thwart parental expectations. As the youth feels less dependence upon parents and turns increasingly to the judgment of peers and to ostensible values conveyed by media stars, parents must find different and more compelling motivating devices to make socialization effective and to avert the erosion of their authority.

How authority is exercised in the home can be more clearly seen by exploring two different theories of socialization: symbolic-interactionist and modeling theories. The symbolic-interactionist theory stems from the early growth of sociology and social psychology in the respective writings of C.H. Cooley and George H. Mead.[33] Cooley developed the concept of "the looking-glass self" in which the individual envisions viewing his face, figure, and dress in the mirror, taking an interest in the reflection by being pleased or displeased, and in his imagination perceives how another would view and react toward him. By learning to take the role of others, one can respond to others from their perspective and become an object to oneself.

For Mead, although animals have intelligence and also social life, they do not have mind and hence are not self-conscious. Emerging in the process of human social life is what Mead calls "significant symbols"; such symbols are linguistic in form and result from gestures and responses to gestures. Thus gestures become significant when they arouse in others the same response that they have for the initiator of the gesture. Here humans differ from animals by being able to take the role of the other, which makes language and communication possible. The self emerges in the communication process that enables the individual to view himself from the perspective of others. The individual's ability to respond to significant symbols presupposes that he can grasp the attitudes of the social group ("the generalized other"); consequently, what Mead calls the "me" arises as a set of attitudes acquired from others. The other phase of the self—the "I"—makes possible the response. Thus the "I" can respond to the "me" in novel ways and thereby assure that action need not be merely repetitive or imitative. The self, however, cannot develop adequately where attitudes and roles are unstable because language lacks a stable meaning.

Erving Goffman, by using a dramaturgical metaphor, shows how the person does not merely initiate roles but can exploit the possibilities for improvisation and play beyond the necessities for correct behavior.[34] In other words, once the child has embraced a role by showing attachment to it, exhibiting the capacity to perform it, and being actively involved in doing it, the child, by the age of five, can actually begin distancing himself from the role by showing that the task is too easy and that he can perform it in more than one way (as in assuming different postures in riding the merry-go-round).

The symbolic-interactionist theory has the strength of depicting humans as actors as well as reactors. The newborn, through social interaction, gradually creates a social self usually within the family. Thus nonsupportive or nonresponsive parents create an environment that impedes the young child's efforts to influence his environment and develop a self-concept. The unresponsive home environment discourages the child from acting and reinforces a sense of incompetence.

A second view of socialization is Bandura's modeling-identification theory.[35] While this theory recognizes that learning can occur through direct experience, it emphasizes that learning also takes place by observing the example of others. Based on the principle of modeling and imitation, a child observes a person (model) perform an act and is more likely to behave in a similar manner (imitation). Repeated trials may be unnecessary; the child can learn the behavior merely through observation. If a child watches a dummy being kicked and is placed in the room with the dummy, he is more likely to kick the dummy than if he had not seen it kicked, even if he is not rewarded for kicking it or seen the model rewarded; however, reinforcement of the model or the child, while it created no new learning, did increase the frequency of the child's performing the act.[36] The child needs to be attentive to what the model does, admire the model, and have the capability of performing the modeled act. Other than parents, the model the child is most likely to emulate is one who can reward him, control the consequences of his behavior, and who possesses high status. Modeling fosters learning of different kinds of behaviors such as play patterns, aggression, language, and many social behaviors. The theory stresses a reciprocal influence between the individual and his environment.

Each theory tends to explain certain forms of behavior that the other neglects, and therefore, employing only one may provide an inadequate picture of the socialization process. The principal advantage of the symbolic-interactionist theory, however, is that it offers a compelling explanation of how the self-concept is formed and utilizes a more dynamic model in which the child is as much an actor as a reactor.

Turning from explanations of socialization to describe rules, the question arises, For what role should the child be socialized? Should they be the ones especially suited to childhood or those similar to or continuous with those she will be expected to assume in adulthood? Some sociologists claim that since adult roles are mainly work roles of one form or another, childhood socialization that develops attitudes and experiences favorable to work are likely to promote adult roles. And where there is extreme permissiveness and an absence of work opportunities for children, childhood socialization lacks continuity with adulthood and may result in the youth's refusal to accept adult roles or cause the transition to adulthood to be traumatic.[37] In many ways the history of the family illustrates a continuity of roles when the home itself was an economic unit and children were sent to work in mines and factories alongside adults. It might be thought that with the advent of universal education, compulsory-school-attendance laws, and child-labor laws, this continuity lapsed because children were increasingly segregated from adults and experienced a protracted period before they could assume adult responsibilities. Yet academic study can be viewed as an occupation, a form of work, because it involves a specific set of duties and a highly structured time schedule. Moreover, much schooling is oriented to vocational preparation, as career education and related curricular developments demonstrate.

Yet educators since the time of Rousseau have admonished society against making childhood merely a preparation for adulthood. Warning fathers not to fill with bitterness the fleeting days of childhood, Rousseau urges parents to love childhood and indulge its pleasures, sports, and instincts.[38] Dewey notes that when education is conceived as a preparation for the future, it fails to take advantage of the needs and possibilities of the present; it loses its motive power because children focus on the present, and therefore the future, for them, lacks urgency. The mistake is to make the future the basis of present effort rather than providing conditions for making best use of the present capabilities of the child.[39]

Some variation in socialization is ascribed to social-class background and to the advent of new theories of child rearing. A shift toward more permissive practices can be observed from 1940 to 1960 as more of the new ideas of infant and child care were accepted by middle-class parents. Middle-class mothers tend to use discussion and love withdrawal as disciplinary measures while lower-class mothers were more likely to use physical punishment.[40] A comparison of the values of white-collar and blue-collar workers revealed that the former group tends to prize internal standards of control for children, such as curiosity, self-motivation, and consideration for others, while the latter group ranks more highly on conformity to external standards.[41] Thus some of the differences in values can be attributed to what the parents have found useful in the occupational world. Blue-collar workers may be more likely to punish the child directly for his misbehavior while white-collar workers may tend first to seek the child's motives or intentions.

Although in chapter 4 I objected to physical punishment on several grounds, when such punishment does not result in injury, love withdrawal may be a more damaging form of discipline for the child (perhaps considerably less so for the adolescent because her self-concept has had more of a chance to form and the reference groups are more likely to be peers and media stars). Love withdrawal manifests parental disapproval with the implication that love will not be restored until the misbehavior is rectified. Love withdrawal may take the form of coldness, disappointment, ignoring or isolating the child, and outright rejection. Since healthy emotional development depends considerably on a warm, caring relationship with at least one adult, love withdrawal during childhood is one of the most severe and inadvisable forms of discipline. The child is unlikely to recognize love withdrawal for what it is—a stop-gap measure of a desperate parent who lacks adequate parenting abilities—and perceive instead that her emotional world is built on sand or suffer the guilt that she is a "bad" child and unworthy of her parent's love. Probably just as emotionally damaging and undesirable is the parental threat to desert the child if she does not behave. Thus neither middle- nor lower-class parents hold a monopoly on sound disciplinary practices.

Who exercises the greatest authority and the actual distribution of family power have considerable effect on the socialization process. One way to uncover these processes is by use of resource theory. Using a probability sample of wives from 731 Detroit-area families, Robert D. Blood and Donald M. Wolfe obtained responses to key questions about decision-making in the home.[42] The husband's power, they found, was greatest when he worked more than forty hours per week and the wife was not employed. Thus the power to make decisions derives from the ability to meet the needs of one's spouse and to upgrade one's decision-making skills.[43] Thus power parallels economic and other resources that each spouse brings to a marriage.

In testing resource theory internationally, Hyman Rodman found that it applied in France as originally formulated but not in Greece and Yugoslavia.[44] Whereas in the United States and France the husband's educational and occupational status and income are positively correlated with authority, in Greece and Yugoslavia they are negatively correlated. In Greece and Yugoslavia it is less a contest between spouses over resources; the more education a man has, despite a patriarchal culture, the more likely he is to grant the wife more authority.

David M. Heer proposes instead that each spouse compares, overtly or covertly, the benefits to be gained in the marraige as opposed to possible alternatives, to the desirability of roles if the marriage were dissolved.[45] The greater the benefits or rewards provided by one's spouse and the less satisfactory the alternatives to one's present marriage, the more dependent one is upon one's spouse and the greater the power the spouse who is depended upon. Thus when the husband's earning ability is slight or decreases, his home power is low; whereas if the wife's earning power were as low as a single person's and her prospects of remarriage to a man of high status were slight, her marital power would be low.

Resource theory and its variants, other than cross-national differences, may have some explanatory shortcomings. The theory emphasizes instrumental and symbolic criteria to the neglect of affectional ones. It may explain why some abused wives remain in a marriage, but it does not explain why those wives who do not find love or companionship in a marriage, despite dim earning power and remarriage prospects as a single person, still seek divorces. With the rise of more egalitarian relationships and the shift toward companionable marriages, both women and men began to expect more affectionate ties and deemphasized economic and related reasons for marriage.

Another difficulty with resource theory is that it assumes that the couple will evaluate the alternatives to their present arrangement and make a decision whether to continue the marriage. But a number of couples claim that they have never seriously considered alternatives to their marriage. John F. Cuber and Peggy B. Harroff studied couples whose marriages had lasted for ten years or more who said they had never considered divorce or separation.[46] These couples were classified into five types based on ways of adjustment in marriage; one type is a conflict-habituated mode in which there is much tension and conflict, though largely controlled, based on what some psychiatrists would say is a deep need to engage in battle. Despite the persistence of these conflicts, such couples insist they have never seriously considered alternatives to marriage.

In any case, for those couples who consider alternatives, the spouse who commands the resources will likely have his values prevail in the socialization process, even if the partner is primarily responsible for child rearing. The socialization process, however, is seriously threatened when violence is substituted for usual disciplinary procedures. The next section will look at characteristics and effects of family violence, and the last section of the chapter will discuss what can best be done to change family policy.

Violence in the Family

Although it is not a popular topic and has yet to receive as much publicity as violence in society at large, violence in the family is far more common than is generally believed. Violence occurs between spouses, between spouses and kin, and between parents and children. Our concern is with the last relationship, but it should be noted that violence is not unilateral—from male to female—but there also are homes in which women inflict violence not only on their children but on their husbands.

Violence with children may take the form of corporal punishment and child abuse. Although many adults may claim to disapprove of the latter, the fact is that corporal punishment is widespread; therefore, evidently, most parents see nothing wrong with using it. Spanking of children is done by at least 93 percent of all parents.[47] Of course, some parents seldom spank whereas others resort to it frequently (as social-class differences indicate). But, in view of the definition of violence given in chapter 5, not all corporal punishment could be classified as violence. Violence was defined as a sudden and extremely forceful act that causes physical harm or suffering to persons or animals. Most forms of corporal punishment of offspring would likely be sudden and forceful; those acts that are milder or more deliberate may be examples of force. Not all such acts would cause physical harm or suffering, in which case they could also be classified as force. Those that cause excessive physical harm, once reported to public authorities, would constitute child abuse. Thus parental use of corporal punishment with their children consists of three types: force, violence, and child abuse. Although our concern is primarily with the latter two types, a word needs to be said about the use of force in child-rearing practices.

Since force need not cause physical harm or suffering, why should it be of any concern? Why should it not be an option that all parents have without experiencing any remorse? From the standpoint of discipline as developed in chapter 4, force is not a form of discipline but a method of control. Whether control techniques can eventually lead to discipline would depend upon the situation and the intention of the parties involved; yet too frequently it merely serves a stop-gap measure to alleviate parental frustration rather than promote discipline. When parents have permitted the behavior of the child to get out of hand, it is understandable, but not necessarily wise, that they resort to force; yet they may be even further away from establishing genuine discipline if such control measures become habitual and the child expects to be treated in this manner.

Although some of the harsh child-rearing practices of the past would be illegal today, the home is still a violent place. Earlier civilizations may have rationalized some of the violence as the best way to prepare the young for battle or exploration. Whatever the merits of such explanations, they are not valid for preparation in today's occupational world, which, in some instances, demands independence of judgment and creative ability; in other instances, perseverance and high boredom tolerance. A general cultural approval of corporal punishment persists; its acceptability leaves it as an option that can lead to severe injury of the child. The Supreme Court's ruling on corporal punishment in schools reflects the cultural acceptability of these practices. The Court concluded that neither the Eighth Amendment's prohibition against cruel and unusual punishment nor the Fourteenth Amendment's right to due process is violated by school disciplinary procedures that permit paddling.[48] But courts can intervene if parents cause injury to the child or the punishment is inflicted with a "malicious desire to cause pain."[49]

Why is corporal punishment so widespread? One explanation is that it stems from frustration. It may be that the mother, having several young children to care for, is unprepared for the responsibility and the demands they make; therefore, she becomes frustrated and, in an attempt to stop a whining, crying, or misbehaving child, uses corporal punishment to alleviate the frustration and attempt to regain control. Or it may be that the father has been laid off his job and uses displaced aggression on his children. Some evidence indicates that where the husband is unemployed or not achieving well in the wage-earner role or has status characteristics lower than the wife's, he will likely experience goal blockages that lead to violence.[50]

The frustration-aggression hypothesis states that aggressive behavior presupposes the existence of frustration, and the occurrence of frustration leads to some form of aggression.[51] This hypothesis has been demonstrated under laboratory conditions but little has been done to test it in the home environment. A further difficulty is the inability of the hypothesis to provide an operational definition of *frustration*. Individuals differ in what they find frustrating and how they respond to such situations. Frustration tolerance differs considerably and is likely the result of cognitive and emotional factors based on past experiences with similar situations. Even when conditions are defined as frustrating, prolonged or intense frustration may lead to flight rather than aggression.

Actually, it is not necessary to invoke the frustration-aggression hypothesis to explain widespread use of corporal punishment in the home; it can be explained quite simply by cultural norms that sanction it. But when parents move from force to violence and from violence to abuse, further explanations are needed.

It may be thought that aggression in the home should not be suppressed because its suppression will lead to personality disorders and that its expression has a salutary cathartic effect that diminishes the likelihood of severe violence. Psychoanalytic theory holds that violence is part of human nature; since it cannot be eliminated, it should be channeled in nondestructive expression. Those who believe in catharsis may encourage children to participate in aggressive play activities, instigate aggressive behavior in psychotherapy playrooms, or have children watch aggressive acts on television. Catharsis (for aggression) is accepted by a number of psychoanalysts and followers.[52] But a considerable body of research findings fails to support the cathartic hypothesis and even suggests that participation by children in aggressive activities may actually increase aggression.[53]

Child abuse occurs whenever acts of violence used by parents in punishing their children cause severe injury or threaten the child's life or safety. Child abuse ranges from death or permanent brain damage to bleeding around the skull, severe bruising, mutilation, broken bones, bites, cigarette burns, and scalds. Children under age four are most in danger of abuse. Reported cases of child abuse range from six to ten thousand cases per year, but these are only the most severe cases that are officially reported. Sample surveys that asked people about cases they know suggest that the figure exceeds two million each year.[54] In England officially reported cases show 4,600 children are abused each year; 700 will die and another 400 will be left with permanent brain damage.[55]

A psychological explanation holds that such parents are suffering from serious emotional or personality disturbances. Ascribed to these parents are a host of maladies: schizophrenia, character disorders, impaired impulse control, grossly immature personalities, chronic aggressiveness, rigid and detached personalities, and the mother's jealousy that the child is a dangerous rival for her husband's affection.[56] Without denying that some abusive parents suffer from some of the preceeding pathologies or maladies, attempts to identify a single personality type have been unsuccessful and such parents do not fit neatly into classification schemes currently in use. Moreover, few studies attempt to test their hypotheses. Thus while psychological explanations cannot be ignored, they need to be supplemented by social and cultural explanations.

Of the social characteristics, both middle and lower classes are represented among child abusers but the lower class is disproportionately represented. It may not only be that lower-class abuse may more likely be reported than that of the middle class; it has earlier been observed that the two classes inculcate different values in child rearing and settle disputes differently. Unwanted pregnancies and children out of wedlock are more likely to lead to abuse. Parents who were raised in violent homes are also more likely to be violent with their children, as the parents unthinkingly adopt the role model found in their own early socialization. The husband's unemployment, a source of frustration and anxiety, may lead the father to take more extreme measures than ordinarily in controlling offspring. More child abuse is by women. Women spend more time with children, have more opportunities to perceive the child is threatening or interfering with the mother's goals, self-esteem, or freedom.[57]

Thus child abuse is based on a complex set of interacting psychological and social factors. How many of these variables must be present and in what combination is difficult to say, but enough of the variables are known that we could speak of predisposing personalities to violence and possible child abuse. It is easy to explain the widespread use of corporal punishment by its general cultural acceptance. But why do some parents escalate from force to violence, and still others from violence to abuse? We can hypothesize that a trigger mechanism could fire, exploding from violence to abuse. But, to continue the metaphor, why does the safety catch work for some parents but not for others? Once a combination of critical variables mixes, an explosive episode of abuse ensues. Which combination of critical variables would cause the explosion would differ among individuals; however, the limited number of key variables previously mentioned can be present only in a finite number of combinations, and therefore being cognizant of these variables as early-warning signals and taking proper preventive action would be wise.

It could be further hypothesized that among child abusers, two predisposing types might be observed: a group that does not overtly accept norms that should lead to child abuse but succumbs from weakness of will or personality disorders; a second group whose norms or role models tacitly accept violence and abuse. The first group may have a desire to raise the child properly but because of poor impulse control, ability to be threatened by the child, immature personalities, and other psychological problems yield to some combination of these traits mixed with some other volatile social or psychological variable. The second type, lacking the norms and role models for adequate parenting, will probably become abusive early in the child's life, and the spouses are likely to settle their own differences through violence, leading to the battered husband or wife syndrome.

The next section therefore will discuss what can be done to alleviate violence and child abuse. Many other problems have also been raised earlier in the chapter, and thus proposals are made for the types of policies and programs needed to reshape and sometimes restructure the family.

Family Policy and the Structure of Authority

One of the most important things that can be done to reduce violence is to remove the legal sanctions for the use of corporal punishment. The Congress and state legislatures could outlaw the use of corporal punishment in public schools, juvenile courts, correctional institutions, and other child-care facilities. By doing so, the normative public consensus would be undermined, the unacceptability of this practice would be communicated, the fear of legal sanctions would arise, and, after a probable transition period, the use of force in child-rearing practices would be largely abolished. And if these outcomes should accrue, would not violence and abuse eventually be eliminated? Not necessarily. It may at best only be reduced. On the 93 percent of parents using force, a smaller percentage would escalate to violence, and a still smaller group (as previous figures indicate) would become child abusers. In order to reduce a hard core of violence and abuse, additional steps must be taken.

Violent role models need to be greatly diminished. These models pervade the media and are available for children as well as adults, despite sporadic attempts to improve programming. The average child spends between two and four hours a day watching television, which is equivalent by age sixteen of watching twenty-four hours a day for fifteen to twenty months.[58] Children and youth frequently adopt role models from television and films. The National Coalition on Television Violence found that the average prime-time program had six violent acts per hour, whereas four times as much violence was found on children's programming.[59] Although what the coalition called "violence" would in some instances be force, according to our definition, the figures are still alarmingly high. The irony is that though more parents are concerned about violence in children's programs, far fewer raise questions about widespread violence in the media in general and the role models portrayed for youth and adults to emulate. Of course, this goes back to the long history of violence in American society and the anachronistic frontier mentality still found in some quarters today.[60] What is needed is a great reduction of violence depicted in the media; and when violence is shown, it should not be gratuitous but emerge naturally from the context portrayed; it should be presented realistically by displaying the suffering that it causes rather than as a quick solution for everyday problems or a smart, efficient way to handle difficult people.

Reductions in many forms of child abuse, violence toward children, and some reduction in spouse violence would likely result from adopting the parenting proposals suggested earlier. Some potential parents could be divided roughly into three groups: those who meet basic competencies; those who presently lack needed competencies but have the potential and the desire to acquire them; and those who, as a result of chronic disability, could not become competent. Obviously, the first group is ready for parenthood (assuming finances, housing, and related problems are under reasonable control); the second group would be licensed for parenthood upon demonstrating needed competencies; while the third group would be strongly discouraged from parenthood by the use of sanctions. Certainly not all forms of child abuse and violence could be ascribed to incompetent parenting; many of the causes are complex and deep-seated, as our previous analysis indicated. Adequate parent-education programs could screen out those parents whose abusive tendencies spring from some type of psychopathology (which may be the largest group of offenders). While sound parent-education programs may not eliminate abusive behavior that stems from some mix of social and cultural problems, policies and proposals that will shortly be presented will address these problems. It should be noted that some violence between spouses arises from conflicts over seriously mishandling offspring; since parent education will help overcome such problems, it would greatly diminish violence from this source.

In identifying those who are poor risks for parenting, it would not only be those adults with some chronic psychopathology but those whose parents abused them since there is considerable likelihood that they would adopt such a role model in their own home unless intervention occurred early enough to overcome such role models. It is not known, however, the extent to which such intervention would be successful; but whenever such role models are combined with psychopathology, prognonis is poor because, most psychiatrists believe, successful treatment of the sociopath or psychopath is rarely successful.[61]

Many abused children are products of unwanted pregnancies: the pregnancy was either out of wedlock or inconvenient.[62] Contraceptives should be available to minors who seek them as one means of reducing unwanted pregnancies. Some parents worry that such a practice will encourage promiscuity; their fear, however, may manifest a lack of confidence in their own offspring and their effectiveness as parents. It also overlooks the number of unwanted pregnancies under present constraints. Coupled with access to contraceptives should be sound programs of sex education and family living in public schools that enable youth to develop an understanding of total sexuality in the context of scientific and moral perspectives as it relates to the family and interpersonal relations. Since sex education has frequently been entirely absent from the home, incomplete, or presented too late, public schools and private agencies will need to assume greater responsibility for it. Sensitive, skilled, understanding teachers are needed for such programs, and resource persons—medical specialists, social workers, counselors, and others—should be utilized in planning and programs. Some parents who eschew sex education in the home strenuously object to its being taught in the schools; however, parental education as previously outlined and greater cooperation between parents, teachers, and other resource persons should alleviate the problem. The White House Conference on Families recommended that such programs include human development, parent education, marriage and the family, interpersonal relations, and human sexuality.[63]

Earlier it was noted that the mother is more likely to abuse the child than the father. Women are given primary responsibility for child rearing, are in contact with offspring much more than the father, and some experience more frustration and thwarting as a consequence. The mother's identity and self-esteem is more closely tied to child rearing, and therefore the child can more readily threaten the mother's personality and emotional balance.

Obviously, some mothers are ill prepared for parenthood and, at least for some, this deficiency could be ameliorated by sound parent-education programs. But the frustration experienced by women moves us to a consideration of women's rights. Thus in the remainder of the chapter, we will be addressing changing family and societal policies to improve the overall condition of the family rather than strictly to reduce violence and abuse (even though the policies may also have a positive effect on these problems as well).

Changing Family and Societal Policy

The percentage of married women with children ages six through seventeen who worked outside the home rose from 20 percent in 1950 to 57 percent in

1978. In 1978, 42 percent of all married women with children under six were in the labor force.[64]

Although ratification of the Equal Rights Amendment may not be successful, affirmative-action programs, regulations against sexual harassment, and an emphasis on equal pay for equal work have appreciably improved working conditions for women, even though further improvements need to be made. Various court decisions have also eliminated some discriminatory practices against women. Courts now require employers to demonstrate the need for discriminatory practices (as in those jobs for men only that are allegedly too strenuous or physically demanding for women). Legislation now prohibits wage differentiation based on sex; where such differences are found, employers need to show that such differences are based on merit or seniority. Though job opportunities and wages for women are not presently equal to men, the necessary legislation exists to bring about nondiscriminatory practices.

Resistance to mothers' working arises from traditional views of a mother's responsibilities, the notion—quickly fading in the face of rapid inflation—that an adequate father earns enough that the family can be supported at a desirable standard of living without the mother's working. Research evidence suggest that the mother's working does not necessarily cause disadvantages for the child.[65]

The problem of adequate child care for working mothers has yet to be settled despite a variety of programs and proposals that include daycare, maternity and child-care leaves, in-home care, and prekindergarten and nursery schools.[66] The question arises, however, of whether a minimum-income system should be established to provide sufficient income for one or the only parent to choose not to work outside the home. In other words, in such a plan, a minimum floor above the poverty level would be established for all families.

Families differ in the problems they face, not only because they obviously are confronted with divergent conditions and have varying degrees of resources for coping with the conditions but also because families themselves differ. No single plan could fit everyone because of the numerous types of families: two parent, married; two parent, contractual; one parent, divorced; one parent, separated; one parent, widowed, one parent, unmarried; a grandparent and a child; relatives and a child; a guardian and a child. The likelihood of living below the poverty line is greater for people over sixty-five and under eighteen than other age groups, for female-headed families with five or more children, and for black and Spanish-surnamed female-headed families.

It is estimated that from a quarter to a third of American children are born into families where the income level will cause basic deprivations for the children.[67] Children from impoverished homes suffer higher rates of infant mortality, bad health, and inadequate nutrition, which is likely to adversely affect intellectual and physical development. In terms of income distribution, if capital gains and tax-exempt bonds as well as income reported are considered, the top fifth of families receive 48 percent of all family income and the bottom fifth slightly less than 4 percent.[68]

Poverty can be reduced by lowering unemployment, providing public employment or retraining programs for those of limited skills and chronically unemployed, or by redistributing income. Earlier it was indicated that a source of male violence toward one's spouse or children was unemployment (for those who want to work). Some who are willing to work have been discouraged by discrimination, lack of opportunity, or unemployability in the present market because of inadequate skills or skills no longer in demand. It is debatable whether the government is capable of offering employment for at least one parent in every family that has a child. Through deficit spending, greater business tax incentives to hire more people, and the creation of jobs by government, unemployment could be reduced. Since more parents, for physical or psychological reasons, are incapable of holding a full-time job that would place them above the poverty level, it behooves us to seriously consider income redistribution.

Any plan for income redistribution should be equitable for the middle class and not reduce motivation and incentives on which the economy relies. Additionally, poor but childless families should not be discriminated against; it would not only be unfair but might encourage a rise in unwanted children for them to qualify for benefits. The plan should provide a strong incentive to work by reducing the program benefits gradually for those who take a job and disquality from benefits those not taking care of children who are able to work but do not actively seek a job. The plan should assure that no child should have a family living standard less than half of the median family income for any substantial period of time. Such support could be provided by revamping the tax system or using some form of tax credits or negative income tax.

Poverty will be reduced some by earlier plans for restricting parenthood, parent education, sound sex-education programs, and the widespread distribution of contraceptives. But because of present income distributions and the use of power in the economic system, an income-redistribution plan will be needed while also devising workable plans for lowering unemployment and providing retraining programs. In this way the lives and opportunities for healthy growth and development of one-forth to one-third of American children will be appreciably improved.

Children will be aided educationally if relations between home and school can be improved. Present relations will be examined in the next chapter along with the need for new patterns of authority likely to foster desirable changes and greater educational benefits for children and youth.

Notes

1. Michael D. Bayles, "Limits to A Right to Procreate," in Onora O'Neill and William Ruddick, eds., *Having Children* (New York: Oxford University Press, 1979), p. 14.

2. Herman Kahn and Anthony J. Wiener, "The Next Thirty-Three Years: A Framework for Speculation," *Daedalus* 96 (summer 1967):727.

3. Lester R. Brown, "An Overview of World Trends," *The Futurist* 6 (December 1972):225.

4. *Information Please Almanac 1981*, 35th ed. (New York: Simon and Schuster, 1980), p. 131.

5. J. Bryan Hehir, "Population Ethics: Religious Traditions: Roman Catholic Perspectives," in Warren T. Reich ed. *Encyclopedia of Bioethics,* (New York: Free Press, 1978), vol. 3, pp. 1254-59.

6. See Ronald L. Meek, ed., *Marx and Engels on Malthus* (New York: International Publishers, 1954), and Mahmood Mamdani, *The Myth of Population Control: Family, Caste and Class in an Indian Village* (New York: Monthly Review Press, 1972).

7. Philip M. Hauser, "Population," in Foreign Policy Association, ed., *Toward the Year 2018* (New York: Cowles, 1968), pp. 142-43.

8. James H. Weaver and Jon D. Wisman, "Smith, Marx, and Malthus: Ghosts Who Haunt Our Future," *1999 The World of Tomorrow*, edited by Edward Cornish (Washington, D.C.: World Future Society, 1978), pp. 9-19.

9. Kingsley Davis, "Population Policy: Will Current Programs Succeed?" in *Readings on the Family System* (New York: Holt, Rinehart and Winston, 1972), pp. 451-72.

10. Representative examples of this school of thought: Paul R. Ehrlich and Anne H. Ehrlich, *Population, Resources, Environment: Issues in Human Ecology* (San Franciso: Freeman, 1970); Garrett Hardin, "The Tragedy of the Commons," *Science* 162 (1968):1243-48; and William Paddock and Paul Paddock, *Famine—1975! America's Decision: Who Will Survive?* (Boston: Little, Brown, 1967).

11. See the predictions about famine in Paddock and Paddock, *Famine—1975!* and various ecological predictions in Paul R. Ehrlich, *The Population Bomb* (New York: Ballantine Books, 1968).

12. These values are discussed in Robert M. Veach, ed., *Population Policy and Ethics: The American Experience* (New York: Irvington Publishers, 1977), part I.

13. Ibid., pp. 47-52.

14. Ibid., pp. 169-180.

15. Alice S. Rossi, "Transition to Parenthood," in *Readings on the Family System*, p. 306.

16. Urie Bronfenbrenner, "Children and Families: 1984?" *Society* 18 (January/February 1981):38-41.

17. Kenneth Kenniston and The Carnegie Council on Children, *All Our Children* (New York: Harcourt Brace Jovanovich, 1977), p. 197.

18. United Nations, General Assembly Resolution 1386 (XIV), November 20, 1959, published in the *Official Records of the General Assembly, Fourteenth Session, Supplement* No. 16, 1960.

19. Rossi, "Transition," pp. 312-313.

20. *Prince* v. *Massachusetts*, 321 U.S. 158 (1944).

21. Philippe Aries, *Centuries of Childhood: A Social History of Family Life* (New York: Vintage Books, 1965).

22. Ibid., chs. 2 and 5.

23. John Demos, "Myths and Realities in the History of American Family-Life," in *Contemporary Marriage: Structure, Dynamics, and Therapy* (Boston: Little, Brown, 1976), p. 12.

24. Jean-Louis Flandrin, *Families in Former Times* (Cambridge: Cambridge University Press, 1979), ch. 3.

25. John Demos, "Images of the American Family, Then and Now," in Virginia Tufte and Barbara Myerhoff, eds., *Changing Images of the Family* (New Haven: Yale University Press, 1979), pp. 43-60.

26. Edward Shorter, *The Making of the Modern Family* (New York: Basic Books, 1975), ch. 5.

27. Flandrin, *Families*, pp. 136-137.

28. Christopher Lasch, *Haven in a Heartless World* (New York: Basic Books, 1979), pp. 4-6.

29. Bernard Wishy, *The Child and The Republic: The Dawn of Modern American Child Nurture* (Philadelphia: University of Pennsylvania Press, 1968), ch. 5.

30. David Riesman (with Nathan Glazer and Reuel Denney), *The Lonely Crowd* (Garden City, N.Y.: Doubleday, 1953).

31. Orville G. Brim, Jr., "Socialization Through the Life Cycle," in Marvin B. Sussman, ed., *Sourcebook in Marriage and the Family*, 4th ed. (Boston: Houghton Mifflin, 1974), pp. 102-109.

32. Erving Goffman, *Encounters: Two Studies in the Sociology of Interaction* (Indianapolis: Bobbs-Merrill, 1961).

33. C.H. Cooley, *Human Nature and the Social Order* (New York: Charles Scribner's Sons, 1902), and George H. Mead, *Mind, Self, and Society* (Chicago: University of Chicago Press, 1934).

34. Erving Goffman, *The Presentation of Self in Everyday Life* (Garden City, N.Y.: Doubleday Anchor, 1959).

35. Albert Bandura and R.H. Walters, *Social Learning and Personality Development* (New York: Holt, Rinehart and Winston, 1963), and Albert Bandura, *Social Learning Theory* (Englewood Cliffs, N.J.: Prentice-Hall, 1977).

36. Albert Bandura, "Vicarious Processes: A Case of No-Trial Learning," in L. Berkowitz, ed., *Advances in Experimental Social Psychology*, vol. 2 (New York: Academic Press, 1965), pp. 1-55.

37. F. Ivan Nye and Felix M. Berardo, *The Family: Its Structure and Interaction* (New York: Macmillan, 1973), pp. 403-404.

38. Jean Jacques Rousseau, *Emile*, translated by Barbara Foxley (New York: Everyman's Library, 1972), p. 43.

39. John Dewey, *Democracy and Education* (New York: Free Press, 1966), pp. 54-56.

40. Urie Bronfenbrenner, "Socialization and Social Class Through Time and Space," in by Eleanor E. Maccoby, T.M. Newcomb, and E.L. Hartley, eds., *Readings in Social Psychology* (New York: Holt, Rinehart and Winston, 1958), pp. 400-425.

41. Melvin L. Kohn, "Social Class and Parent-Child Relationships: An Interpretation," *American Journal of Sociology* 68 (January 1963):471-480.

42. Robert D. Blood, Jr., and Donald M. Wolfe, *Husbands and Wives: The Dynamics of Married Living* (New York: Macmillan, 1960).

43. Ibid., pp. 40, 44.

44. Hyman Rodman, "Marital Power in France, Greece, Yugoslavia, and the United States: A Cross-National Discussion," *Journal of Marriage and the Family* 29 (May 1967):320-335.

45. David M. Heer, "The Measurement and Basis of Family Power: An Overview," *Journal of Marriage and the Family* 25 (May 1963):133-139.

46. John F. Cuber and Peggy B. Harroff, *The Significant Americans* (New York: Appleton-Century-Crofts, 1965), pp. 43-65.

47. Rodney Stark and James McEvoy III, "Middle Class Violence," *Psychology Today* 4 (November 1970):52-65.

48. *Ingraham* v. *Wright*, 430 U.S. 651 (1977).

49. Alan Sussman and Martin Guggenheim, *The Rights of Parents* (New York: Avon Books, 1980), p. 50.

50. John E. O'Brien, "Violence in Divorce-Prone Families," in Suzanne K. Steinmetz and Murray A. Straus, eds., *Violence in the Family* (New York: Dodd, Mead, 1975), pp. 65-75.

51. John Dollard, et al. *Frustration and Aggression* (New Haven: Yale University Press, 1939), p. 1.

52. See Bruno Bettelheim, "Children Should Learn About Violence," *Saturday Evening Post* 240 (May 11, 1967):10-12; William C. Menninger, "Recreation and Mental Health," *Recreation* 42 (1948):340-346; and Dorothy W. Baruch, *New Ways in Discipline* (New York: McGraw-Hill, 1949), pp. 35-45.

53. Bandura and Walters, *Social Learning* pp. 254-258.

54. Steinmetz and Straus, eds., *Violence*, p. 205.

55. Sydney Brandon, "Physical Violence in the Family: An Overview,"

in Marie Borland, ed., *Violence in the Family* (Atlantic Highlands, N.J.: Humanities Press, 1976), p. 1.

56. Letitia J. Allan, "Child Abuse: A Critical Review of the Research and the Theory," in J.P. Martin, ed., *Violence and the Family* (New York: Wiley, 1978), p. 48.

57. Richard J. Gelles, "Child Abuse as Psychopathology: A Sociological Critique and Reformulation," in Steinmetz and Straus, eds., *Violence*, pp. 190-204.

58. Kenniston, *All Our Children*, p. 51.

59. "TV Violence Unabated," *The Daily Texan* (December 1, 1980):8.

60. See National Commission on the Causes and Prevention of Violence, *Violence in America: Historical and Comparative Perspectives*, vol. I (Washington, D.C.: Government Printing Office, 1969).

61. Henry C. Kempe, et al., "The Battered-Child Syndrome," *Journal of the American Medical Association* 181 (July 7, 1962):17-24.

62. E.H. Bennie and A.B. Sclare, "The Battered Child Syndrome," *American Journal of Psychiatry* 125 (1969):975-979.

63. White House Conference on Families, *Listening to America's Families: Action for the 80's* (Washington, D.C.: The Conference, 1980), p. 48.

64. Ibid., p. 178.

65. See Alison Clarke-Stewart, *Child Care in the Family: A Review of Research and Some Propositions for Policy* (New York: Academic Press, 1977).

66. Economic problems of daycare and similar programs are presented in Mary Jo Bane, *Here to Stay: American Families in the Twentieth Century* (New York: Basic Books, 1976), pp. 82-85, and National Research Council, *Toward a National Policy for Children and Families* (Washington, D.C.: National Academy of Sciences, 1976), ch. 5.

67. Kenniston, *All Our Children*, pp. 26-27.

68. Ibid., p. 44.

7 Patterns of Authority in School-Family Relations

The family and the school are the two institutions most concerned with the growth, socialization, and education of the young. Whenever these two institutions fail to discharge their responsibilities, the larger society is ill-equipped to compensate for the losses, and an entire generation suffers. The school and family sorely need a sound working relationship based on mutual understanding and cooperation. Yet many old and new conflicts still impede progress.

This chapter first explores parents' authority for home instruction and for decisions once the child enters school in light of de facto and de jure forms of authority. Increasing parental choice is next investigated in terms of alternatives in public education, the voucher plan, and libertarian education. Turning then to issues about parental responsibility and participation in schools, theories of representative and participatory democracy help in understanding these issues, especially as reflected in controversies over proposals for community control or decentralization. Finally, as parents' participation in schools increases, it is important to know whether their responsibility also increases for their child's school disciplinary problems. Some plans, approaches, and procedures are also explored, including community education, for increasing parent participation in schools.

Parental Authority in Formal Education

Every state but one (Mississippi) has compulsory-school-attendance laws, which usually cover the ages of six or seven to sixteen. This educational requirement, however, may be fulfilled either at home or at school in some states; but if parents choose to educate their children at home, the burden is on the parents to demonstrate that the instruction and curriculum they offer meet acceptable state standards. Other states require that children attend some school, either public or nonpublic. The state, although it cannot require parents to send children to public schools (as opposed to private), is not obligated to pay for the student's private schooling unless sent there by the state.

In the preceding chapter the problems of adequate parenting were outlined. It was suggested that the number of inadequate parents is far larger than the number convicted of neglect and abuse. Of the adequate parents, few of these are likely capable or motivated to handle home instruction successfully—and the small number who have been approved are a reasonably accurate indication of instructional competence (rather than unfair state standards as some aspiring parents allege).

But why do not more of the many adequate parents offer home instruction? One reason is motivation. With a larger percentage of women working full time than ever before, it is unlikely that many new parents would apply for home instruction as long as this trend continued. Many parents also rightfully believe that they are not capable of home instruction; they recognize that they lack the requisite specialized skills and abilities. Dissatisfied parents, rather than applying for home instruction, usually send their child to a different school (when family finances permit).

Parenting is chiefly caught up with socialization rather than education. Socialization processes instill proper social rules and thereby help preserve social institutions. Education, on the other hand, is usually designed to change and improve individuals and society by providing requisite knowledge and reflective abilities. This is less true in the early grades in which the acquisition of skills and a rudimentary knowledge of the cultural heritage are emphasized. This is not to say that the home fails to exercise an educative function; the point is that the family is primarily a socializing and nurturing institution whereas schools continue socialization but strive to be primarily an education institution.

Since both the school and the home are heavily involved in socialization, this would seem to be the nexus where parents and teachers could more readily communicate about the child's early education. Where parents can see continuity between socialization in home and school, they are likely to elicit sympathy for the program; yet because of the range of social-class and ethnic differences represented in school, discontinuities frequently arise.

Where does authority lie once the child enrolls in school? Do parents relinquish all authority, or do they share it with school officials? State laws permit, prescribe, and proscribe; it is within the framework that the laws establish and the courts adjudicate that authority is duly exercised. It would be misleading to seek a sovereign body because authority is divided between the different levels of government and a system of checks and balances are operative. Since power over education was not delegated to the federal government nor prohibited to the states, it was, according to the Tenth Amendment, left to the states. Education today is principally a state function. It is conducted by the education provisions in state constitutions, through state legislatures that establish schools and regulate their operation, and through state boards of education that formulate educational policies for the control, supervision, and implementation of statewide functions. The state, through its discretionary authority, delegates functions to local school districts; these functions are carried out by the local school board and the superintendent of schools.

The parent still has considerable authority despite the laws and regulations just cited. Parents, for instance, can make the ultimate choice as to the type of education their child will receive: home instruction, a public, private, or parochial school. This statement, however, needs qualification because such a choice is not economically feasible for lower-class families and even the lower-middle class (unless the latter class is prepared to make considerable financial sacrifices). In other words, the higher social classes do have more options in their children's education, and consequently, public schools will likely enroll all children from the lower socioeconomic classes. Those who have the option of sending their child to a private school but elect to keep him in a public school are likely exhibiting their satisfaction with public education, whereas it is less certain with parents from lower socioeconomic backgrounds.

Thus the question arises of whether it is fair that some parents can exercise greater authority in the choice of their child's education. Two solutions have generally been offered: the voucher plan and greater alternatives in public education.

But before exploring these alternatives, let us inquire what sort of authority parents are exercising here. Is it a case of de facto or de jure authority to say that parents can choose for their child either home instruction or a public, private, or parochial school? Technically, parents do not have an office but base their authority on a legally recognized role that resembles de facto authority. In other words, parents have been legally authorized to exercise such authority. Parents also exercise de jure authority except when adolescent offspring persistently object to parents' educational decisions. One type of restriction on parental authority was earlier defeated. The Compulsory Education Act in Oregon, which required parents or guardians to send children only to public schools, was struck down in *Pierce v. Society of Sisters* (1925). The Court recognized that "the child is not the mere creature of the State" and that those who nurture him have a right and duty to "prepare him for additional obligations."

But is it wise to grant parents this authority if their expertise is limited? A parent does not fit the profile of expert authority very well because an expert appeals principally to epistemic claims and provides evidence and grounds for their support, whereas a parent uses coercion and power much more than an expert. Moreover, in light of the previous discussion of parental education, actual expertise and specialized parenting skills are quite limited. The parents' authority is not based primarily on expertise but on a de facto role that the state recognizes in order to preserve the family as an institution and to protect and nurture the young. But since such crucial education choices may likely be improved by greater knowledge, it should be kept in mind throughout this chapter that there are ways to enhance parents' knowledge and understanding, as discussed in the following section.

Increasing Parental Choice

The government has given parents the legal right to choose the type of education their child will receive, but it has largely used a negative, rather than a positive, conception of freedom. The negative form is freedom from restraint; the positive is an ability to exercise a power. Thus someone not restrained is free to move about and go where she chooses (negative freedom), but she may still not be free to travel wherever she chooses because of inadequate income (a lack of positive freedom). All socioeconomic classes enjoy negative freedom in parental choice (of the type of education), but only the higher classes have the economic means to fully exercise their choices. The question is whether the government should make some provision to enlarge the choices of lower-income parents. No pretension is made that the government could literally equalize in the sense of providing identical opportunities; for even if doing so were desirable—and an equality of opportunity does not demand it—the cost would be prohibitive and probably an unfair burden to the higher classes. Even egalitarians do not interpret equal as identical where the government would somehow equalize family incomes, home and neighborhood conditions, and genetic endowments. The egalitarian may want some income redistribution but would not likely believe in a literal equality, which would obviously stifle individuality, initiative, and be strongly coercive. What is sought here is that children from lower-income families are not unduly and unfairly penalized, that they are afforded basic opportunities to develop their potentials in a healthy learning environment that provides some choices of programs and teachers.

The voucher plan is one proposed solution to this problem. It is based on enlarging the freedom of parental choices rather than attempting to directly equalize opportunities. Early voucher plans were essentially unregulated and posed threats of violating the separation of church and state and increasing segregated schooling.[1] In contrast, Christopher Jencks and others have developed a highly regulated voucher plan that seeks to overcome the serious shortcomings of the earlier proposals.[2]

The Jencks' plan would create an Education Voucher Agency (EVA) at the community level for receiving government funds for financing schools. It would be locally controlled and would resemble a board of education except that it would not operate any schools of its own; responsibility for operating schools would be retained by public and private local boards. The EVA would determine the eligibility of public and nonpublic schools to participate in the plan.

The purposes of the voucher plan are to provide more education options, break the "monopoly" of the public schools, and enable poor parents to have the same choice as wealthy parents as to where they can send their children to school. The voucher would be regulated by schools offering each applicant roughly an equal chance of admission. Each school would announce every spring the number of students to be enrolled the following academic year; each school would be required to take everyone who applied, except when the number of applicants exceeded the number of places, in which case a lottery would be used to fill half of its places. Each school, in order to avoid increasing segregation, would have to show that it had accepted at least as high a proportion of ethnic-group students as had applied. Discrimination against the poor could be avoided by requiring each school to accept the voucher as full payment for a student's education; otherwise, wealthier parents could attempt to supplement the voucher. In fact, vouchers from children of lower-income families would have higher redemption value because their education would likely be more costly. Additionally, EVA would pay the transportation costs of all children in order that low-income families would not be inordinately burdened.

EVA would disseminate information about all schools in the area to enable parents to make intelligent choices. A real danger exists, unless this service is provided, that some parents will be unable to choose wisely because of misleading advertising circulated by schools and erroneous information circulated by citizens.

The Office of Economic Opportunity made grants to several communities to study the feasibility of the voucher plan, but only the community of Alum Rock, California, with the aid of a federal grant, decided to try the plan. Alum Rock's plan, however, differed from Jenck's by using only public schools and providing alternative programs within them, and using the board of education in lieu of EVA. After four years of operation, it was found that teachers, students, and parents liked the plan but standardized-test scores were either equivalent to national norms or had in some instances dropped below them.[3] In any case the Alum Rock program, since it differed significantly from the original plan by involving only public schools, does not actually test the original plan but explores a new option instead.

Excluding Alum Rock, a number of serious deficiencies can be found in voucher plans.[4] A basic tenet of voucher proponents is that public schools constitute a monopoly, and consequently, the use of vouchers would open many new options to parents. Voucher advocates frequently use the free-marketplace analogy that vouchers would do for education what free enterprise has done for the economy and its productivity. Schools, however, are relatively decentralized and do compete with private schools and with each other: in their sports program, for teachers, appropriations, special projects, and the like. The market analogy is misleading insofar as profit-making firms sell their products to anyone who has cash or credit, whereas private schools are selective and not open to everyone. Moreover, to provide the options claimed to result from using vouchers, nonpublic schools would have to be far more innovative and experimental in their programs and organization, as only a small number exhibit these characteristics.

Once nonpublic schools accept substantial state funds, they would likely be more thoroughly regulated. It may mean that parochial schools would no longer be able to offer sectarian religious courses, and all nonpublic schools may be subject to desegregation rulings. Voucher plans make no provision for eliminating discrimination in the hiring of teachers. Nonpublic schools may also be required to observe judicial standards of academic freedom.

Public schools, under a voucher plan, would unlikely receive additional tax funds but nonpublic schools would be free to increase their endowment, thereby leading to greater inequities. The voucher system would increase public costs by paying nonpublic-school tuitions, staffing and operating the EVA, creating new buildings and facilities for private schools and underusing those of public schools (because of decreased enrollment, increased transportation costs, and inefficient use of tenured public-school teachers).

Thus, in view of the substantial shortcomings of the voucher plan, it may be wiser to offer greater curricular alternatives in public schools. Alternative schools, which are designed to provide options to the traditional model or comprehensive high school, usually have more comprehensive goals than traditional schools, greater curricular flexibility, and are smaller and less bureaucratic than the comprehensive high school. Examples of alternative schools are open schools, schools without walls, magnet schools, and multicultural schools.[5]

On the other hand, greater alternatives in public education does not eliminate the discrepancy in educational opportunities between wealthier and poorer families, though it does reduce the gap. Actually it is unreasonable, as earlier noted, to expect to provide identical opportunities since it is neither feasible nor consonant with the principle of equality. Nevertheless, greater opportunities might still be provided by taking a libertarian approach to education. Although not all voucher proponents are libertarians (Jencks, for instance), most libertarians would either advocate or else not object to vouchers (though vouchers may not be their first choice). But libertarians also have other ideas and proposals that should be explored.

Libertarian Education

Philosopher and 1972 libertarian presidential candidate, John Hospers, has stated some essential libertarian principles.[6] All human beings have the right to be free to make their own choices as long as they do not interfere with the choices of others. Thus all individuals have rights to their own life and property and have a duty to refrain from violating the same rights of others. It is through property rights that the individual's work is rewarded, goals can be achieved, and future plans can be confidently made. Rights are violated through the use of force, and government is the principal culprit;

therefore, the role of government should be limited to the protection of life, liberty, and property. Libertarians would reject laws that require people to help one another, such as unemployment compensation, social security, minimum wages, rent ceilings, and the like. And they would usually oppose laws regulating pornography, alcohol, and drugs.

Libertarians generally exhibit suspicion and distrust toward the government's role in education. Many libertarians are acutely dissatisfied with public education, object to the coercive power of government, and believe it has usurped parents' rights, consider the state's role to be at times detrimental to private education, and offer legislation and plans for reducing what they consider to be government interference and for granting parents primary authority in the formal education of their children. This education might be conducted exclusively in the home or in public, private, or parochial schools; the main point is that parents (or guardians) would choose the education best for their children.

The Dangers of Government Coercion. Libertarians strenuously warn about the dangers of the state's coercive power. The power of government, Murray N. Rothbard asserts, has been used to enforce uniformity and obedience through compulsory school attendance; public schools have been used to drive out thought of violence and rebellion among the lower classes.[7] Government coerces, according to Gerrit H. Wormhoudt, whenever it decides who must attend school, what is to be taught, who will teach, and how the funds will be allocated.[8] The government standards complement compulsory attendance laws to give the government a near monopoly of schooling.

But some libertarians see the problem of coercion somewhat differently. E.G. West believes that compulsion should be used selectively rather than universally: government powers should be directed at those parents who are irresponsible in providing for their children's education.[9] Thus selective compulsion would not penalize parents who are properly handling their educational responsibilities, but the state would intervene only in cases of negligence.

Libertarians do not always distinguish whether their objections are principally to compulsory-attendance laws or to a compulsory curriculum and school activities, although it seems that their objections are directed to the former. For instance, libertarians should make it clear whether they favor either repeal or modification of these laws. If they seek to amend these laws, the possibilities are virtually endless. Some possibilities would be to modify the age requirements or the daily and hour time requirements; to increase the opportunities for youth to work rather than attend school; and to permit various home-study arrangements. Each of these plans involves legal, financial, and educational ramifications that would require considerable exploration before adoption.[10]

Libertarians, however, may have misinterpreted the coercive characteristics of compulsory-attendance laws. Laws create obligations and embody standards; the standards justify demands for compliance, and therefore compulsion is a secondary rather than a primary factor in the way that laws function. Persons tend to talk about the state's coerciveness, claims M.S. Katz, only in connection with laws of which they disapprove; and since most (American) parents accept compulsory schooling, they would use the standard built into the law to criticize those who deviate from it.[11] It is a mistake to ascribe a connection between compulsory school attendance and the substantive results of schooling because the legal requirement in itself does not tell us anything about the content of education, the operation of programs, and teaching practices. Thus there is no logical connection between the two and, if there is an empirical connection, libertarians have not shown it.

Certain social outcomes are probable should compulsory-attendance laws be abolished. Gerald Reagan has observed that some who have profited from advanced schooling may favor the repeal of these laws because the benefits of schooling would be less widely distributed and therefore competition would be reduced.[12] The poor and disadvantaged would likely suffer the most should compulsory schooling be abolished.

Increasing Parental Options. The other reasons that libertarians generally offer for the changes they propose, in addition to their desire to reduce the state's coerciveness, are that public schools are performing inadequately and that parents should be accorded greater freedom of choice in educating their children. The most systematic and sustained critique of public schooling by a libertarian was made by the economist E.G. West.[13] His study, however, was conducted during the 1960s and focused on schooling in England and Wales; nevertheless, some of the principles he develops may well be applicable to American public education. In response to the libertarians and other critics, some educators and social scientists have attempted to demonstrate the accomplishment of public education.[14] An independent observer would probably conclude that public education faces serious problems, that some libertarian criticisms are sound, but that many accomplishments of public education have been obscured since the Coleman Report, and that recent studies may likely redress the balance. Libertarian proposals for improving education seem to be less connected to specific criticisms of public education than to their fears about government coercion and the consequent abrogation of parental freedom. Thus the libertarians' case is based more on philosophical grounds rather than specific empirical claims; in other words, libertarians attempt to show what a more ideal education would look like in view of their principles and assumptions about human nature and the good society.

The chief plank of the libertarian education platform is to increase parental choice. Libertarians oppose the state's coercive powers and its alleged monopoly over education, especially its fiscal power. But the most significant consequence of these powers is the restrictions placed on parental choice in educating their children. Parents, libertarians contend, are responsible for choosing food, shelter, and clothing for their children but not their children's education. Protection of children against malnutrition or starvation are as important as protection against ignorance, but laws are not passed for compulsory and universal eating. Not all parents are expert dieticians, but they can get advice and instruction, if necessary, and choose appropriate foods for their children; similarly, with the help of expert advice, parents could choose wisely their children's education. Thus complex decisions about food, rest, and other important matters are left to parents. "Only when it comes to education," Coons and Sugarman insist, "has the state, deliberately or otherwise, virtually emasculated the family's option."[15]

Since the preceding argument by analogy is frequently made by libertarians and much is made of it, let us look momentarily at analogical arguments to see if libertarians have established their case. Analogical arguments are not valid in the sense that the conclusions follow from the premises with logical necessity; rather, *probability* is all that can be claimed. One pertinent criterion for assessing analogical arguments is the number of respects in which the things involved are said to be analogous. Parents, we are told, make the final decisions regarding their children's food, shelter, clothing, hours of rest, and other important matters. But in what way are these functions similar to education other than their obvious importance and that adults—whether parents or educators—choose for children? Educational functions are more complex than the other ones enumerated, greater expertise is required, and it is a fact that more parents are competent to fulfill the other functions than educational ones; this is substantiated by the few parents who qualify to educate their children at home.[16] The other functions that parents fulfill do not require them to understand cognitive processes, how learning takes place, how to develop instructional objectives, select content and structure learning experiences, and evaluate learning experiences and outcomes. Thus there are many dissimilar tasks between education and the other functions and thus the analogical argument has a *low probability* of being sound.

But libertarians might claim that they are not actually advocating that most parents take over the day-to-day responsibility of educating their children; instead, they want parents to be vested with final authority for choosing the education best for their child—whether public, private, or parochial school, or home education—and to be granted the necessary financial support to exercise control effectively. Thus the original argument, with the preceding modifications, is now weaker: it holds that parents, with access to sufficient information, expert advice, and adequate funding, could and should make the decisions as to how their children can best be educated.

John Coons and Stephen Sugarman have developed more thoroughly than any other libertarians the grounds for family control of education.[17] They seek to discover what is in the best interests of the child; they find, beyond the acquisition of a few basics, a lack of consensus and no agreement on the means to achieve these objectives. Despite this lack of consensus, public schools have a certain sameness that emphasizes technology, uncontroversial information, and neutrality. The question, they believe, is converted into whom the state shall empower to decide the best interests of the child. The agent best qualified to decide should be willing to listen, have appropriate knowledge about the child, and have sufficient concern for the child's interests. Educators have knowledge about classes of children but parents have intimate knowledge about particular children. And there is a question of whether anyone other than parents really cares about children. Even those teachers who are altruistic and caring, the nature of their role causes their caring to remain "cool and abstract." The child is usually with a teacher no more than a year, but she is with her family for many years, and therefore the family is in the best position to observe the outcome of educational decisions over long periods of time.

Coons and Sugarman posit autonomy as the eventual goal of the child. The autonomous person is intellectually and morally independent, a coordination of intellect and responsible action. But the public schools, they believe, tend to develop the "conditioned man" rather than the "autonomous man"; they promote the "true American," a person without distinctive qualities. And since most faculties are constituted by teachers of similar socioeconomic background, students are not confronted with a range of different views and values. Under a family-choice system, the average child of twelve should be able to participate with parents in school choices and thereby promote personal autonomy.

Many of the things that Coons and Sugerman say about family choice is plausible. Yet they say nothing about eliminating poverty—the greatest obstacle to improving the child's life chances. They also tend to overlook the value of impartiality, objectivity, and expertise in decisions about a child's education. History is filled with cases of parents who sought to fulfill their own frustrated ambitions through their children or who failed to recognize the significance of dormant talents and punished their children for expressing them. The American family is also going through a turbulent period of increased violence, high divorce and desertion rates, lack of parental supervision, transient and ambiguous sex roles, and a host of other problems, as discussed in the previous chapter. It does not appear that the family would be presently prepared to assume these greater responsibilities; however even if families were capable of doing so, they still may not be the logical choice. For instance, it is not clear why some families would be willing for children to increasingly participate in decisions about their education or why some families would not likely have their child indoctrinated in the ideology of some fanatical cult.

Autonomy, a worthy aim, does not seem self-sufficient. Without an emphasis on morality, autonomy is undesirable; great criminals are autonomous agents. Autonomy needs to be reconciled with morality and consideration for others. And without respect for truth, the attempt to exercise autonomy is likely to lead to frustration and failure. In chapter 2 it was shown that emotional autonomy is not an entirely appropriate goal because it reflects certain culturally unacceptable character traits, while both cognitive and moral autonomy are too demanding for most people and are suitable only for an elite.

While libertarians should be commended for their attention to the child's interest, they are at the same time amazingly silent about the public interest. Yet public schools were established not only to fulfill the child's interest but the public interest as well. *Public*, as opposed to private, refers to that which has no relation to a particular person or persons but concerns all members of the community without distinction. Thus a hall is said to be public not because every member of the community chooses to visit it but because it is open to any person who chooses to enter.

The public interest can be supported by either positive or negative actions. Positive actions would provide goods and services; negative actions would be taken to prevent harm. Public schools would be an example of the former and police acts of the latter.

Public schools, according to R. Freeman Butts, are public in terms of purpose, control, support, access, and commitment to civic unity.[18] A public school serves a public rather than a private purpose; it is not maintained for the personal advantage of teacher, proprietor, student, or parents. The public schools are designed to serve the welfare of a democratic society by assuring the imparting of knowledge and understanding needed for citizenship responsibilities.

But the support of public education does not mean turning one's back on the child's interest because it is in the child's interest—at least in the larger, longer view—to have a strong system of public education. All too often an artificial opposition is erected between individual and public interests. Not only in many cases will individual and public interest coincide but the life chances of each person depend on more than just increasing options. Life chances—opportunities for individual growth and realization of talents—are a function, Ralf Dahrendorf claims, of two elements: *options* and *ligatures*.[19] Options are possibilities for choice in the social structure on which personal choice depends. These could be choices in terms of occupation, living conditions, goods and services, and the like. On the other hand, ligatures are bonds and linkages: forefathers, nation, community. Ligatures give meanings to the place the individual occupies, create an anchoring and a foundation for action. Although ligatures without options would be oppressive, options without ligatures would be meaningless.

A critical problem facing American society is ostensibly the erosion of ligatures, which carries with it a loss of values and a sense of pointlessness. Although public schools have usually been thought of as functioning to increase options, an overlooked function is its preservation of ligatures. In other words, it transmits certain values, traditions, and principles of citizenship—and there is less assurance that family control of education will offer the ligatures needed in a balanced combination with options to maximize life chances. Thus neither life chances nor the public interest is likely to be served best by the plan of family control.

Parental Responsibility and Participation in Schools

Two major positions on democratic participation are important for educational policy: representative democracy and participatory democracy. The former position is what actually takes place in most school districts, while the latter is more frequently advocated today in the literature. Representative democracy envisions the citizen's role as determining who shall represent him as a result of the election process. Thus democracy could be defined as an elective system in which majority influence is assured by elective and competitive minorities to whom the system is entrusted.[20] Political leaders, says Robert Dahl, are more likely to defend democracy, even if voters should prefer some other system, because democratic procedures regulate conflicts and protect their position of leadership.[21] V.O. Key, Jr., agrees that the health of democracy consists of the standards and competence of influentials and political activists.[22]

Thus the theory limits the citizen's role to the selection of political leaders; since each citizen must make wise political choices, education should make one knowledgeable about government and prepare new political leaders. This position, held by a number of groups, can be seen clearly in essentialism. The essentialists are opposed to making schools miniature democracies, whether by expanding the social studies, introducing life-adjustment education, or by injecting socializing procedures into an enlarged vocational program. Essentialists generally agree that the basic task of the schools is to develop the mind by transmitting the cultural heritage; this will equip the young with the knowledge, skills, and ideals needed to contribute to the stability and perpetuation of society.[23]

Schools help to prepare leaders by serving to screen and sort people for political and economic life. Both essentialism and pragmatism contributed to meritocratic goals by the former's emphasis on preserving the culture through preparation in basic subjects, while the latter stressed the use of experts in evaluating truth claims.

Proponents of participatory democracy[24] hold that the representative theory is largely an accurate description of American politics today; however, they add that this is not the way the system *should* operate. What the system should do is to offer the widest possible participation to all citizens, as individuals should participate in decisions that significantly affect their lives. Politics, they hold, is not limited to government but extends to any institutions and agencies in which power is used. Representative theory, however, would reject the extension of the political arena because of the dissimilarity that institutions other than government do not have the right to use force; in addition, to extend the term so widely tends to vitiate it.[25]

Participatory democrats do not believe that democratic institutions will survive without a redistribution of power and a greater sharing in decision making. They also deny that representative democrats are more interested than the common man in preserving the system—especially when doing so conflicts with their interests.

One type of participatory democracy in education is the view that democracy is a way of life. Even though Dewey's cultivation of epistemic experts may have contributed to the growth of a meritocracy, Dewey's ideas are more generally in the participatory vein. Dewey viewed democracy as more than a form of government; it is primarily a mode of associated living.[26] He established two tests for the worth of social life: the number and variety of interests shared by a group, and the freedom of interplay with other groups.[27] Undesirable societies establish barriers to the free exchange and interplay of ideas, whereas a democratic society makes provision for all members and utilizes their thinking to help make changes in social life.

Dewey believed that schools should provide an understanding of social forces and the resources needed to cope with social problems. An understanding is needed of how things work and what must be done to get them to work properly. Thus knowledge has to be connected to social action. This could be accomplished in the curriculum by utilizing the social studies to show how society operates and what changes need to be made; in science, by indicating the social consequences of scientific discoveries; and in vocational education by providing an understanding of industry and the professions.[28]

Dewey was also concerned that teachers, either directly or through representatives, participate in the formation of educational policy. In the late thirties, he found that democratic methods of dealing with students had made more progress than similar methods of dealing with teachers and thereby urged that teachers can best develop decision-making skills by having an opportunity to use them.[29]

Dewey concluded that democracy rests on a faith in human nature, intelligence, and cooperative experience. Yet this faith, which was shattered in the 1960s, came under question in his own time. His contemporary, Walter Lippman, proposed instead that creative statesmanship be nurtured by giving leaders real rather than nominal power; the statesman in turn must be prepared to control people for social purposes by appealing to their myths or creating new ones that enlist their sacrifices in the right causes.[30]

A more serious challenge to Dewey's theory of democracy as a way of life was the emergence of political science on more empirical grounds and the young discipline's tendency to apply psychoanalytic findings to political behavior. Political scientists pointed out nonrational influences and illogical sources of political belief so as to raise serious doubts about the application of intelligence in political life.[31] Harold Lasswell argued that ostensible rational motives and behavior in political processes are actually a displacement of libidinal drives.[32]

Community Control

Probably a less Freudian approach to political life, without denying nonrational forces, would admit that not only political leaders but the average citizen is capable of making rational decisions. Community-control advocates, in fact, believe that citizens can make better educational decisions than professionals. These advocates believe that when central bureaucracies can be bypassed in the education of their children by turning decision making over to a representative lay board in the community, the inefficiencies, neglect, and favoritism attributed to bureaucratic school systems will be overcome.

Community-control advocates cite discriminatory policies in the employment of black teachers and administrators, point to a curriculum that fails to relate to black needs, and to white teachers who are unprepared to teach ghetto children. The clash of black interests with the central school administration and the local teacher's union became a momentous struggle in New York City's Ocean-Hill Brownsville dispute.[33] Struggles also took place in other metropolitan areas.[34] Thus centralized, bureaucratic school systems have been unresponsive to the demands of parents and local citizens. Many of these changes have at one time or another been borne out by studies of metropolitan school districts.[35]

Through community control, black history and black studies could be taught by those who best understand the black experience; this would lead to the development of greater black pride and overcome middle-class bias found in many schools. Community control would allow blacks and other minorities and neighborhood groups to have their own schools; it would mean that they would operate their own school district, establish lay boards, and hold school personnel accountable for learning outcomes.

How did so much centralization come about? The growth of metropolitanism has been accompanied by the centralization of all municipal services. Centralization in education was designed for better administrative practices, to reduce inefficiency and provide more equitable arrangements, and to provide more up-to-date services. Shortcomings of the small school district had been thoroughly documented by educators, and for the past several decades school-district consolidation has been pressed by state departments of education. It was found, for instance, that high schools with less than a hundred students in the graduating class could not provide a curriculum with sufficient range and depth of course offerings.

A number of arguments have been advanced against community control. It is claimed that community control will undermine personnel standards and violate professional autonomy. Through the central administration, uniform and equitable personnel standards are developed and enforced; whereas in the history of school practices, small school districts have usually had the lowest standards and were most likely to employ unqualified personnel. Community-control proposals also place teachers and administrators under the supervision of lay persons. While schools should be responsive to community needs, such supervision violates professional autonomy, may lower the educator's effectiveness and create a serious morale problem.

Some centralization proponents would more likely admit that a plan of administrative decentralization poses fewer problems than community control. In such plans principals and field administrators are granted more authority for planning and program design. Legislative action has divided New York City and Detroit school systems into a number of separate and relatively autonomous districts. These decentralized school districts, however, may still serve a population as high as three or four hundred thousand. Parents may find that decentralization adds another level of administrative bureaucracy and, by creating further confusion as to where decisions are actually made, interferes with effective participation. Community-control advocates, however, would claim that this is administrative decentralization but not political decentralization.

Community control may also duplicate services and increase costs. Despite allegedly greater efficiencies from centralization, it has not always been borne out in practice. Although community-school programs will likely differ considerably from suburban schools, it is still unavoidable that some services will have to be duplicated by such an administrative arrangement.

Community control, opponents add, not only runs against the tide of school-district consolidation but would require state legislatures to create new school districts—an unlikely prospect today in most states. It may also lead to increased community segregation. While community control may alleviate pressures, it may also be a way of accommodating the demands of a small number of militant groups to keep pressures from getting out of control and to satisfy a desire for change without investing great resources in schools or neighborhoods.[36]

Research evidence fails to show that decentralization or community control improves education by raising achievement-test scores.[37] Not surprisingly, a survey of superintendents' views in 399 school systems showed that the superintendents were more positive about citizens' advising professionals on school policy than having citizens actually determine school policy.[38] Most administrators, teachers, and teacher unions have resisted community control because it demands that they relinquish their authority and that they take orders—in areas that they perceive as their expertise—from lay persons. It is unlikely that professional educators will change their attitudes markedly toward community control; however, it is more likely that they will, in some school districts, accept increased citizen participation and advice on school policy.

Increasing Parent Participation in Schools

Schools and families are engaged in complementary tasks, according to one observer, but find themselves in sharp conflict with one another.[39] The ideal parent from the teacher's viewpoint is one who accepts the teacher's expertise, shows appreciation for the teacher's efforts, gets the child to obey the teacher, and accepts blame for the child's weaknesses. The ideal teacher from the parents' perspective is one who recognizes the child's special aptitudes and abilities, develops these so that the child moves to or near the top of the class, and recognizes that the child's best qualities were inherited from the parents.[40] Thus as long as parents and teachers hold these or similar attitudes, conflict and frustration are likely to result. Instead, both groups need to seek a rapprochement by which they view their task as working as cooperatively as possible for the good of the child.

Looking again at representative and participatory democracy, the former is found when citizens vote in school-board elections and leave decision making and participation largely to elected board members; the latter is exemplified in community control and in the free-school movement in which parents organized small private schools based on neoprogressive principles and usually engaged in the administrative problems of selecting a suitable building, finding qualified teachers, raising funds, and participating in curricular decisions. Many public-school educators then would accept a form of participation intermediate between the representative form and either community control or free schools.

Parents can be involved as an audience, as a teacher at home, as a school aide, as a paid volunteer, and as a decision maker.[41] Parents as audience is a familiar pattern, but this pattern could be improved by schools' communicating more effectively to parents and the larger public. The parent as teacher at home can tie in with the discussion in the last chapter about parent education and the contributions schools can make by providing information, guidance, and programs. The parent as a paid volunteer would pay parents to attend school to learn techniques for teaching their child. In contrast, by parents becoming school aides, teachers are relieved of routine tasks; parents learn first-hand about school operations; and teachers, by working more directly with parents, may change their attitudes toward them. As for parents' participating in decision making, most federal legislation since the early 1970s mandates citizen participation in terms of consulting and advising. There are about 14,000 district-wide Title I Parent Advisory Committees and 44,000 building committees with a total of almost 900,000 members; moreover, an additional 150,000 persons serve on Follow Through, Head Start, and other groups.[42]

Another way to increase participation is through community education. Wherever there is a community school, education is designed to serve the entire community and provide varied learning activities for adults as well as children. Schools would be open from early morning to late at night on a year-round schedule with programs ranging from basic literacy to weight reduction. Opportunities may be provided for improving vocational competencies and for dealing with commmunity problems such as crime, delinquency, and drug abuse. Services are provided for persons from all socioeconomic levels, and the curriculum evolves from the problems and needs of the community. Not only could community schools provide information about child care, nutrition, and consumer affairs, they could also be a center for an integrated view of family care.

Some problems, however, have been encountered in community education. Programs are expensive, most teachers are not equipped to conduct such programs, the services offered expand the role of the school and may overtax it, programs for adults may compete for funds with those regularly scheduled for youth, and low-income groups are difficult to get involved in such programs. To avoid these and other pitfalls, community education programs will have to be carefully conceived, soundly planned, adequately supported financially, and implemented by the joint cooperation of educators, youth, and adults.

Increased Parent Participation and Responsibility for Discipline

As parent participation in schools increases, can parents be held more responsible for the discipline problems of their children? In other words, it would seem that in those school districts in which parental participation is minimal, schools would be largely responsible for discipline problems, even though some of the problems originated in the home, because parents had little or no opportunity to participate in school decisions designed to alleviate the problems. Yet it is not just the amount of participation or time parents spend in school activities; it is the type of participation that makes a difference. Parental power in decision making is not increased significantly when parents volunteer, serve as paraprofessionals, or utilize grievance procedures established by school officials. Committees that are assigned only one or two tasks may not transfer much power to parents; but citizen participation on boards that determine policy, select personnel, approve budgets, and determine the quality of services would provide citizens with an effective voice. A Rand study concluded that citizen participation can increase citizen influence without hurting program effectiveness.[43]

Thus we can conclude in determining responsibility that not merely the amount but the type of participation is important. When parents participate in policy decisions on school discipline and these policies fail to work out as planned, then the decision makers would assume responsibility for the decisions—though not necessarily for the failures in implementation (which may stem from certain inadequacies of teachers and school officials)—and seek to develop more effective policies.

Can parents be held responsible for restitution? In other words, if their offspring was found guilty of vandalism or of striking a teacher, should the parents themselves be held responsible for restitution?

As more courts recognize that constitutional rights apply to students, the *in loco parentis* doctrine has weakened. In trivial disciplinary matters, du process is not called for; an informal hearing is required in cases of short-term suspensions and when the offense could be entered on the student's record; and extensive due-process proceedings are required where long-term suspension or suspension during final examinations are proposed. Generally, school discipline is within the jurisdiction of local school boards and school officials. Parents are limited in their right to intervene in school disciplinary policy: parental objection to the school's use of corporal punishment is insufficient to prevent its use if the state allows it.[44]

Other than the special interest and bias most parents have toward their children and the generally limited interest in others' children (except as they affect their own children), parents are not inherently interested in school discipline. As noted in the previous chapter, parents use both instrumental and expressive requirements in their role. Instrumental requirements consist, among others, of the ability to manage time and energy; consistency and firmness; training the child in body controls, language and motor skills. Expressive requirements include spontaneity, flexibility, tenderness, love, and sensitiveness to childhood fantasies. Teachers have many instrumental requirements, both in socialization and formal instruction, but it is ambiguous and unclear as to what exactly are their expressive requirements. Teachers are caught between universal and individual standards. Universal standards apply to impersonal standards of competence and achievement for all students, such as norm-referenced tests, while individual standards apply to the particular student, as in criterion-referenced tests. The teacher's professional role frequently demands the application of universal standards to assure fairness and impartiality; yet the human dimension in learning and individual differences also calls for individual standards and the fulfillment of expressive requirements. Many parents probably would like individual standards and expressive requirements used with their child but universal standards applied to other people's children. Universal standards are objective and measurable; expressive requirements are not; yet they also ostensibly place great demands on overburdened teachers, and many are incapable or unwilling to deal with them fully. Thus some parents expect teachers to show special consideration and empathy in disciplining, teaching, or evaluating their children.

But can parents be held responsible in school disciplinary cases for restitution? Generally, parents cannot be held liable if the accident or damage was caused by the child's carelessness or lack of judgment. But parents may be held liable if the act occurred while the son or daughter was employed by the parents, as in the family business, or if the parent directed the child to cause the damage or sponsored the child's actions. In several states, parents have been found liable where they failed to exercise adequate control or supervision over the child and had knowledge that injury to another was a possible outcome of the child's behavior. And when parents recognize that the child has destructive tendencies but do not exercise proper control, they can be found liable. Many states now hold parents financially liable, up to certain limits, for their children's willful damage or injury to others.[45] A model statute has been proposed that would hold parents accountable for delinquent children on the grounds that the youth is a burden to the state. Yet such plans may cause conflict in the home by parents' retaliating against children who get them into trouble or by the youth, who wants to cause problems for parents, performing harmful or injurious acts. Parents, moreover, may strive to establish in court their youngster's innocence even though she may need rehabilitation.[46]

Parents can be held financially liable for their child's acts of school vandalism, and students can be charged with assault and battery for their violence.

Yet, as noted earlier, discipline is generally under the aegis of the local school board and school officials. Parents may be encouraged to participate in various school activities and school personnel will likely confer with parents whose child is having a persistent disciplinary problem; however, the basic responsibility lies with the school. Nevertheless, greater cooperation and understanding between the school and the home will alleviate some of these problems.

The next chapter will look more closely at how authority can be restructured in the school to overcome some of these problems. It will be shown how authority figures can reconstruct their attitudes and thinking and how their roles and relationships with children and youth can also be modified.

Notes

1. For some of these early plans, see Virgil C. Blum, *Freedom of Choice in Education* (New York: Macmillan, 1958), and Milton Friedman, "The Role of Government in Education," in Robert A. Solo, ed., *Economics and the Public Interest* (New Brunswick, N.J.: Rutgers University Press, 1955).

2. Christopher Jencks, et al., *Education Vouchers, A Preliminary Report on Financing Education by Payment to Parents* (Cambridge, Mass.: Center for the Studey of Public Policy, 1970); also by Jencks, "Education Vouchers," *New Republic* 161, no. 1 (1970):19-21.

3. Jim Warren, "Alum Rock Voucher Project," *Educational Researcher* 5 (March 1976):13-15.

4. See George R. LaNoue, "Vouchers: The End of Public Education?" *Teachers College Record* 73 (December 1971): 304-319.

5. See Mario Fantini, ed., *Alternative Education* (Garden City, N.Y.: Anchor Books, 1976), and Vernon H. Smith, *Alternative Schools: The Development of Alternatives in Public Education* (Lincoln, Neb.: Professional Education Publications, 1974).

6. John Hospers, "What Libertarianism Is," in Tibor R. Machan, ed., *The Libertarian Alternative* (Chicago: Nelson-Hall, 1974), pp. 3-20. Also see his *Libertarianism* (Los Angeles: Nash Publishing, 1971).

7. Murray N. Rothbard, "Historical Origins," in William F. Rickenbacker, ed., *The Twelve-Year Sentence* (LaSalle, Ill.: Open Court Publishing, 1974), pp. 11-32.

8. Gerrit H. Wormhoudt, "Supreme Court Decisions," in Rickenbacker, *The Twelve-Year Sentence*, p. 64; also see Joel Spring's argument against compulsory schooling in Rickenbacker, *The Twelve-Year Sentence*, pp. 155-157.

9. E.G. West, "Economic Analysis, Positive and Normative," in Rickenbacker, *The Twelve-Year Sentence*, pp. 171, 187-188. An occasional libetarian will support compulsory schooling, however. See Robert L. Cunningham, "Education: Free and Public," pamphlet (Wichita, Kan.: Center for Independent Education, n.d.), p. 2.

10. For further discussion, see Lawrence Kotin and William F. Aikman, *Legal Foundations of Compulsory School Attendance Laws* (Port Washington, N.Y.: Kennikat Press, 1980), ch. 12.

11. M.S. Katz, "Compulsion and the Discourse of Compulsory School Attendance," *Educational Theory* 7 (Summer 1977): 179-185.

12. Gerald M. Reagan, "Compulsion, Schooling, and Education," *Educational Studies* 4 (Spring 1973):1-7.

13. E.G. West, *Education and the State* (London: The Institute of Economic Affairs, 1965).

14. Herbert H. Hyman, Charles R. Wright, and John Shelton Reed, *The Enduring Effects of Education* (Chicago: University of Chicago Press, 1975); Harold Hodgkinson, "What's Right With Education," *Phi Delta Kappan* 61 (November 1979):159-162; Arthur J. Newman, ed., *In Defense of the American Public School* (Berkeley, Calif.: McCutchan, 1978); George F. Madus, Peter W. Airasian, and Thomas Kellaghan, *School Effectiveness: A Reassessment of the Evidence* (New York: McGraw-Hill, 1980); and Herbert H. Hyman and Charles R. Wright, *Education's Lasting Influence on Values* (Chicago: University of Chicago Press, 1979).

15. John E. Coons and Stephen D. Sugarman, *Education by Choice: The Case for Family Control* (Berkeley, Calif.: University of California Press, 1978), p. 10. The same argument is also presented by other libertarians: West, *Education and the State*, p. 13; and Cunningham, "Education: Free and Public," p. 6.

16. Richard A. Bumstead, "Educating Your Child at Home: The Perchemlides Case," *Phi Delta Kappan* 61 (October 1979):97-100.

17. Coons and Sugarman, *Education by Choice*, chs. 3-5.

18. R. Freeman Butts, "The Public Schools: Assaults on a Great Idea," *The Nation* (April 30, 1973):553-560.

19. Ralf Dahrendorf, *Life Chances* (Chicago: University of Chicago Press, 1979), pp. 30-39.

20. Giovanni Sartori, *Democratic Theory* (Detroit: Wayne State University Press, 1962), p. 126.

21. Robert A. Dahl, *Who Governs? Democracy and Power in an American City* (Chicago: University of Chicago Press, 1956), pp. 311-325.

22. V.O. Key, Jr., *Public Opinion and American Democracy* (New York: Alfred A. Knopf, 1961), p. 558.

23. Isaac L. Kandel, *Conflicting Theories of Education* (New York: Macmillan, 1938), pp. 77-88.

24. Some representative works of participatory democracy: Students for a Democratic Society, "Port Huron Statement," in Mitchell Cohen and Dennis Hale, eds., *The New Student Left* (Boston: Beacon Press, 1967), pp. 9-16; C.B. Macpherson, *The Political Theory of Possessive Individualism: Hobbes to Locke* (London: Oxford University Press, 1962), pp. 271-277; Robert Paul Wolff, *In Defense of Anarchism* (New York: Harper Torchbooks, 1970); and Peter Bachrach, *The Theory of Democratic Elitism: A Critique* (Boston: Little, Brown, 1967), ch. 7.

25. Arguments against the tendency to politicize nongovernmental institutions and social life are found in Mary Anne Raywid's "The Politicalization of Education," *Educational Theory* 23 (spring 1973):119-132.

26. *Democracy and Education* (New York: Free Press, 1966), p. 87.

27. Ibid., p. 83.

28. Challenges of Democracy to Education," *Progressive Education* 14 (February 1937):79-85.

29. "Democracy and Educational Administration," *School and Society* 45 (April 3, 1937):457-462.

30. Walter Lippman, *A Preface to Politics* (New York: Kinnerly, 1914).

31. William B. Munro, *The Invisible Government* (New York: Macmillan, 1928); and Peter Odegard, *The American Public Mind* (New York: Columbia University Press, 1930).

32. Harold D. Lasswell, *Propaganda Techniques in the World War* (New York: Knopf, 1927), and *Psychopathology and Politics* (Chicago: University of Chicago Press, 1930), ch. 10.

33. Differing interpretations of this bitter dispute can be found in Maurice Berube and Marilyn Gittell, *Confrontation at Ocean-Hill-Brownsville* (New York: Praeger, 1969), and Martin Mayer, *The Teachers Strike, New York 1968* (New York: Harper & Row, 1969).

34. Reports of the struggles in Detroit, Washington, D.C., Los Angeles, and Philadelphia are given in Harry L. Miller, *Social Foundations of Education: An Urban Focus*, 3rd ed. (New York: Holt, Rinehart and Winston, 1978), pp. 374-381.

35. See such studies as Peter Schrag, *Village School Downtown* (Boston: Beacon Press, 1967), and David Rogers, *110 Livingston Street* (New York; Vintage Books, 1969).

36. George R. LaNoue and Bruce L. Smith, "The Political Evolution of School Decentralization," *American Behavioral Scientist* (September 1971):73-93; and Martin Schiff, "The Educational Failure of Community Control in Inner-City New York," *Phi Delta Kappan* (February 1976): 375-378.

37. Allan Ornstein, "Research on Decentralization," *Phi Delta Kappan* (May 1973):610-614; and David Selden, "The Future of Community Partic-

ipation in Educational Policy Making,'' in Carl A. Grant, ed., *Community Participation in Education* (Boston: Allyn and Bacon, 1979), p. 76.

38. Harriet Talmage and Allan C. Ornstein, ''School Superintendents' Attitudes Toward Community Participation and Control,'' *Educational Research Quarterly* (summer 1976):37-45.

39. Sara Lawrence Lightfoot, *Worlds Apart* (New York: Basic Books, 1978), p. 20.

40. Mary E. Bredemeier and Harry C. Bredemeier, *Social Forces in Education* (Sherman Oaks, Calif.: Alfred Publishing, 1978), p. 276.

41. Ira J. Gordon, ''Toward a Home-School Partnership Program,'' In Ira J. Gordon and William F. Breivogal, eds., *Building Effective Home-School Relationships* (Boston: Allyn and Bacon, 1976), ch. 1.

42. A review of mandated citizen participation can be found in Luvern L. Cunningham et al., *Improving Education in Florida: A Reassessment* (Tallahasse, Fla.: Select Joint Committee on Public Schools, 1978), pp. 215-295.

43. Robert K. Yin et al., *Citizen Organizations: Increasing Client Control over Services* (Santa Monica, Calif.: Rand Corporation, 1973).

44. Louis Fischer, David Schimmel, and Cynthia Kelly, *Teachers and the Law* (New York: Longman, 1981), pp. 198-212.

45. Alan Sussman and Martin Guggenheim, *The Rights of Parents* (New York: Avon Books, 1980), pp. 63-64.

46. Roberta Gottesman, ''Restitution and Parental Liability as Alternatives to School Discipline,'' *Education Digest* 47 (October 1981):25-28.

8 Improving School Discipline

Students cannot learn when inhibited by fear of attack or vandalism, and teachers are distracted and anxious when faced with threats or the possible outbreak of violence. Safe schools are sorely needed throughout the country. But safety is only the first step. Schools should be healthy environments that promote learning. Thus in this chapter it is important to be clear about purposes and to determine how these purposes can best be achieved.

What are the ultimate purposes of any system of school controls? To help create the conditions for a sound learning environment for all students, and to provide a setting in which teachers and other educators will be free of the fear of violence and be able to utilize their professional abilities.

How can these purposes be attained? Several questions will need to be answered, and the relevant ideas developed in response need to be tried. The first question is, How can we bring under control the most serious problems of violence, disruptions, and vandalism? In other words, until these stressful conditions are brought under control, much of the school program's effectiveness is jeopardized as well as the safety of students and faculty.

Then we need to look more closely at authority. How does authority exercise a significant role over student behavior? In explaining this question, it will be shown how a normative network of rules and regulations are established and why such networks are not always effective. Then when disruptions occur, what are the long-term objectives in the application of sanctions, and what type of sanctions are most likely to realize those objectives? Also, would it be desirable to try to change the way chronically disruptive students think about authority, or would it be better to change the way school authorities relate to these students? Or perhaps some combination of both approaches? Thus several different types of students are presented, and it is shown how best for educators to relate to each type.

The final two sections of the chapter offer some suggestions for improving classroom discipline and show the relation of discipline and sound study habits.

Creating Safe Schools

Statistics on disruption, crime, violence, and vandalism were cited in chapters 1 and 5. Although the data seem to indicate that the most serious offenses peaked in the mid-seventies, the problem is still critical in some school districts, and those schools with a relatively safe atmosphere want to avoid the disruptions found in the other districts. As late as 1978, the National Institute of Education's "Safe School Study" still found around 6,700 schools seriously affected by crime.[1] Not only the disruptions and the dangers of physical harm and property damage are threats in some schools but, as a consequence, fear increases and inhibits a healthy learning environment. The Safe School Study found that 20 percent of the students were sometimes afraid of being hurt, while 3 percent said they were afraid most of the time. This meant that these students avoided restrooms and several other places in school where they may likely confront danger. And 12 percent of the secondary teachers, some 120,000, hesitated to confront misbehaving students.[2] Thus until the actual safety of both students and teachers can be more fully assured, these schools will not be healthy learning environments, and teachers will spend an inordinate amount of time fearful of attack or preoccupied with serious control problems.

Security Systems

How then can the most serious problems of violence, disruptions, and vandalism be brought under control? The most seriously affected schools have tried a host of measures: security guards, undercover police, electronic-alarm systems, electronic surveillance, guard dogs, architecturally redesigning schools to reduce vandalism and theft, paid community security aides, and voluntary security help.[3] Before any of these measures are undertaken, it is best for principals to assess their possible overall effects. The use of uniformed police in schools may alienate or antagonize some students and make the school scene like an armed camp. Some electronic devices may invade students' privacy. And undercover police posing as students may arouse suspicion and distrust once discovered, develop tensions between students and administrators, and undermine free social relations among the student body.

Thus what principles should be observed, apart from the relative effectiveness of the different measures to reduce violence and vandalism, in deciding on the adoption of any security measure? Keeping in mind that conditions in some schools are not sufficiently serious to adopt any of the preceding measures, any measures undertaken should not violate the rights of students, teachers, and other school personnel. Security guards or police, in preventing or quelling disorders or violence, should not, except when unavoidable, use violence. (Chapter 5 made an analysis of the grounds for the justification of violence.) Thus force, *ceteris paribus*, is preferable to violence, coercion to force, and negotiation to coercion. Finally, any security measures should be applied fairly and equitably. This principle does not mean that security measures cannot be introduced that could fall heavily on groups or gangs that thave committed acts of violence or vandalism; it only means that security agents and principals should not apply standards unevenly so that certain groups such as minorities are more likely to be apprehended or singled out as disrupters or delinquents or, when apprehended, be given more severe penalties than other students.

Some publications about security measures overlook principles that countermand their use and make decisions instead on the relative effectiveness of the measure to reduce violence or vandalism; our approach, in contrast, suggests that some measures cannot be sanctioned. Inadequately trained guards may use violence to quell violence (when unnecessary) or single out certain minority students for especially harsh treatment. Electronic-surveillance equipment, dogs to sniff out drugs, and undercover agents all raise serious legal questions as to their violation of students' right to privacy and security from searches.

Many architectural and building changes may prove effective in reducing theft and vandalism without violating any of the principles stated here: new multistrength windows that have many times the strength of regular glass, electronic-alarm systems, changing school buildings to reduce vandalism (roofs with plastic domes instead of skylights, bricking up openings in storerooms and basements that have an entry problem, more sophisticated door and window hardware, and so on).

Assigning police or security guards may create more problems than it solves. The constant presence of uniformed and armed police can create friction with students, most police are not especially trained to work with youth, and the stationing of police in school presents an image of an armed camp. When security guards are employed in schools, they should be identifiable but not wear police uniforms; they should also have special training in psychology and human relations so that they can work effectively with students, faculty, and parents. Whether to use paid community aides and volunteer help would depend on their qualifications and the tasks assigned them. Guard dogs to intercept vandals and uncover drugs may pose problems of invading privacy, may give the school district a bad image, and could pose problems of liability if they interfere with persons not linked with an offense. Better to employ specially trained security guards without guns and establish a functional liaison between the local chief of police and the principal.[4] In a survey of school districts with more than 10,000 students, it was found that less than half of the school districts that employ security officers have a formal training program and that most of the training is on the job.[5] Although there may be a role for untrained community volunteers who live in the school neighborhood to report potential vandals, security guards need special training for the security system to be effective.

School security includes not only the more common acts of violence, vandalism, and theft but should include training for handling violence at school sports events, violent gangs, arson, and bomb threats.

Roving gangs pose a threat in some school districts. Gangs have been periodically a feature of American metropolitan life; but after a quiescent period in the late sixties, they have risen again in a more virulent criminal form. Gangs conduct a wide variety of criminal activities, including robberies of businesses and homes, protection rackets, and for some, involvement in drug traffic. Many gangs have access to a range of weapons—from automatic rifles and pipe bombs to bazookas—and this availability of weapons has increased the lethal nature of gang violence. Since most gang members are of school age, it is natural that they would be found in school areas for purposes of recruitment, sharing information, and planning activities. A conservative estimate is that gangs are responsible for more than half of the vandalism in Los Angeles schools.[6] The activities of gangs on school grounds create a climate of fear that reduces school attendance and inhibits learning. In Philadelphia a coordinated program has stemmed the tide of gang activity by involving school officials, community leaders, churches, recreational centers, neighborhood crisis-intervention teams, and informal parents' councils.[7] Thus since gangs, as do some other school problems of violence and vandalism, grow out of conditions in the larger community, school officials need to solicit the cooperation and support of key persons and relevant agencies in the larger society.

Smaller schools may pose fewer security hazards than larger ones. Although larger schools are somewhat less expensive to construct on a per-pupil basis, the savings may be negated by the greater amount of vandalism in the larger schools. As schools and classes grow in size, teachers have more difficulty relating to students on an individual basis, and students may have more difficulty in developing close peer relations. One method of reducing size is to divide the student body into smaller, self-contained units.[8] Since violence is consistently higher in schools with large classes, whenever financially feasible, class size could be reduced or teachers in the junior high and middle schools could be responsible for teaching in more than one subject area to enable them to work with one group of students for a longer period of the day.[9]

cf. apprenticeship

Authority and the School's Normative Network

School systems, as well as all but the smallest and youngest organizations, are regulated by a policy network. School officials initiate an ongoing system of formulating, disseminating, implementing, and evaluating policy. Although some policies may be tacitly understood, the basic policies are eventually formulated and usually disseminated to faculty and staff. The various policies are related to one another in a policy network by which an observer can gain a profile of the school's overall operations. The policy network, however, is not developed from a rationalistic model of basic axioms and postulates or universal principles from which subsidiary principles could be deduced. Policy seems to be derived and organized in a more informal, functional manner.[10]

Policy networks can be better understood and explained through functional models. These models use purposive explanations in which the purposes are sought for the object, activity, or policy. Thus when the functions can be discovered for certain acts, it may be possible to discover the social structures that help maintain the institution. Since there are unanticipated and unintended consequences of actions, not all acts serve a cultural function. For instance, when corporal punishment of students is used for reform rather than retribution, it might have the unintended effect of causing the offender to become violent against classmates or teachers. Thus some acts are no longer functional (as chaperones on dates) or may be dysfunctional (as the effects in some cases of corporal punishment).

Of course, school policies regulate more than discipline: they regulate finance, buildings and facilities, curricula, and other aspects of a school system. In exploring the interrelationship of functions that policy serves, the way that functions complement, reinforce, or obstruct one another enables one to determine whether policy outcomes contribute to or impede the attainment of systemwide goals. Thus if certain school-security goals are established, a set of policies, after given sufficient time to take effect, are evaluated for their effectiveness in promoting the goals and, as a consequence, the policies are either continued, modified, or a new set is introduced.

Policy regulates classes of actions rather than specific acts, for it is not in the interest of policymakers to attempt to regulate the enormous number of specific acts performed in large school systems. Many minor acts—tying one's shoe, exchanging greetings, and so on—are not in the interest of the system to regulate. Moreover, since a number of related acts need to be regulated, policy is stated in the form of a covering rule.

When policymaking is undergirded by general norms, it provides a broader context for its development. General norms emerge from a culture's value system and serve as moral principles and ideals by means of which the general rules of conduct are constructed. General norms are universal and noncontextual in scope insofar as they apply to persons of various situations and circumstances. A prohibition against murder applies to everyone. Policies, in contrast, are context dependent because they regulate the activities of a particular institution or subunit of the institution at a particular time and place and apply only to the persons who come under the framework of the policy network.

Policy serves several functions: it regulates institutions and organizations and provides orderly guidelines for day-to-day operations and thereby ensures continuity; it also specifies guidelines governing the introduction and application of innovations. Policy states what is prescribed, prohibited, or permitted in a system. And for personnel, it provides a set of expectations and directives that define the performance of roles.

Policy, as noted, can be understood as a form of rule. A rule is a type of generalization used to prescribe conduct, action, or usage. A distinction can be made, as John Searle indicates, between regulative and constitutive rules.[11] Regulative rules regulate antecedent or independently existing forms of behavior. Constitutive rules not only regulate but also create or define new forms of behavior. Etiquette, for example, is a system of regulative rules; whereas sports and games, such as football, are based on constitutive rules because the rules make their playing possible. In other words, constitutive rules create the game, whereas regulative rules control preexisting forms of behavior.

Regulative rules generally take the form, "One ought to do *X* in circumstance *C*." These rules are usually stated in the imperative mood ("Grades in each course are due forty-eight hours after the final exam").

Constitutive rules take the form, "*X* counts as *Y*." Policy specifies guidelines to govern the introduction and application of innovations within organizational systems. That an innovation counts as a policy within certain contexts and that in the context there is nothing preexistent to regulate means that the innovation is an example of a constitutive rule.

Rules are one of the control structures governing student behavior. Most of these rules are of the regulative types, but some are constitutive rules insofar as they define and make possible new activities. Duke and Meckel state that the use of rules involves the following steps and procedures: rule development, determination of sanctions, enforcement, rule adjudication, and sanctioning.[12]

Rule development, as indicated, stems from the development of school policy. However, even though teachers observe school policies that affect teaching and classroom management, specific rules are also established by teachers, or through teacher-student planning, to handle classroom situations. If rule development is to be effective, how can it best be conducted?

Rules should not violate student rights; in fact, the normative network of schools should protect rights of speech, assembly, association, due process, and others. Students are more likely to assent to and comply with rules in which they have a hand in development; consequently, they should participate in formulating classroom rules whenever their understanding and responsibility are sufficient that their participation will enhance rather than detract from promoting a sound learning environment. The student council or some other governing body should work cooperatively with the principal and other officials in improving school policy, and each district should elect a student representative who should be able to serve on the school board as a nonvoting member. The representative will present and interpret the students' positions, explain group viewpoints within the student body, and urge or discourage the passage of certain legislation.

In classrooms, it would be wise to have as few rules as possible and eliminate those that fail to contribute to educational objectives. Students should understand the reasons for each rule, and every rule should be stated positively. Above all, rules should be enforced promptly, firmly, and fairly.

With fewer rules, it is not only easier for students to understand them but easier to enforce. Enforcement is also made difficult when some students believe partiality is involved in sanctioning (the imposition of penalties on those found to violate norms); thus resistance will be strengthened and some student groups may likely deliberately seek to undermine the school's normative network. Before sanctioning, a disciplinary function of rule adjudication is used whereby the guilt or innocence of persons is determined. Students, in contrast to constitutional provisions for the judicial system, usually have to prove their innocence when accused of wrongdoing.

Sanctions

The determination of what sanctions to employ is a critical function that significantly influences the school's system of controls. To determine sanctions, it is necessary to keep in mind various objectives sanctions might serve: protect others from danger, restore order, retribution, punishment, restitution, and reform.

Without protection of the safety of students and faculty, little learning can take place. Teachers also need the cooperation of school administrators in disciplining or expelling violent students and for preparing official reports of assaults on teachers; otherwise, teacher morale will be low, some teachers will seek to transfer to another school (which their principal may not permit), and still others will drop out of teaching altogether. A psychiatrist's evaluation of 575 teachers referred to him between 1972 and 1979 suffering extraordinary and continuing stress bore a striking resemblance to "combat neurosis" among the psychiatric casualties of World War II. Many of these teachers had unconsciously expected their students to see them as wise parental figures and could not understand why violence was directed at them.[13] The school-security features and the types of sanctions mentioned earlier in the chapter, along with firm support and leadership of the principal, should largely assure the safety of faculty and students and prevent many of these psychiatric cases.

Sanctions should also help to restore order but not just any kind of order. Disorder is not only created by rule infractions but by organizational and instructional changes. Even a change in the entrance and egress from a school building could cause disorder. Yet order can also be related to methods of instruction. According to a study by Elizabeth G. Cohen and others, as instructional activities become more complex, order is more likely threatened; consequently, methods of supervising tasks undergo basic changes, and the teachers' conception of order also changes.[14] Thus order is functional, contextual, and depends on tasks. But what these authors overlook is that a decision to adopt more complex instructional strategies depends on more basic decisions about the attainment of instructional objectives and whether new objectives are warranted. Moreover, one's educational philosophy will determine what one will accept as order and how much weight will be given to it. Essentialists, for instance, stressed order more than did progressives, and the former group defined order more traditionally.

Decisions on the complexity of instructional tasks may be made not only on the basis of instructional objectives but individual differences. The more creative students will likely prefer complex tasks in which they are given much independence, whereas the average students may be attracted to simple tasks, detailed instruction, and careful supervision. Highly creative people prefer tasks that are asymmetrical and complex as opposed to the symmetrical and simple.[15] Thus the creative person can tolerate more disorder—or what looks like disorder to the less creative—in learning tasks and problem solving; consequently, the amount of disorder tolerated in assignments and projects would be a function of individual differences.

The important point then is that order in itself is not the key variable. Bureaucracies, prisons, and detention centers may be orderly without much learning taking place. Our objectives are to create a sound learning environment for all students and a place where teachers and other educational personnel are free from fear and can utilize their professional abilities. It is not "order" in the abstract but, instead, functional forms of order that may be needed in some situations but inadvisable in others.

More serious than the problem of order is the violation of rules, though not all types of rules. Some rules are no longer functional and should be dropped; their violation creates no problems. Just as there are laws still on the books in some states to regulate the horse and buggy, school systems have their own horse-and-buggy rules. But the violation of functional rules may interfere with the teaching-learning process.

Thus sanctions are needed to protect others from harm, but their use in restoring order would depend on the situation. Sanctions have also been used for retribution. This use of sanctions administers punishment for a wrong done or, occasionallly, reward for a good done; it stresses strict justice when merited punishment is administered.

But what is the purpose of punishment? It is to accomplish the goals stated earlier by discouraging the wrongdoer from repeating his misbehavior. Is punishment (in the form of retribution) a justifiable sanction?

Retribution theory holds that pain or loss should be caused to those who have done wrong. Kant says that punishment is not inflicted to achieve another good but *only* because the person has committed a crime. Punishment for wrongdoing, Kant insists, is an absolute duty of society if a system of justice is to be preserved. The amount of punishment should correspond to the moral turpitude of the offender.[16]

The retributist believes only the guilty should suffer, but it may be a more effective deterrent to punish parents for their children's wrongdoings than to punish children, or to punish both. The retributist would say that such practices would be unjust; yet is the purpose of sanctioning only to punish the guilty or to deter future offenses? The two may not be synonymous.

An assumption of the retributist is that the wicked ought to be less well off than the virtuous; otherwise, a system of justice would not prevail, and society would be seriously undermined. But it is actually not the general function of either the courts or the school's disciplinary system to see that the virtuous triumph; rather, those who are apprehended for violating specific laws or rules may be punished. Some ignoble but prudent persons may not have broken the laws and some noble ones may have done so.

The retributist also believes that the infliction of pain on the guilty is mandatory without offering further justification why the deliberate infliction of pain on anyone is warranted. Does the school or the community actually benefit by causing pain? Does doing so help reform the offender, prevent him from committing similar offenses in the future, and deter others from like offenses?

In contrast, utilitarianism considers punishment an evil. Jeremy Bentham states that punishment ought to be excluded except where doing so would cause a greater evil.[17] The immediate ends of punishment are (1) to control the acts of the offender by making him legally incapable of committing further crimes or by rehabilitation, and (2) to influence others through example.

But it might be objected that if the purpose is to deter crime or wrongdoing, what is to prevent the utilitarian from punishing innocent people (for example, parents of youth for the youth's offenses) or by fabricating a tale of apprehending a notorious criminal or incarcerating innocent people suspected of a crime if doing so would deter crime or wrongdoing. Bentham says that we should pursue the greatest good, or the greatest happiness, of the greatest number. Happiness is defined as pleasure, with the meaning of pleasure varying somewhat from one individual to another, and the assessment of pleasure based on a majority of society. Yet, for Bentham, pleasure was not a simple quantification with each person's pleasure counting the same: Pleasure differed according to intensity, duration, certainty or uncertainty, propinquity or remoteness, fecundity, purity, and extent (the number of people affected).[18] But if it would increase the majority's pleasure by deterring crime by questionable methods previously noted, Bentham's formula does not preclude doing so. Thus it needs to be supplemented with the principle of respect for persons and the refusal to punish without just cause such as the willful violation of just rules or laws.

But even with those additions and qualifications, a conflict of values may be involved. Punishment, in some instances, may deter wrongdoing but violate respect for persons. Respect for persons sounds reasonable enough, but just what does it mean? To respect someone is to exhibit esteem or honor for the person, or show consideration or concern. But if it is said that we should show respect for others just because they are persons, then in many cases we may not show honor or esteem but just consideration (which should be sufficient and is all that the principle demands). Yet we do this because either they are persons like ourselves or we prize the traits of being a person. The notion of a person is a normative concept insofar as being a person is to exhibit such valued traits as rationality, aesthetic sensitivity, refined emotions, moral agency, free will, and the like. Whether these or some other traits are ascribed to persons, it does pose problems as to how human beings who are deficient in some of these traits ought to be treated. Issues surround infanticide of defective newborns, euthanasia, capital punishment, and the obligation of soldiers in wartime to kill enemy soldiers.

Here we only note these issues without pursuing them. Respect for persons, for our purposes, would mean not inflicting avoidable pain, harm, or suffering on others and to see that all people are treated justly by promoting just rules and laws. Since I believe that these same principles, *mutatis mutandis,* should be applied to animals, then respect does not stem from being human but from other characteristics. Animals are conscious beings, exhibit admired emotions and traits (love, affection, sorrow, loyalty), and can suffer pain and deprivation. But to show respect for human beings means something different than showing respect for animals (other than protection and avoidance of inflicting needless pain). Respecting persons may be to see that society makes provision for universal education at public expense and to support a legal system that safeguards basic rights. In contrast, respecting animals may mean protecting their natural habitats, eliminating animal experiments for commercial products and medicine that cause unnecessary suffering, abolishing large-scale animal farms that abuse animals, and promoting vegetarianism.

Punishment may be administered to students on grounds either of retribution or deterrence; however, the infliction of pain, even to those

violating just laws and rules, must always be justified—a weak link in the retributist position. The retributist still may claim that respect for a normative network is best engendered by punishment that causes some type of pain or deprivation that is proportionate to the offense. Assuming that some respect for a network must be gained before compliance can be established, then we may want to consider punishment on these and other grounds of deterrence.

Acts that are punishment for some students, such as school suspension, may be viewed as a reward by other students. Acts then, to serve as punishment, must actually be construed as punishment by the offender. Punishment, or a form of deterrence, has a number of weaknesses: it does not change the reasons for the misbehavior, fails to offer guidance for rectifying conduct, and does not have a long-term effect or transfer outside the immediate situation. Its use can also create undesirable resentment toward authority and jeopardize cooperation. Thus punishment should at best be a stopgap measure where chronic misbehavior leaves no alternative.[19]

Other than protecting people from harm, retribution, and deterrence, sanctions are also used for restitution and reform. As indicated in the last chapter, restitution that demands compensation from the parents of offenders may create conflicts between youth and parents and discourage parents from revealing violations of the law or school rules to authorities; nevertheless, parents can assist with restitution without being held directly responsible for their offspring's actual offense by seeing that their youngster fulfills the terms or contract or any reasonable restitution program they might enter into with school officials. Thus in the case of vandalism, an agreement is reached among officials, the vandals, and the vandal's parents as to what types of work services, repairs, or financial compensation would be reasonable; then parents and school officials can cooperate in supervising and enforcing the restitution plan.

Although restitution is not synonymous with punishment, if it is equated with it by the offender, it may be subject to some of the same criticisms given previously. Restitution is not in itself designed, as is retribution, to cause pain and suffering; yet, like punishment, it is a penalty; but unlike many forms of punishment, it is intended as a constructive penalty in a twofold sense: it provides constructive activity for the offender and direct compensation for the victim. Restitution as a sanction has some technical problems insofar as cases in which the offender is incapable of or severely limited in making restitution, as in the case of an arsonist's destroying an expensive computer system. A poor arsonist lacking job skills is in no position to provide restitution or compensation, though she could be assigned tasks of taking care of school property, which would be a case of rehabilitation or reform.

Thus restitution can be used for reform just as well as some officials may use it as a form of punishment; it lends itself, however, to reform. The purpose of reform is to amend what is defective or corrupt. It also aims to remove an abuse or wrong and to make changes for the better. Reform, which means to correct, amend, or remedy by making something right that is wrong, also implies changing something in order to eliminate imperfections or effect a new form of character. Though reform does not imply that punishment cannot be used, the idea of reform with juvenile delinquency is to change behavior or character so as to overcome delinquency; in so doing, retribution is ruled out as an objective. Thus reform has proven successful whenever it rehabilitates most chronic offenders. But since it is also necessary that new offenders not join the ranks, an effective deterrence system is needed. Reform too would need to observe the same principles stated earlier regulating deterrence. In the more serious and chronic cases, schools may be incapable of reforming the offenders and will have to refer the students to juvenile courts or other outside agencies.

Turning from the objectives of sanctions to the act of sanctioning, before such acts can be effective, a system of enforcement that includes rule adjudication needs to be established. Enforcement would be based on a system of authority established in each school system. Each teacher would usually be expected to manage ordinary classroom discipline problems and establish a system of rules and sanctions; but more serious disciplinary cases would need an unequivocal set of guidelines enforced by the principal so that teachers would know precisely what to do and where to seek help when they are under extraordinary stress. The guidelines should clearly state who will be involved in handling serious cases of discipline and the respective responsibilities of the various parties.

Any system of enforcement can improve rule adjudication by observing the preceding recommendations and fulfiling the following tasks: stating all rules clearly and precisely; seeing that all parties affected are informed about the rules in advance; checking again to determine whether the rules and penalties are understood; and enforcing penalties for rule infractions swiftly, firmly, and fairly. Rules that infringe on or violate student or teacher rights must be eliminated and due process must be observed according to the latest legal requirements.

Sanctioning, the process of applying sanctions, involves a knowledge of permissible sanctions, the types of infractions for which they can be applied, who is authorized to apply them, and the conditions that should be observed in applying them. For instance, suppose corporal punishment is permitted by the state and is used in local school districts. Teachers need to know that corporal punishment is permissible, whether it can be used for handling any disciplinary problems or only certain types, who can administer the punishment (teachers as well as the principal, or only the principal), and the conditions to be observed (Must the student first be warned before punishment? Do witnesses have to be present? What degree of force is permitted?).

Disorders and Personality Theory

Given similar circumstances, why is it that some people violate rules or laws or become violent and other persons do not do so? For instance, in cities where riots broke out in ghettoes during the 1960s, only about 15-20 percent participated in the riots.[20] Applying the frustration-aggression hypothesis does not help explain these figures because living under the extreme duress and stress of ghetto life is frustrating to all residents. But since ghetto conditions also produce a pervasive sense of powerlessness and helplessness, those who experience these feelings are unlikely to take action; rather, those who take action are the more successful residents who have not lost all hope and thereby expect their action can lead to social and economic improvement.[21] Thus the difference between the two groups lies in expectations, attitudes, and thought processes.

Students may violate rules whenever they believe that a rule is unwarranted; therefore, it is important that students understand why the rule was established and why it is important to comply with it. Of course, it is usually not necessary to single out each rule for justification but only those contested or frequently not observed; it is usually sufficient instead to provide a rationale for the overall policy network.

Another way of viewing attitudes toward rules, we can postulate, is to explore the use of excuse making whenever rules are violated by four different personality types. Type *A* is a conscientious student who has an active super ego and is motivated by a strong sense of obligation. *A* tries to be firm but honorable in those instances in which he makes moral judgments about others. *A* is scrupulous in making excuses; therefore, when in doubt, he usually feels an obligation to accept responsibility and to voluntarily take blame or punishment; as a result, his conscientiousness is mixed with guilt whenever violating a rule.

In contrast, whenever *B* is blamed for misbehavior, she is likely to try to excuse herself; and she is likely to interpret intentions and consequences liberally so that she will receive the most favorable judgment in terms of responsibility for acts. In making cases when accused by the teacher of misbehavior or disruption, *B* will attempt to justify the act; when that fails, she will turn to a form of excuse making that *A* would be reluctant to use. Though when asked by the teacher she claims she would like to comply with the rules, she finds herself frequently in dispute with her teachers and other authority figures and tends to resist their overall evaluation of her behavior. In *B*'s case the controversy centers over how the rules governing excuse making can actually be used.

C seeks immediate gratification of his desires and will take aggressive action against those who stand in his way. Owing to impulsiveness and an inability to tolerate frustrations, *C* cannot defer gratification or plan for distant goals. *C* lacks a concern for facts and has difficulty in conceptualizing time. In some instances he becomes fixated on a particular idea or principle and shows fanatical devotion to it. *C* is usually not able to modify his actions on the basis of success or failure. When found guilty of violating a rule and when punished for doing so, he interprets it as an attack and reacts by counterattack. *C* aspires to overturn his negative world view by depriving the distrustful adult world of its power and to make himself invulnerable. In sharp contrast to *A* and *B*, *C*'s attitude toward excuse making is to refuse excuses, demand proof of guilt, and make authorities justify their acts. *C* will not confess to an act he knows he committed but will place the onus of blame on the evaluator. Though he recognizes that others are caught and punished, he believes that he is smarter and will not be apprehended. Since *C* operates at the Freudian pleasure-principle level of the Id personality, he is unable to defer gratification, and therefore any thwarting or frustration is likely to turn to rage and then to violence. He views the school as another aspect of a hostile adult world in which he usually feels compelled to take aggressive action.

D, the fourth type, is a student who finds a cause, is an aggressive, unconventional activist, and is usually intellectually able with leadership potential. Such rebels with a cause may wear black armbands to protest the Vietnam war, lead demonstrations, petition school officials against censorship of the student newspaper, and protest school dress codes. Though these students are first likely to employ nonviolent protest, their provocative, militant behavior may polarize various segments of the student body and sometimes lead to violence. Although *D* may not be the first to engage in a violent act when confronted with hostile opposition, she may be strongly accused of inciting the violence.

In comparing the four types, most teachers would hope to have a classroom of potential *A*s, even though *B*s would be common in many classrooms and some *C*s and *D*s could be found in various school systems. *D*s would likely always be a small minority, while *C*s may be a significant minority in schools that have experienced high levels of disruption. *A* can learn from past experience, and the teacher is likely to respect *A*'s judgment. *A* is under control and is in a sense disciplined, though he defers too frequently to authority rather than generating his own direction; he is capable of improvement as a result of instruction and example. The teacher can appeal not only to *A*'s reason but to his image of a conscientious person and his sense of responsibility toward others. The teacher can also show *A* how to examine more carefully grounds for excuse making.

On the other hand, *B* poses more problems for the teacher. It is not that the teacher must convince *B* of the need for proper behavior and compliance with the rules, as *B* claims she wants to do so. Rather, the problem is to get *B* to examine her excuse making while the teacher maintains respect for *B*'s integrity and judgment. Here the teacher must believe that *B* has the capacity to recognize eventually her tendency to enlarge the range and scope of excuse making. Thus the teacher needs to give *B* opportunities for realistically assessing and reappraising what would constitute reasonable excuse making and, in light of such reappraisals, adjust behavior accordingly.

In *C*'s case, sound discipline is highly unlikely until remediation is effected. The teacher cannot appeal to *C*'s intellectual integrity and independent judgment because they are lacking. Nor can the teacher, as in the case of *B*, work through excuse making because *C* always seeks to justify acts and to project guilt onto the teacher. Ordinary disciplinary measures will prove ineffectual, but therapy and rehabilitiation may be helpful in certain cases. Until such students can be referred to agencies that are better equipped than schools to cope with and help them, the schools will have to maintain a tight security system to protect the safety of others.

It is surprising that more *D* types did not arise prior to the 1970s when student rights were less protected. *D* may sometimes attempt to justify violence or its incitement in others when her rights are denied. It would be necessary for *D* to show that her rights are being denied, that this denial is not based on conflict with other rights that have priority in such cases, and that the securing of the denied right could not be achieved or would be inordinately protracted by nonviolent means that would cause less harm. The teacher, while recognizing *D*'s fervent commitment, needs to show *D* that most school rules are sound and should be complied with, and that this can be done while contesting those few rules *D* considers unjust.

Improving Classroom Discipline

In any discussion of everyday classroom-discipline problems, type *C* will have to be excluded (for reasons previously indicated); but the other three types of students can be worked with in the usual classroom setting.

To improve classroom discipline, it is important to keep in mind some conclusions reached in chapter 4. That chapter distinguished our conception of discipline from order, coercion, control, reward, and punishment. Discipline was viewed as an active process (''proactive'' rather than passive or reactive); the person is the doer of the action; the process employs tasks and is goal directed; it may refer to individuals, groups, or teams; activities are usually discontinuous rather than continuous; it features constitutive rules and instruction; rules and standards are refereed or evaluated. A disciplined person has orderly habits, is able to observe rules of conduct, follows instructions properly, and exercises self-control in learning tasks; this person also manifests appropriate intellectual development by completing desirable tasks successfully and fulfilling worthwhile standards.

Although teachers need to exercise control over their classrooms, control is not discipline because it does not fit the preceding criteria and may be induced by coercion. As indicated in chapter 3, not only punishment but rewards as well may have coercive features. In some instances control may be bought at too high a price so that genuine discipline is precluded; yet if the teacher recognizes that control is just a temporary stage that has to evolve into a more fruitful classroom environment, the stifling of genuine discipline can be avoided.

But how does this higher level evolve? Assuming that overall school security is under control and students are not generally fearful for their safety, they therefore focus on classroom tasks and learning objectives. Under these conditions students need to become actively involved in pursuing learning tasks and assume increasingly greater responsibility for their classroom activities. But to be involved means to be motivated—and the motivation should not be external from the anticipation of rewards or punishment. The student would be involved in the learning tasks either because doing so would likely lead to other worthwhile learning activities (as learning to type might help one to write more effective letters) or desirable for its own sake (typing viewed as an enjoyable pastime). Activities to build the persistent dispositions and attributes associated with discipline would not likely be accomplished by rewards because rewards, when they have a coercive effect, deny self-agency and, when withdrawn, the behavior usually collapses, if not immediately, after a period of time when the student finally recognizes that reinforcement is not forthcoming.

But how could teachers generate this kind of motivation? Obviously, many students have little interest in their studies and would drop out of school except for compulsory-attendance laws. Some of these students cause disruptions; others become passive and apathetic. When students see that what they are studying is meaningful, that it has some bearing on either their present or future concerns, then they are likely to become more involved and take greater responsibility for their learning. But since there may be many aspects of the curriculum needed for a sound education but for which the young, because of immaturity or other reasons, are not prepared to apprehend the value, how can these important subjects still be offered and achieve the type of motivation previously described? Of course, one solution is to state emphatically that certain subjects or classics should be taught only to those who can appreciate them. This may be best, but we might also underestimate how many people can come to appreciate them if only they are organized more in terms of how any particular group of learners are likely to learn best and are taught effectively. Motivation can be enhanced by emphasizing transfer of training: showing the precise connection between the material and situations outside the classroom and giving the student opportunities to practice making essential connections.

Yet, other than emphasizing transfer, each student, it might be thought, could provide his own rewards and avoid the possible coerciveness of rewards imposed by authority figures. Since in genuine discipline the process is proactive, then the use of self-reward may motivate the student to act in his own behalf. The rewards could be a commercial product (buy himself something he wants) or a privilege or treat (go to the movies if he completes the assignment on time). But there are some technical problems: more affluent students have a wider array of rewards and to ask one to administer his own system of rewards in a judicious and nonindulgent manner assumes the presence of the type of discipline that the teacher is seeking to instill. Moreover, unless this self-reward plan is merely a temporary measure, it may become habitual, and consequently the student would refuse to undertake a desirable activity unless a reward could be found. Thus while a self-reward system may be superior to one externally imposed, it cannot in itself be an indication of sound discipline; however, for especially onerous tasks, it may be the best way to approach them should ordinary disciplinary processes fail.

Discipline utilizes tasks and is goal directed. The fulfillment of the tasks would contribute to goal achievement; but wherever the goal is complex, tasks cannot be lined up in a mechanical way in a step-by-step process to attain the desired goal; the goal, instead, must be approached creatively and experimentally. For instance, if the child's goal is to learn to add numbers, then the tasks can be established serially; however, if an advanced science student seeks to solve a theoretical problem, specific tasks cannot always be laid out because the steps involved in the solution are unknown.

But in some cases a student may accept the learning goal as worthwhile but still not exhibit sound discipline in approaching it. How could this be explained? One reason this question is of interest is the assumption earlier that part of the problem of discipline is inadequate motivation; here, however, it is assumed that some form of motivation is present but is insufficient to enable the student to achieve the goal One obvious explanation is that the teacher or the student herself has set goals beyond present abilities, either because of an inaccurate assessment of abilities or overambitiousness. Another, but less common, explanation is weakness of the will.

With weakness of the will the student knows what is the right thing to do, believes it is right and has a desire to do it, yet fails to do so. Would this be no more than another example of lacking the ability to perform the task, or would there actually be some sort of personality or character deficiency? Here the deficiency may be a lack of conscientiousness. Conscientiousness arises from one's conscience in fulfilling one's duties; it is the attitude toward one's obligations and the manner in which they are fulfilled. A person is conscientious when she seeks to find what she is supposed to do and is faithful in fulfilling it. One accepts the principle: "Do one's duty" or, better, "Perform one's obligations faithfully." Thus one may then accept and fulfill obligations, whether derived by the agent or externally imposed; and one may also conscientiously believe that she has a duty to disobey duly constituted authority whenever conscience dictates and she is willing to assume public responsibility for disobedience.

The content to assist in cultivating conscientiousness is studies of authority and fairness (in relation to authority). The student can begin by considering his or her own authority relations with parents, teachers, law-enforcement agents, and other significant figures; then the student needs to evaluate any personal concerns about these relationships. Practice is needed in examining one's own actions and attitudes toward authority figures and one's successes and failures in acting conscientiously. Experience could be provided in working with authority figures. To achieve balanced views, students could conduct interviews with individuals and groups engaged in dissent. As progress proceeds, case studies of authority, its fair and unfair use, drawn from world history and the social sciences will enlighten debate, stimulate the imagination, and provide paradigms for discussion. Finally, the student needs to consider her own political obligations and their ethical basis. This means that opportunities, both in class an community, should be provided for practicing conscientious action and expressing dissent on controversial issues.

Recalling the four types of students previously presented, types *A* and *D* both fulfill certain key criteria of conscientiousness and would not be afflicted with weakness of will. They exhibit conscientiousness, however, in different ways: *A* complies more with the dictates of authority figures and earnestly seeks to fulfill his obligations, whereas *D* has a penchant for questioning and disobeying authority whenever her conscience dictates. In contrast, *B* and *C* have, among other problems, lack of will. *C* lacks sufficient impulse control and is unable to plan for distant goals or show concern for facts. He is not ready even to begin the exercises to improve conscientiousness until most of his more acute problems are brought under control. In contrast, *B* would like to be more conscientious but generally does not succeed. In her case the program previously outlined may be helpful. Since the number *B*s in some classrooms is substantial, prospects for improving conscientiousness would not only be a boon for the student but alleviate teacher frustration, reduce disruption, and generally enhance class morale.

Earlier it was indicated that a disciplined person exhibits appropriate intellectual development by completing desirable tasks and fulfilling worthwhile standards. The tasks and standards would vary according to the curriculum and the learner's level of intellectual development. Ultimately, teachers endeavor to help students develop skills in learning how to learn; such skills are some of the characteristics of discipline found in intermediate and advanced learners. According to R.F. Dearden, such skills are a cluster of second-order learning skills having wide application to first-order operations.[22] Specific content learning is a first-order operation; second-order learning consists of activities such as investigating how to investigate and thinking about how to think effectively.

Learning how to learn, he claims, consists of four types of second-order skills: information-finding skills; general substantive principles (scientific principles, moral principles, or other types); formal principles of inquiry (that is, methods of inquiry in the various disciplines); and self-management skills. Information-finding skills and self-management skills seem especially to be part of our concept of discipline. Information-finding involves such skills as learning how to ask questions to gather needed information, learning how to listen carefully, and learning how to pay attention and concentrate on the task at hand. One cannot complete tasks successfully or achieve goals—essential characteristics of a disciplined person—unless one has gained the rudiments of acquiring and utilizing information, listening and concentrating on the immediate task. Thus to teach these second-order skills and to model them for students will likely promote some of the elements of sound discipline as well as stimulate academic achievement.

Discipline and Study

Since study is an essential process in most forms of academic learning, it may prove helpful to clarify it and show the role discipline plays in promoting it. Experienced teachers have long recognized that a student sitting at a desk with a book in front of him and looking preoccupied may not necessarily be studying. Nor is being surrounded by some of the tools that are generally associated with studying—books, maps, globes, blueprints—assurance that a student is studying. On the other hand, it would seem strange to claim that one is studying but not concentrating, trying, or focusing on a task. Thus studying seems to involve a trying, doing, undertaking, attempting. It may also involve attending, observing, relating, organizing, reciting, and reinforcing. But we should not look for a specific cognitive process to identify studying. Though thinking may be associated with studying, other activities are also related: reciting, memorizing, rule-following, rehearsing, and imitating (as in studying one's lines for a play).

To say that "I studied" does not mean that one was entirely successful (that is, learned the material according to the prescribed standards). One can engage in the activity of studying (fulfill the criteria of what counts as studying) but in the particular episode fail to fulfill the learning assignment. A student may say, "I studied the math assignment for two hours, but I still didn't really understand how to work it." Many factors are involved in successful study—a requisite academic background, proper tools for study, a quiet area, and so on; however, part of the success could be credited to sound discipline that is a necessary condition in virtually all forms of study.

One can study effectively or ineffectively, concertedly or halfheartedly, but one does not study unintentionally. Thus to say that someone is studying is to imply intent. But intent must have a direction, something that is intended; this something is an intent to focus on a task. A task, which can either be self-initiated or assigned, usually refers to a piece of work that needs to be completed. Study tasks can be self-imposed or assigned by others, and the difficulty and complexity of the tasks vary. The intent is to focus on the tasks in such a manner that the designated goal can be achieved. To achieve the goal involves learning. *Focus* means to fix or settle on one thing, to concentrate by bringing something to the center of one's attention by directing one's thoughts and efforts—in this case to the task.

There is no act of studying in general; rather, study is a task activity, and the notion of "task" is contained in the concept of study. What one is studying is determined by the task and the goals to be achieved [for example, *X* is studying a homework assignment on the binomial theorem (task) in order to fulfill the assignment (goal 1) and to learn more about algebra (goal 2)]. The process of study comprises the following dimensions:

Task Methodology Goals Outcomes

We have already discussed study as task oriented and can look more closely now at the other features. The methodology is influenced by the student, materials, and the situation. As for the student, ability, learning style, motivation, and other factors are pertinent, and all these affect how well the task can be handled and what methods are most appropriate.

Materials can be divided into what is studied and what is used in helping one study. What one studies is the content of the task: an architect studies blueprints, a conductor studies a musical score, and a navigator studies a map. The materials that may facilitate study may range from pen and paper to the latest computer. Thus what is studied is materials, and what facilitates study in such contexts becomes instruments.

The situation usually influences methodology because the method's effectiveness is partly a function of the situation. Students, for instance, who wait until the night before the test to begin serious study have eliminated the use of certain methods employed by students who study daily. Another feature of the situation is whether its overall effect facilitates or inhibits learning.

The goal provides an overall sense of direction and enables the student to evaluate his success in the study episode. Studying, in contrast to original research, does not usually lead to the discovery of new knowledge but, rather, when successful, to new learning experiences and the achievement of new goals.

Studying, although for purposes of analysis can be demarcated into discrete episodes, should be so organized as to provide continuity from one session to another. Knowledge of the relative success of goal achievement allows feedback either to the next task or to try again on the same task if previously unsuccessful. Thus present-study outcomes can be used to determine future study tasks and how best to approach them.

The preceding description and analysis of study may sound familiar insofar as the characteristics of discipline and study overlap. Certain elements of discipline, however, are also needed in building a fence, painting a picture, composing a song, conducting a scientific experiment, and even in writing a book about discipline. The reason that study was singled out for analysis lies not only in the similarity of certain elements but the critical and essential role that study plays in the learning process. Moreover, when students are able to study successfully, they are exhibiting certain features of sound discipline; and when they fail to complete a study task it may or may not indicate a breakdown of discipline. Thus a reasonable level of sound discipline is at least a necessary, but not sufficient, condition for successful study.

Some of the features of the study can also be found in students' successful participation in everyday classroom activities. Thus studying and classroom participation involve in varying degrees trying, doing, undertaking, and attempting; they also include attending, observing, organizing, relating, reciting, and reinforcing. When students study together, their activities increasingly resemble features of classroom activities. The class period, for instance, may be divided into segments in which instruction is presented and either special student projects are worked on or students study their assignment alone or together with teacher assistance. The qualities of discipline earlier enumerated are needed in order to participate effectively in any of these activities. The rewards for exhibiting these qualities need not be provided by the teacher or the student; the growth in abilities is sufficient reward and fulfillment.

The next chapter shall take a look at the future of authority relations and its effects on discipline by exploring a number of plausible scenarios.

Notes

1. National Institute of Education, *Violent Schools—Safe Schools*, vol. 1 (Washington, D.C.: Department of Health, Education and Welfare, 1978), p. 3.

2. Ibid., p. 5.

3. National School Public Relations Association, *Vandalism and Violence: Innovative Strategies Reduce Cost to Schools* (Arlington, Va.: The Association, 1971), pp. 18-39.

4. See E.J. Keller, "School Security: The Role of the Police," *Law and Order* 20 (December 1972):50-52.

5. E.L. Creekmore, "How Big Cities Train for School Security: A Nationwide Survey," *Security World* 11 (January 1974):28-29.

6. Committee on the Judiciary, *School Violence and Vandalism*, U.S. Senate, Subcommittee to Investigate Juvenile Delinquency (Washington, D.C.: Government Printing Office, 1976), p. 152.

7. Ibid., pp. 341-369.

8. Birch Bayh, ed., *Challenge for the Third Century: Education in a Safe Environment*, Committee on the Judiciary, U.S. Senate (Washington, D.C.: Government Printing Office, 1977), pp. 83-84.

9. NIE, *Violent Schools*, pp. 132-133.

10. See David Braybrooke and C.E. Lindblom, *A Strategy for Decision* (New York: Free Press, 1963). The authors substitute for the rationalistic model their version of "disjointed incrementalism" as more closely corresponding to the way policy is actually developed.

11. John Searle, *Speech Acts* (Cambridge: Cambridge University Press, 1969), pp. 33-42.

12. Daniel L. Duke and Adrienne M. Meckel, "Disciplinary Roles in American Schools," in Keith Baker and Robert J. Rubel, eds., *Violence and Crime in the Schools* (Lexington, Mass.: Lexington Books, D.C. Heath, 1980), pp. 104-105.

13. Alfred M. Block and Ruth Reinhardt Block, "Teachers—A New Endangered Species?" Ibid., pp. 82-83.

14. Elizabeth G. Cohen, Jo-Ann K. Intili, and Susan Hurevitz Robbins, "Task and Authority: A Sociological View of Classroom Management," in Daniel L. Duke, ed., *Classroom Management*, 78th Yearbook, Part II, of National Society for the Study of Education (Chicago: University of Chicago Press, 1979), pp. 116-143.

15. See Frank Barron, *Creativity and Personal Freedom* (Princeton, N.J.: Van Nostrand, 1968).

16. Immanuel Kant, *The Philosophy of Law* (Edinburgh: T. and T. Clark, 1887), pp. 194 ff.

17. Jeremy Bentham, *Introduction to the Principles of Morals and Legislation* (London: Hafner, 1948), ch. 13.

18. Ibid., chs. 3 and 4.

19. Malcolm Saunders, *Class Control and Behavior Problems* (Berkshire, England: McGraw-Hill Book Company United Kingdom Limited, 1979), pp. 82-83.

20. W. McCord and J. Howard, "Negro Opinion in Three Riot Cities," *American Behavioral Scientist* 11 (1968):24-27, and D.D. Sears and J.B. McConahay, "Participation in the Los Angeles Riot," *Social Problems* 17 (1969):3-20.

21. N.S. Caplan, "The New Ghetto Man: A Review of Recent Empirical Studies," *Journal of Social Issues* 26 (1970):59-73, and T. Crawford and M. Naditch, "Relative Deprivation, Powerlessness, and Militancy: The Psychology of Social Protest," *Psychiatry* 33 (1970):208-233.

22. R.F. Dearden, *Problems in Primary Education* (London: Routledge & Kegan Paul, 1976), pp. 69-74.

9 A Look to the Future

The future will not wait. Time moves on inexorably. It causes some people to hold tightly to infrequent moments of joy; others to seek a real or imagined idyllic, former age; and a few to attempt to anticipate future developments and devise ways to cope with them intelligently.

Families and schools have always had the task, in one form or another, of preparing youth for the future; however, this task is probably more difficult today than in the past. Both the rate and magnitude of change are unprecedented, while social institutions have often proved ill-prepared in anticipating, planning, and coordinating changes. The inadequacies of existing institutions and the beliefs and values upon which they rest have been drawn to public attention more vividly and forcefully than ever before as a consequence of electronic developments that have made instantaneous and virtually worldwide communication possible.

This chapter will look at possible futures to the year 2000, their opportunities and hazards, in terms of likely changes in authority patterns in American schools and homes. Some of the findings about authority uncovered in earlier chapters will be brought forward to help us analyze the scenarios. Four different scenarios will be presented: Technotronic Society; The Hegemony of Private Education; The Family and Pluralistic Life Styles; and Ecohumanistic Organic Community. These scenarios will be partly imaginative constructs and partly based on various types of futuristic studies. They differ in their probability, but all have a reasonable degree of probability during the time frame indicated.

Scenario 1: Technotronic Society

Although the United States and some European nations experienced a recession during the early 1980s, new technology and expanded resources by the mid-eighties improved economic prospects. For several years governments instituted systems of rationing, credit controls, and wage-and-price restraints; however, these were largely removed by the late 1980s. As new sources of energy were developed, the accomplishments of scientists, engineers, and planners were publicly acknowledged, and a technological elite arose with all the perquisites of a special class. The public recognized their new heroes and heroines and accorded them as much attention as formerly given to movie and television stars. Attempts of environmental groups during the 1980s to establish a new environmental ethic based on conservation rather than exploitation diminished as more abundant sources of energy were developed.

Electronics continued to produce many innovations: computers to assist in medical diagnosis; access to library holdings on microfiche with readable computer printouts; ordinary books available to the blind by computers converting printed English into natural-speech sounds; portable computer terminals and telephone-plus-computer systems for allowing managers thousands of miles away to keep in touch with several employees simultaneously through computer terminals; and most homes equipped with a computer terminal for shopping, voting, and for increasing numbers who will be employed in their home at their computer console.[1]

Both the family and formal education were affected by these electronic developments. By the 1990s the family became increasingly an "electronic cottage," but not to the extent that Alvin Toffler predicted. Mainly those who were early in their careers and eager to advance were willing to foresake the traditional workplace of office and factory for a return to the home. Such work in the home consisted of monitoring distant manufacturing processes, typing electronic correspondence, writing a pamphlet, or programming a computer. For couples, whether married or living together, the reemergence of the home as an economic unit presented new opportunities. Those couples who had formerly pursued separate careers outside the home could now forge closer relations by their greater amount of time together and joint-work responsibilities. On the other hand, it posed for couples married for more than a few years a serious adjustment problem not entirely unlike a retirement from the work force. As Toffler had predicted, some families did take on more functions and reverse the trend of family functions increasingly assumed by other institutions.[2] Yet he underestimated how many more traditional workplaces could still be found in the early 1990s. The American family merely became more diverse. In the electronic cottage, however, parental relations with children became more technocratic: structured, preplanned, hierarchically organized in terms of rules and standards. This was all in keeping with the technocratic mentality (which will be discussed shortly).

Earlier forms of education technology was expanded and perfected during the 1990s. Instructional and educational television, dial-access systems for automated information retrieval for individualized instruction, microteaching, computer-assisted instruction, and computer-managed instruction became common features in public schools. Instruction followed the premise stated by Weingartner in the 1970s that everything can be done better by adopting electronic information-handling systems. The computer, he claimed, is synergistic, and everyone can learn more efficiently this way than by traditional instruction.[3]

With the decline in public-school enrollments, resistance to school bond issues, and the growth of the technotronic outlook, schools were ripe for shifing instruction from teachers to pupils.

One bold prediction that did not materialize was that since teachers would be freed from covering content, they could be primarily concerned with the affective domain.[4] Instead, teachers during the 1990s had to devote themselves to discipline, supervision, programming, program development, evaluation of programs, and the like; thus not only was little time available for the affective domain but most educators did not consider it a responsibility of public education. Problems of hostility, estrangement, and anxiety in learners were explained either as a failure to get the proper fit between individialized programs and students or else inadequate teacher management of automated instruction.

Educational thought was turbulent during the 1990s. Freud became passé, especially as more derogatory biographical data were unearthed and the last vestige of followers sought vainly to defend him; Piaget was mentioned less and less frequently and was no longer *de rigeur* for doctoral research. Instead, educators became embroiled in fervent debates, siding with either one of the two prominent figures of the decade. S.T. Thompson, a protégé of B.F. Skinner, developed behavioral technotronics to explain laws of learning, mastery, and efficiency in the use of electronics in education, politics, and management. Most American educators sided with Thompson. The other theorist was Rudolph Wilhelm Hurtzmann, the German philosopher-psychologist, who made a synthesis of cognitive psychology, phenomenology, and hermeneutics for explaining the life-world of Western educational technocracy and its alleged hegemonic propensities when introduced in Third World countries. A small but vocal group of radical graduate students renounced the prevailing views and turned to Chaung-Shih, a Chinese educator, who claimed that all natural events proceed by spontaneous creativity without effort, and once one harmonizes his thought with the eternal order, one's educational activities will unfold effortlessly.

All societies honor certain traits and personality types and ignore, deemphasize, or punish the expression of undesired traits. Different historical periods have recognized different types: innumerable societies have recognized the conqueror and military man; ancient Athens cultivated the democratic political type among its male citizens; the Romam Empire revered the orator and encouraged the development of engineers and administrators to handle the affairs of the vast empire; in the Christian and Islamic Middle Ages, as well as various periods in India and China, the holy man was dominant; the universal man of the Renaissance; the Englightment man of Reason; the individualist and frontier men and women in nineteenth-century western America; the capitalistic entrepreneur in

America and other industrial nations; and the loyal member of the Politburo in the Soviet Union. The technocratic society emphasized a narrow band of skills, though perhaps no narrower than some types previously enumerated. When other traits emerged that ran counter to technotronic man and woman, these traits were not so much punished by making their expression a crime as by using social disapproval and refusing to open employment and career advancement to these other types. Although the technotronic society exhibited less racial and ethnic discrimination than in America of the early 1980s, there was less tolerance for diverse life styles, especially those that deviated from the technotronic ideal. Thus social pressure was brought against bohemian types, artists, beatniks, counterculturists, anarchists, and others to the extent that they either converted to the dominant ideal for survival or decided to emigrate to a more hospitable country.

Of the different forms of authority, expert authority was the prevailing mode. An elite of scientists and engineers was the honored group, as Daniel Bell noted earlier about postindustrial society.[5] Bell envisioned three routes to power: the historic one of inherited property; the acquisition of political office through the political machine; and through advanced education to gain professional skill. The last route was the dominant one to power in technotronic society. The technical elites also aligned themselves with other influential groups in business and politics who could help them acquire and maintain power. The expert authority of the technical elites was sorely needed by society for planning and decision making (through linear programming, path analysis, program budgeting, and systems analysis). Thus the norms of applied scientific professionalism supersede the norms of economic self-interest. But an advanced education in the fine arts, humanities, and cognate areas of inquiry that were not directly applicable to technotronic networks were not routes to power but unemployment. During the mid-1990s, however, some composers and artists were commissioned to create music and art that glorified the values of computerization and automation; the new elite increasingly mandated an official type of culture promotive of technotronic values and labeled as "degenerate" any other forms in the arts. Although objections were raised against the ensconcement of an official cultural line, the threat of job cutbacks and other economic reprisals silenced all but the most audacious and zealous iconoclasts.

Sex differences in the workplace were reduced to a minimum. During the late 1980s the former wage differentials between men and women were virtually eliminated, discrimination in hiring and promotions based on sex were overcome, and the belief that men and women are inherently different in language-learning and mathematical aptitude was ascribed strictly to environmental influences. Since by the early 1990s no significant differences between the sexes were popularly acceptable and sexual discrimination and harassment had largely been eliminated from all forms of employment, any residual sexual attraction such as as flirtation and romantic attachment were rigorously discouraged. Jan Merideau, who get her start in the 1980s as a designer of lavish evening gowns, fashioned a loosely fitting but neat one-piece unisex outfit for the workplace that minimized physical differences between the sexes; its functionality instantly caught on with the managers and became required dress in all automated industries. Men and women were also expected to wear hairstyles of similar short length and to remove facial and bodily hair; for bald men, toupées were required.

The control mechanisms of technotronic society were not only exerted through the expert authority of the technocrat but also by moral persuasion, coercion, and power. Through the socialization process in school and home and later socialization in the workplace, the ideals of the society were inculcated, and citizens were urged to live up to them. Alternatives were sometimes discussed but were shown to be morally and socially inferior. A technotronic ethic emerged gradually and was refined by technicians and government officials; it was expected that the ethic would be taught in all schools and homes. To see that the ethic was made concrete and workable, many rules were devised to regulate the different institutions. The rules were employed in a coercive manner insofar as inducements to comply (through the use of sanctions) were strong and choices were limited to a spectrum within the framework of the rules. As for power, it was earlier mentioned that economic reprisals were used to induce others against their will. Technocrats, however, preferred to use influence and moral persuasion rather than power; however, when the former devices failed, coercion, which still permitted some choice, was used before power was employed. Influence was usually exerted by the public appeal of the technocrats based on their expertise, status, and their contribution to society.

Violent crime steadily diminished. Only those for whom socialization had failed and who were totally lacking inner controls committed violent crimes because of the high probability of arrest and conviction. People could be watched everywhere, and privacy was virtually nonexistent. More lenient laws permitted wiretapping and bugging, and conversations in public could easily be recorded at a distance by the new audioears perfected by a Japanese firm, and any public acts could easily be photographed or recorded on a television monitor by ubiquitous electronic devices. Computer and industrial crimes, however, could not be entirely eliminated despite increases in security because those committing them were ostensibly erstwhile disgruntled computer experts. Those apprehended for computer crimes were sent to a special training program that employed behavior modification and were reindoctrinated in the approved system of ethics; they were also required, through various projects, to make restitution for damages committed. In contrast, those committing violent crimes were usually incarcerated and placed on drugs. The work week in 1994 was reduced to thirty hours; the additional leisure time was used to enjoy the free media entertainment, available twenty-four hours daily, that had been carefully programmed to serve as an outlet and catharsis for any latent hostility and potential antisocial acts.

Decades earlier Lewis Mumford had warned about the dangers of automation, but he was not heeded by the new experts. Mumford, looking at the historical record, insisted that autocracy and technocracy are twins, that they suppress variety and autonomy and pressure people to conform to the controls of the autocratic designer.[6] He added that the media of communication, although evidently a great improvement over earlier, cruder models, fail to provide needed information about their own performance, or when the information is available, refuse to accept it by blocking its transmission and attempting to cover up its own errors.[7] The system is only interested in quantitative increases; where automation has taken command, it has made dialog, social cooperation, and moral evaluation difficult. Thus human beings need the freedom to accept, modify, or reject the new technology and should gain the understanding necessary by which those discussions can be intelligently made.[8]

As Jacques Ellul said, man has no moral, intellectual, or spiritual reference point for judging technology because he is born into a technological society, a distinctive milieu in which he finds himself, without being fully conscious of this environment and the way it shapes him. In this environment, the individual is prepared for professions that require a knowledge and use of technology; entertainment and advertising hypostasize the environment and depict leisure in terms of using technological things and devices. Thus there is only one way to satisfy desires—the technological way.[9] And although technology frees humans from many former restraints, the range of fundamental choice is limited. Choices are expressed in terms of objects and have no ethical content; but what is to be produced or eliminated, the choice among investments, the ones that determine consumption, are not open to the consumer. The system reduces choices either to faster or slower growth. Thus both the choices and the intellectual systems are expressions or justifications of technology.[10]

But citizens of technotronic society were not fully cognizant of these dangers because they had no firm place to stand apart from the system itself. Consequently, in the world of the 1990s, criticism of technocracy was in terms of growth patterns (insufficient growth in some sectors and overly rapid growth in others) or distribution of rewards (some segments of the population claimed that they did receive sufficient compensation for their services). Society was rushing pell mell toward greater growth of technocracy and the encapsulation of citizens in the intellectual systems and life styles that emerge from and are consonant with this type of society. On the one hand, some earlier prophecies did not materialize in the 1990s: economic collapse as a consequence of unmanageable population growth; alterations of the balance of power between the rich and poor nations as the latter learned to wage nuclear war; and the inability to maintain industrial growth as a result of resource limitations and pollution problems, leading to the destabilization of democracies and the rise of authoritarian states.[11] Yet no alternate technology, as urged in the 1970s and based on a steady-state economy and ecologically sound practices,[12] could be found in the United States during the 1990s or even seriously entertained.

Scenario 2: The Hegemony of Private Education

Public-school enrollments began to decline in 1972, and by 1974 private-school enrollments began to rise out of the decline of the 1960s and continued their increase until 1991. Many reasons could be adduced for these changes. During the 1970s public attitudes exhibited less confidence in public education; and the middle class, formerly the bulwark of public education, increasingly sent their children to private schools. The 1980s witnessed the continued growth of private schools—traditional parochial schools, Christian academies, segregated and integrated college-preparatory schools, free schools, fundamental schools, and other types. The private-school movement was given a boost during the 1980s when tax exemptions were once again allowed for organizations that discriminate racially; consequently, some segregated private schools that earlier were scarcely able to survive began to prosper, and a multitude of new segregated schools, both black and white, sprang up around the country.

Both black and white middle-class families strove to send their children to private schools—and many were succeeding in doing so, if not for the child's entire education, at least for a substantial part. This was made possible, despite continuing inflation, by smaller families, delay of childbearing, and both husband and wife working outside the home in over 50 percent of two-parent families.

Despite vigorous efforts by proponents, various voucher plans floundered. Instead, tax credits or deductions for children sent to private schools were legally approved at the federal level, followed by a significant minority of state legislature providing credits in state tax plans. Thus the road opened wide for financial compensation long sought by some parochial school leaders. Just as some private higher-education funding had long been provided, transfer payment of public funds either directly to private and parochial schools or in the form of tax credits provided a vast expansion of nonpublic schools in the late 1980s. Certification for nonpublic schools was nonexistent in some states or considerably below the standards for public schools in other states. As different types of nonpublic schools proliferated, their standards and the quality of preparation of teachers varied enormously.

In the meantime public schools began to change dramatically. The schools of the poor were now the public schools. But since the poor usually posed greater educational problems than middle- and upper-class youth, many teachers sought positions in nonpublic schools, and the turnover rate, as could be expected, was higher in schools for the poor. Some states, lacking other inducements or unwilling to initiate them, lowered certification requirements and issued large numbers of emergency certificates for public-school teachers.

The curriculum of most public schools was designed to meet minimum competencies, used many types of compensatory-education programs, and emphasized fundamental skills and some vocational preparation. Diverse, enriched, and alternative programs could be found almost exclusively in nonpublic schools. Most nonpublic schools defined their role and objectives in more limited terms than the comprehensive high-school or the omnibus public-school programs of the 1970s by focusing on either religious education, college preparation, programs for exceptional children, or some other specialized program. Nonpublic school educators, by supporting tax credits rather than a voucher plan, were able to avoid many of the regulatory activities that vouchers entailed and thereby enjoyed largely a free reign in developing their programs, hiring teachers, and deciding which students would be admitted.

By the late 1980s the former ideals that animated public education were little more than curious relics. Public schools had been extolled for serving the public in terms of purpose, control, support, access, and commitment to civic unity; these schools, it was proclaimed, were designed to serve the welfare of a democratic society by assuring the imparting of knowledge and understanding needed for citizenship responsibilities. Despite failures to fully fulfill those ideals, the ideals were eclipsed by the shift to nonpublic schools, with their diversity, lack of common offerings, neglect of citizenship preparation, and the growth of class consciousness. A student was stigmatized for attending public schools; even among private schools elaborate informal distinctions were made so that attendance at a certain school would signify not only social-class standing but one's likelihood of entering one of the more prestigious careers or professions. Thus the net effect of the nonpublic-school movement of the eighties was to create a more highly stratified society with fewer common bonds except superficial ones imparted through the mass media. These changes, along with higher unemployment rates of public than nonpublic-school graduates, led to the growth of a relatively permanent underclass, social tension and instability, and higher levels of violence and street crime.

With the proliferation of different types of nonpublic schools, authority took the form of many so-called experts proclaiming the educational virtues of their school system. This seemed inevitable once it was realized that each program would need widespread publicity and effective promotion in order to recruit students and maintain desired enrollment levels. Local media were filled with advertisements of schools, and televised debates of experts, each with his own facts and figures undergirded by an ideology, appeared nightly for several weeks prior to the registration for a school term. Parents and other interested observers tuned in as much for the entertainment value as for information, as many of these experts were no longer ponderous and pedantic figures but sought to appeal to a wide audience. A few education experts, in fact, became so popular that they changed careers and became media personalities. Some parents who would not think of their children becoming classroom teachers encouraged them to become education experts, though most parents still urged their children to become technotronic executives.

The problems of control and discipline were mitigated for nonpublic schools in which there was a close match between the students' interests and aptitudes and the educational program. Unfortunately, parents did not always understand their children or the programs well enough to choose wisely. Many schools still had some problems of vandalism, theft, classroom and school disorders; however, the incidence of disruption in nonpublic schools was lower than in the public schools of the early 1970s. After reductions in violence and vandalism from this 1970 period, that level was again reached by public schools in the late 1980s. The difference for this later period was that, with advanced electronic devices in use, levels of detection and apprehension of offenders was greatly increased, and student suspension and expulsion rates escalated to all-time highs. Yet expulsion intensified and exacerbated the problems of the underclass, which was already faced with high unemployment rates, an unsympathetic middle class that jealously guarded its limited opportunities, and technotronic managers who would hire only those with the latest, advanced technocratic skills.

Scenario 3: The Family and Pluralistic Life Styles

Some of the trends cited in chapter 6 about the family continued in the late 1980s and early 1990s. Specifically, although the nuclear family persisted, an increasing number of different types of family and intimate arrangements were tried and tested in American life.

The strong sense of community, a common value system, and stringent sanctions characteristic of some aspects of earlier America were no longer to be found. Although organized religion, especially Christianity, was once a force to help maintain the nuclear family and monogamous relations, religion's hold over secular affairs greatly diminished despite the recrudescence of fundamentalist sects during the early 1980s. The inability of the nuclear family to satisfy many human desires in a rapidly changing, unstable society led to the growth of multiple alternatives to conventional structures.

Since 1970 most people no longer lived in the conventional nuclear family but as single households, single-parent families, dual-working-parent families, childless couples, or postchildbearing couples. By 1994 attitudes toward being single had changed markedly. Where once social pressure was exerted to marry and to raise a family, now being single carried little or no stigma, and little social pleasure was applied to marry for the first time or to remarry. As the number of singles grew, they found strength in numbers by establishing their own social clubs and organizations to promote their interests.

Cohabitation (unmarried couples either of the same or opposite sex living together for sexual and/or other reasons) increased to 17 percent in 1994 of the total U.S. adult population. Research on heterosexual couples who later married failed to establish definitively that such relations led to greater marital stability. In most cities restrictive housing covenants were repealed that denied housing to unmarried couples.

Much less frequently found were triads and communes. Although the life spans for both men and women were extended as crippling and fatal diseases were gradually conquered and a larger percentage of the population observed sound health habits, the female's longevity span exceeded the male's by six years. With the graying of America, some women opted for triad relationships rather than to live alone. In these relationships two women would live with one man who was still in reasonably good health. These relations were found occasionally in 1994 and generally accepted. Less frequently would the triad consist of one woman and two men. Triads of this type were formed when men would attach themselves to successful and powerful women in politics, entertainment, or the media industry.

Some communes emerged that were based on radical political philosophies or religious sectarianism. One reason that communes remained sporadic was that radical political ideas were difficult to propagate in a technotronic society. Another reason was that the general economic prosperity did not foster a need for communes or collective living. Earlier experiences with communes, especially in the late 1960s, showed that problems frequently arose in the group over carrying out a division of labor in sharing economic tasks and in handling sexual relations among members. In some cases communes in the 1990s did not purport to be organized for sexual fulfillment but for either economic or political purposes.

In contrast to communes, which usually recruited college students and arose out of religious or utopian philosophies, multiadult households emerged from intimate groups or networks of persons in their thirties or older who still remained part of the mainstream culture. Usually these groups started by two couples' joining forces; most of the multiadult households numbered eight or less, including children. These households, in some respects, resembled the earlier extended family insofar as they partially took on some functions—educational, economic, religious—that the nuclear family turned over to other institutions. Some households were monogamous while others were sexually free. Children were the main beneficiaries insofar as they had more adult role models which, if the role models were desirable and nurturing, enabled children to see the world in a broader, more balanced perspective. Still, the number of people living in multiadult households in 1994 was less than one million nationally, and even this figure was larger than membership in communes.

Multiadult households emerged both for the rearing of children and to serve sexual and economic functions as well. By 1994 other changes in marriage could be observed. At that time eighteen states had legalized trial marriages, a temporary state in which the partners would sign a contract committing themselves to two years or less together; the contract was renewable after that period of time. This constituted an intermediate step between cohabitation and regular marriage; it provided de jure approval of a love relationship. Most states in which trial marriages were legalized established it as a prerequisite to marriage: two years of a successful trial marriage were required before a regular marriage license could be obtained. It was believed by proponents that this preliminary step would help assure more successful, stabler, and happier marriages; but as of 1994, no definitive studies were available because these laws had only been in effect for a few years.

Two types of marriage licenses were issued: marriages without children and marriages with children. Standards were lower for obtaining the former license but still higher than those of the early 1980s because in some states they required two years of successful trial marriage and a knowledge of marriage and family relations (demonstrated by passing a test). Those couples either in trial marriages or marriages without children who had children incurred a legal penalty; thus it was expected that pregnancy would be aborted unless doing so would endanger the woman's life.

Marriages in which children were desired not only had to meet all the provisions of marriage without children but required a parenting license. The license was needed essentially because of reasons cited earlier in chapter 6. To meet requirements, potential parents would need to demonstrate not only an adequate knowledge of child development and rearing practices but desirable attitudes toward children. Moreover, they would be required to demonstrate competencies in child care under the watchful eye of child-care and family-life specialists. Regulations governing child abuse and negligence were more stringent than those of the early 1980s, but the incidence of removal of the child from the parental home was still not as high as the former period because of the screening effects of the parental license. As a consequence, younger children, some observers said, were now less prone to violence and less attracted to violence in the media, although it was probably still too early to make that judgment. One mistake that usually was not made in granting parenting licenses was to seek only one model of a good parent; instead, several models were sanctioned as long as the prospective parents observed desired principles and exhibited healthy attitudes.

Partly as a consequence of these changes in child-rearing practices, the incidence of violence in schools abated, and the range of disciplinary problems narrowed. In other words, disciplinary problems arising out of aggressiveness diminished; when they did occur, they no longer would more likely be expected of a lower-class student because the parenting license assured certain uniformities and the observation of certain principles without imposing a single model. Aggressiveness was not discouraged in contests and competitions governed by rules of fair play but was deterred only when it led to actual or potential harm of another. School discipline problems grew out of the distractions of student interests in outside activities and in an overstimulating culture at large; it took the form of an inability to focus or apply oneself to the work at hand by engaging in individual and group diversions that students considered entertaining and a way to pass the time. Thus all sorts of group and individual games, electronic or otherwise, captured the attention of many elementary-and secondary-school students. When electronic games were banned from some classrooms, students invented games that showed an ingenuity that teachers often wished would be displayed in academic work. When some parents and teachers complained to the consumers' union about the saturation of the market and the media with electronic games, the technotronic corporations extolled the games' educational value and claimed, furthermore, that a reduction in their production would lead to considerable unemployment and damage the economy.

The other source of disruption was Congress's passage of a law requiring two years of national service of both men and women at age eighteen. Youth had the alternative of either military or national social service similar to the Peace Corps or Job Corps. Many young women were incensed that although the Equal Rights Amendment failed to pass, this bill would require the same service of women as men, except that women would not be required to serve on the front lines in wartime. Men raised some of the same objections to the bill as were raised during the Vietnam war, except in 1994 there was no war raging (though some eighteen-year-olds thought the bill encouraged a more aggressive military posture and, consequently, expected war to break out any day). In many public and nonpublic high schools and colleges, while the bill was being debated and after it was passed, demonstrations erupted on many campuses, thereby posing a problem for administrators of maintaining some degree of order while protecting civil liberties. In some cases students insisted that their rights to demonstrate were arbitrarily restricted, which in turn led to further protests.

Scenario 4: Ecohumanistic Organic Community

In the year 1997, recognizing the approach of the new century, Marilyn Anne Reynolds, the president of the United States, established the Commission on the Twenty-First Century, a national ad hoc body drawn from the most distinguished men and women from all walks of American life. The charge given the commission was to assess the present status and progress of America with reference to past ideals, principles, and values of the heritage and the emergent values of the twenty-first century; then in light of findings, the commission was expected to present a model of the type of society toward which the country should move and a set of recommendations and policy proposals by which this model could likely be achieved.

The commission established grassroots committees across the country; these committees, after data gathering, deliberation, and debate, would be expected to send delegates to Washington to present their findings. The commission received ample funding, support of Congress as well as the executive branch, and sufficient access to the media.

At the United Nations, delegates from some Western nations planned to introduce a resolution to appoint a study group for the year 2000, but some Third World countries threatened to veto it. The World Council for Peace and Welfare, a new international organization based in Geneva, proposed a plan for world disarmament.

After more than one year of deliberation, several lines of thinking began to come to the fore within the commmission. EOC, or Ecohumanistic Organic Community, a fancy name that one of the commission members dubbed the dominant model, was discussed with much interest and enthusiasm. This model ran counter and significantly differed with the prevailing technotronic model.

EOC called for a new relationship with the environment. It opted for a steady-state environment with zero population growth. One of the reasons that environmental problems were exacerbated was the continued growth of population. Each American consumes five times as much food and sixty times as much energy as the average South Asian.[13] Thus it is hypocritical for the United States to urge population control while both lacking a population policy and failing to curb population growth and the consequent expenditure of economic and environmental resources. Thus EOC called for a national policy that would provide incentives for family-planning, sex-education, and family-life programs in the schools; daycare facilities; maternity leaves; and stringently regulated immigration that would reduce legal immigration to a level approximating emigration. It was urged that states recognize three types of certificates for intimate relations: trial marriages, childless marriage, marriage with children. (The latter would require the conditions outlined in scenario 3.)

Another concern that EOC addressed was the question, How can the state maintain a bond of unity, a civic sense, while still recognizing and encouraging cultural differences? Although the nature and use of the state's laws and power are important determinants of the state's characteristics and its impact on citizens, the state needs to create a sense of authority and obligation in which reliance on force and legal sanctions are minimized so that citizens voluntarily comply with the laws and maintain civic pride, while continuing to preserve their right to dissent. The state can sustain its authority—and hence its legitimacy without resort to force—as long as it is deemed just, satisfies basic needs but does not induce artificial needs, provides sufficient outlets for the nonviolent petition of grievances, and protects other civil rights.

These are large and demanding provisions that the architects of EOC relaized many earlier democratic states had not usually been able to fulfill. The sense of justice, it was held, could best be promoted by the passage of laws that both experts and lay persons believed to be just, the provision of speedy and impartial trials, the reform of the penal system to rehabilitate those who can eventually become useful citizens, the protection of society from recidivists, and maintenance of rights to peaceable protest, and reasonable access to the media to make one's cause known.

Although there was agreement among EOC proponents over basic physical needs, a consensus was not forthcoming on other needs despite the availability of various theories and empirical findings. Since physical needs cannot be met wherever poverty exists, it was proposed that the government would provide a minimum-income floor below which no person would fall. At the same time retraining programs, work incentives, and daycare centers would be provided.

In a democratic society people should be free to pursue a way of life of their own choosing as long as a commitment to this way of life does not persistently violate just laws and the duly established rights of others. Thus EOC eschewed an officially approved way of life, though by advocating certain principles, it was suggesting that certain types of activities would be undesirable. By safeguarding the right to peaceful protest, for instance, it opposed those officials and groups that attempted to stifle dissent. But since EOC values freedom, recognizes individual differences in both abilities and in goals and aspirations, it refused to lay down an officially approved way of life and enforce it with stiff sanctions.

Organic community should represent an outgrowth of semiautonomous communities that share common bonds and interests. But such communities, EOC proponents recognized, may not be feasible in an age in which greater centralized services are needed. In terms of both energy development and social relations, however, more decentralized arrangements were advocated. At the national and world levels, centralized planning would still be needed in trade, resource utilization, population control, and other areas. Yet EOC planning sought to begin with the community and then move out to larger areas among people only when necessary.

Many subcommittees grew out of EOC deliberations. The Education Committee, as one of its first agenda tasks, decided to explore the question of how the educational system could best promote organic communities. Only tentative agreement was reached after numerous sessions. It appeared that the work of the commission and the deadline for final reports would have to be extended if other committees also experienced delay and protracted debate.

The Education Committee tentatively agreed that schools would need to teach the value of developing and maintaining organic communities, to encourage student commitment to such communities while still providing an atmosphere of free inquiry that could ultimately challenge the need for such communities. Also included in the curriculum would be studies of human sexuality, family life, population, ecology, economic planning, international relations, disarmament, and world peace. Students, in order to be effective members of organic communities, would cultivate cooperation, sympathy, and caring relations. Committee members generally agreed that the emphasis should be on humanizing education and cultivating genuine intellectual excitement in learning. Discipline, they added, should arise out of respect for responsive, democratic authority and greater opportunity to engage in proactive behavior, to set meaningful tasks and strive for worthwhile goals. It was a sparkling beginning and augered well for a better and brighter future.

Notes

1. See Stephen Rosen, *Future Facts* (New York: Touchstone Books, 1976), ch. 7, and Alvin Toffler, *The Third Wave* (New York: Bantam Books, 1980), pp. 194-207, 216-221.

2. Toffler, *The Third Wave,* pp. 216-221.

3. Charles Weingartner, "No More Pencils, No More Books, No More Teachers' Dirty Looks," *Educational Futures: Sourcebook I,* edited by F. Kierstead, J. Bowman, and C. Dede (Washington, D.C.: World Future Society, 1979), pp. 71-82.

4. Charles Weingartner, "Schools and the Future," in Theodore W. Hipple, ed., *The Future of Education: 1975-2000* (Pacific Palisades, Calif.: Goodyear Publishing, 1974), pp. 182-206.

5. Daniel Bell, *The Coming of Post-Industrial Society* (New York: Basic Books, 1973), pp. 221, 358-364.

6. Lewis Mumford, *The Myth of the Machine: The Pentagon of Power* (New York: Harcourt Brace Jovanovich, 1970), graphic section.

7. Ibid., p. 183.

8. Ibid., pp. 184-193.

9. Jacques Ellul, *The Technological System* (New York: Continuum, 1980), pp. 311-318.

10. Ibid., pp. 319-325. For an opposing position, see Samuel C. Florman, *Blaming Technology* (New York: Saint Martin's Press, 1981).

11. Robert L. Heilbroner, *An Inquiry Into the Human Prospect* (New York: Norton, 1975).

12. David Dickerson, *Alternative Technology and the Politics of Technical Change* (Glasgow: Fontana/Collins, 1974).

13. Gerald O. Barney, ed., *The Unfinished Agenda* (New York: Crowell, 1977), p. 27.

Index

About the Author

John Martin Rich is professor of cultural foundations of education at the University of Texas at Austin. He is a past president of the American Educational Studies Association and the North Central and Ohio Valley Philosophy of Education Societies. Professor Rich is the author and editor of seven previous books, and his numerous articles and reviews have appeared in professional journals in the United States and abroad. He received the Ph.D. in philosophy of education from The Ohio State University.